# CANADIAN CRIMINAL RECORDS

## AND HOW TO START FRESH

Published in Canada by Fitzhenry & Whiteside, 195 Allstate Parkway, Markham,
ON L3R 4T8
Published in the United States by Fitzhenry & Whiteside, 311 Washington Street,
Brighton, Massachusetts 02135

Fitzhenry & Whiteside acknowledges with thanks the Canada Council for the
Arts, and the Ontario Arts Council for their support of our publishing program.
We acknowledge the financial support of the Government of Canada through the
Canada Book Fund (CBF) for our publishing activities.

Library and Archives Canada Cataloguing in Publication
Canadian Criminal Records and How to Start Fresh
ISBN 978-1-55455-167-5
Data available on file

Publisher Cataloging-in-Publication Data (U.S.)
Canadian Criminal Records and How to Start Fresh
ISBN 978-1-55455-167-5
Data available on file

Interior design by Daniel Choi
Cover design by Tanya Montini

Printed and bound in Canada

# CANADIAN CRIMINAL RECORDS

## AND HOW TO START FRESH

Antree Demakos, B.A., LL.B., J.D.

Fitzhenry & Whiteside

# Contents

# ACKNOWLEDGMENTS

## RCMP and Police Services  (rcmp-grc.gc.ca) (torontopolice.on.ca)

Yves Marineau, RCMP, Access to Information and Privacy Coordinator, and Cpl. Mel Abramovitch, RCMP, for providing me with the raw data for 3 million individual criminal files available in the RCMP database.

To the provincial and municipal police services nation-wide, who have always been generous with their knowledge, and supportive of public education with regards to criminal records. And a special thanks to Chief Bill Blair, Toronto Police Services whose encouragement is much appreciated.

## Correctional Service of Canada and Ministry of Probation and Parole (csc-scc.gc.ca)  (mcscs.jus.gov.on.ca)

Correctional Service of Canada and Ministry of Probation and Parole, for recognizing the value of rehabilitation, and for promoting education through Ian Levine's seminars at their training facilities.

## Courts (attorneygeneral.jus.gov.on.ca)

To the many provincial and federal court officers, and in particular Paul Vincent, Ontario Court, Consulting Manager, Operational Support, who, over the years, have provided detailed answers to my numerous questions regarding court policies and procedures.

And to my friends the Honourable Mr. Justice Marvin A. Zuker, Ontario Criminal Court Judge, and Larry Banack, Certified by the Law Society of Upper Canada as Specialist in Civil Litigation, Bencher of the Law Society, Former Chair of the Law Commission of Ontario, Chair, Board of Trustees of the Law Foundation, for their encouragement and words of wisdom.

### Youth Justice Ontario  (youthjusticeontario.ca)

Don Adam, Executive Coordinator, Youth Justice Ontario, for his insight and help with Chapter 3.

### Parole Board of Canada  (pbc-clcc.gc.ca)

Parole Board of Canada, Record Suspension Division, for their continued help over the years and in particular, for providing valuable information about the practical implications of the new Pardon legislation (Record Suspension).

### Pardons Canada   (pardons.org)

Ian D. Levine, Founder and Board of Advisors; Andrew Tanenbaum, Program Director; Jodi Tanenbaum, Director of Operations; and Marisa Cutter, Director of Policies and Procedures, for providing current information about the effects of the recent legislative changes brought about by Bill C-10, for sharing their statistical data, and for reviewing Chapter 7.

### Canadian Immigration Law  (migrationlaw.com)

Guidy Mamann, Certified by the Law Society of Upper Canada as an Immigration Law Specialist, former Immigration Officer, weekly Columnist and widely Published Author, for his detailed review and suggestions for Chapter 5.

### Statistics Canada  (statcan.gc.ca)

Samuel Bernadin, Information officer /Agent d'information Canadian Centre for Justice Statistics/Centre Canadien de la Statistique Juridique, for providing incident based crime statistics, Canada.

Shannon Brennan, Senior Analyst for the Canadian Centre for Justice Statistics, and Mia Dauvergne, Senior Analyst, Policing Services Program, Canadian

Centre for Justice Statistics, at the Justice and Human Rights Committee, for their comprehensive Crime Report of Police-reported crime statistics in Canada.

Dr. Kent Campbell, Ph.D. for his detailed analytical work with the statistics in Chapter 8; and in particular, for taking the RCMP's raw data and turning it into something we can all understand.

Beth Ellen Rossen, RN, M.Sc., Ph.D., and Arnold H. Rossen, MBA, P. Eng., for their scrutiny of the statistical analysis in Chapter 8, and for making valuable suggestions.


## Omnibus Crime Bill Discussion Panel - 2011

Thank you to the Discussion Panel and the Sponsors for taking the time to conduct an in-depth and comprehensive review of Bill C-10.

## Moderator:  Maureen Brosnahan, CBC

## Panelists:
- Patricia Allard, Deputy Director, Canadian HIV/AIDS Legal Network
- Caleb Chepesiuk, Director, Canadian Students for Sensible Drug Policy
- Eugene Oscapella, Lawyer; Founder, Canadian Foundation for Drug Policy
- Greg Simmons, Prisoners' Rights Expert
- Steve Sullivan, Director, Ottawa Victims Services; First Federal Ombudsman for Victims of Crime
- Krysta Williams, Native Youth Sexual Health Network


**And of course, a heartfelt thank you to Andreas,
for being so *awesome* while I wrote this book.**

# FOREWORD

As Co-founders of Pardons Canada, and having been involved with the *removal of criminal records* for 20 years, Antree Demakos and I have helped more than 250,000 of the nicest "criminals" you'd ever want to meet. Now, with the immeasurable and far-reaching effects of the new *Pardon* law, Antree felt that it was time for her to write this book.

In Canada, 4.5 million adults (1 in 5) have been charged with a crime. More than 500,000 people are charged each year, and in the year 2011, more than 2 million crimes were reported by the police. This means that you, or one of your family members, a friend, a neighbour, or someone else you care about either has a criminal record, has already removed it, or will inevitably acquire one. Therefore, whether directly or indirectly, the ramifications of having a criminal record affect us all.

How is it possible for so many of us to be "criminals"? Are we living in a nation of criminals? Simply put, no. In fact, Canada continues to be one of the safest countries in the world. While a very small percentage are *career* criminals, and an even smaller percentage are *dangerous* criminals, the vast majority of people with records are everyday folk. They are found in all socio-economic strata of society. They have jobs. They are mothers and fathers. They pay taxes. They use one name, not five aliases. They don't own guns, and they don't *hang out* in gangs.

**How did they get into trouble**? Most often, people become afoul of the law in trying to deal with real-life issues: including, being young and foolish, falling in with a bad crowd, suffering from depression, experiencing other mental health issues, having addictions (alcohol, drug, gambling), and coping with relationship problems (e.g., divorce).

Furthermore, it is quite *easy to get a criminal record.* Simply being *accused* of a crime, even where the person *is not* formally charged, will lead the police to generate an *incident* and/or *occurrence* report. If the police *do* lay charges, fingerprints and photographs are almost always taken. Although the charge may not result in a conviction – for example, if the case was withdrawn – much to everyone's disbelief, the criminal record that was created (by the police, the court and the RCMP) will remain on file.

As a result, these reports and records will appear on standard police and RCMP searches. For these people, life as they knew it, is over.

**What are the effects of having a criminal record**? The discovery of a criminal record creates obstacles in many vital aspects of a person's life – including the ability to get a job, be accepted in school programs, become licensed for employment or business purposes, travel to the U.S.A., volunteer, rent or buy an apartment or house, or become a Canadian citizen.

In today's world a *police clearance* is required for most applications. In order to provide a clearance, the police will conduct a search of their records to determine if there is any information on file. A police records search will reveal information from police reports and will list all charges. Even *very old* records will resurface and be disclosed. In such cases, a person who is now middle-aged or older (likely with children, a home and other responsibilities) will once again be punished for the crime. When the record is discovered, and the consequences are realized – such as losing their job, or being turned away at the American border – their lives often fall apart. Similarly, young people, with recent criminal records, are precluded from *starting their adult lives on the right path* when they can't be admitted to school programs or aren't able to get a decent job, after their record is revealed.

The list of problems created by criminal records is endless. Most of all, having a record affects people's self-esteem; which in turn governs how they behave in our society. It is dangerous to allow 20 percent of our adult population to be ostracized, stigmatized and left without hope. As a result, they often feel desperate and are more likely to commit another crime. Whereas, statistics have shown that when people have *Hope* and can *Start Fresh* – by removing their records – the result is tremendous, as less than 4 percent reoffend.

**With so much at stake, what can be done to remove or erase a criminal record?** For the most part, criminal records remain on file indefinitely and keep re-appearing at the most inopportune times. A person with a record, therefore, continues to be punished long after the charges were dropped, or the sentence was served, unless they take steps to clear it. As simply as is possible, Chapter 7 of this book explains the various ways to remove a criminal record.

Why is this book important? Why now? During the past two decades, Antree and I have experienced the outcome of many legislative changes. Now, with *Pardons* being replaced by *Record Suspensions*, people are more confused than ever. Our *central* position in the criminal records system has afforded us first-hand knowledge of how these records are handled within the labyrinth of municipal, provincial and federal government departments. Equally important is that we have the benefit of seeing the long-term effects that befall people entangled in this system.

Armed with her extensive experience and unique perspective, Antree has written this book in order to simplify the law pertaining to criminal records, and to dispel the widespread misconceptions and beliefs about them. This book is beneficial to all who work in the criminal justice system, (lawyers, judges, police, probation and parole officers, etc.); as well as those in the social services (rehabilitation and addiction programs, job placement services, immigration and family services, etc.); and of course, all who have a criminal record, or who care about someone who does.

With straightforward explanations, this book will take you through the life of a criminal record – from its creation to its removal.

*As the Program Director for Pardons Canada (pardons.org), Ian acquired in-depth knowledge about the consequences of criminal records and how to re- move them. He has presented over 400 seminars nation-wide, to all levels of government – including police services, correctional facilities, and probation and parole training centres.*

**Ian D. Levine**, B.A., D.M.A.
**Pardons Canada,** Co-founder, Program Director (1987-2008), Outreach Education Coordinator (2009-2011), Board of Advisors (Current)
**LegalLine.ca**, Co-founder, Director of Government Alliances

Chapter One

# What is a Criminal Record?

## – The Creation and Storage of Criminal Records –

Understanding what criminal records are, when and how they are created, and where they can be stored can often be confusing.

To start with, it doesn't take much to get a criminal record. Police reports about *incidents* or *occurrences* can result in a police file—even if no charges were laid. Once an individual *is* charged, however, a whole new can of worms opens up: the criminal record is stored in many different places within the vast criminal justice system, and can be accessed by police services and other government agencies without the individual's knowledge or consent.

Furthermore, there are multiple systems used to create and store criminal records. Canada has 230 different police services (each with multiple offices) and 750 court offices. Each of these creates criminal records based on their individual record management systems, guidelines, and discretion. There is no consistency as to the type of criminal record information stored at these different government offices, but the information forms the basis for police and court reports.

## 1.  What is a criminal record?

Most people assume a criminal record to be a standard document containing police and court information about their criminal convictions. Those without convictions often assume that they have no criminal record. Both beliefs are wrong.

**For practical purposes, *any* record held at a government office, containing information about a person's criminal activity or involvement is considered to be a *type* of criminal record. This is so because many different types of *criminal* information can be collected, stored, and used against an individual. In essence, if *anything* is on a file, a police clearance cannot be obtained.**

In its broadest sense, a criminal record is a host of fragmented government information about a person's criminal history that could include:

- Personal information
  (names, aliases, date and place of birth)
- Fingerprints and Photographs
- Physical characteristics
  (sex, height, weight, racial group, eye colour, distinguishing marks)
- An indication of whether a DNA sample has been collected
- Whether the person has been convicted of a sexual offence for which a Pardon or Record Suspension has been granted or ordered
- Known associates and connections to organized crime
- Detailed charging information
  (including an offence classification, such as violence, theft, drugs, sex, etc.)
- Cautionary codes warning others about the individual
  (e.g., violence, escape custody, mental instability, attempted suicide)
- Detailed disposition information (including dates and jurisdiction of convictions that have not been pardoned or suspended and non-convictions, as well as sentences)
- Local police records and reports of incidents
  (these incidents may have never resulted in charges, but may include allegations or pending charges)
- A list of law-enforcement and government agencies that have been provided with the criminal record.

In my experience, the most common reasons why people committed crimes were:
- They were young and foolish.
- They got in with a bad crowd.
- They were human and made a mistake.
- They were going through an ugly divorce (very often both the husband and wife are charged with assault).
- The person has a mental-health issue (temporary or long-term).
- The person was suffering from depression.
- At the time of trouble, the individual was an addict (drugs, alcohol, gambling, sex).

Although such detailed information about a person's criminal history can assist police services in protecting the public, it can also have far-reaching negative effects for those everyday folk who had a temporary lapse of good judgment. Inaccurate or irrelevant information, or information that resulted in dismissed or withdrawn charges, will be ultimately disclosed as part of a police records check. Criminal record information, no matter how minor, will negatively influence those reviewing the information, such as prospective employers, Canadian Immigration officials, and American border officers.

## 2. Who can have a criminal record?

Any adult or young person[1] in Canada can have a criminal record—no one is immune. Children under the age of twelve who are engaged in criminal activity do not legally fall under Canada's *Youth Criminal Justice Act*. Therefore, children committing crimes will not be discussed in this book.

Technically, even non-human entities such as corporations or organizations can have a criminal record. The reality is, however, that police will charge human beings because non-human entities cannot be imprisoned, or easily monitored. Indeed, these entities can be changed or dissolved, thereby frustrating law-enforcement efforts to hold them accountable.

## 3. Who creates criminal records?

Criminal records are almost always created when the police charge a person with an offence. After the police lay a charge, the local court with the authority to deal with those charges then creates its own records.

In most cases, the police photograph and fingerprint the individual in addition to laying charges. The charging police service[2] can be a municipal police department, a provincial or territorial one, or federal—the Royal Canadian Mounted Police (RCMP).

In addition to police records, each court creates its own criminal records, distinct from the police and from each other. Courts differ by levels of legal superiority and are separated by jurisdiction (different for each province). Provincial and territorial courts responsible for criminal prosecutions are either considered *inferior* (hearing minor criminal matters) or *superior* (hearing serious criminal matters). Court decisions can be appealed to a higher court, each of which will create its own records.

> Most people are charged with *Criminal Code* offences. A small percentage of charges (5%) are drug offences under the *Controlled Drugs and Substances Act*, and about 1% of the charges are for offences under various other federal statutes.

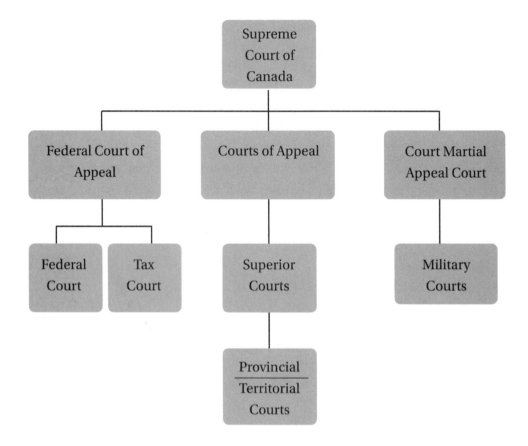

## 4. What is the Royal Canadian Mounted Police (RCMP)?

The RCMP is Canada's federal police. They have authority to act across the entire country. With the exception of Newfoundland and Labrador, Ontario, and Québec, the RCMP is also contracted by the provinces and territories to be their provincial or territorial law-enforcement agency.[3] Additionally, the RCMP serves as municipal police to many Canadian towns and cities. Headquartered in Ottawa, the RCMP:

- Was established as the North West Mounted Police in 1873 by the Canadian government to police vast areas of western Canada
- Officially became the Royal Canadian Mounted Police in 1920 after absorbing the Dominion Police
- Is organized into four regions, fourteen divisions, with a presence

throughout Canada

- Has 26,000 employees and 75,000 volunteers
- Administers or enforces more than 250 federal statutes and agreements
- Is responsible for protective security measures to safeguard designated persons (VIPs), federal properties, and other vital points from security offences and threats
- Administers the Canadian Police Information Centre (CPIC)
- Has over 750 autonomous units.

## 5. What is the Canadian Police Information Centre (CPIC)?

CPIC is a computerized information storage and retrieval system operated by the RCMP on behalf of the nation's policing community. It contains or provides access to various criminal record data banks. It operates on a twenty-four-hour-a-day, year-round basis, and is located at the RCMP headquarters in Ottawa. CPIC provides instant information about crimes and offenders to over 80,000 law-enforcement officers within 2,882 local police departments and to the over 750 RCMP detachments, and federal, provincial, and territorial agencies across the country. The users of this information are called *CPIC network users*. CPIC also allows these network users to post alerts and exchange messages.

CPIC originated in 1966 from meetings between federal and provincial attorneys general concerned about how better to assist the police community. CPIC was approved by the Treasury Board of Canada in 1967 and became operational on July 1, 1972. A national *Advisory Committee,* made up of senior police officers from all three levels of government, oversees CPIC's content, use, and regulation, and approves network users.

CPIC is the only national information sharing system linking criminal justice and law-enforcement partners across Canada. American law-enforcement officers also can access CPIC information via the Federal Bureau of Investigation's (FBI) National Crime Information Centre (NCIC).

Some information is restricted, such as information on young offenders, and is not supposed to be released to the NCIC.

Accurate CPIC records are necessary not only for the capture of offenders, but also in obtaining proper punishments. Although for the most part, CPIC does provide accurate information, it has not been free of controversy. Its effectiveness has come under fire many times, when different police services failed to share information that could have led to the earlier capture of criminals or to more severe punishments. Also, CPIC has been plagued by backlogs of criminal records that have yet to be created or updated by the network users.

## 6. Criminal records are created and stored using more than one system

Criminal records are created according to the laws under which the local police services and courts are governed.[4] The courts and police also use their own internal record management systems and guidelines. Because municipal, provincial, and federal laws differ, and because these laws do allow the various police services and courts to implement processes and, to some extent, use their own discretion in applying the law, a variety of systems has developed over the years. Examples of record management systems used by Canadian police services include:

- Police Reporting and Occurrence System, used by the RCMP
- Police Records Information Management Environment (PRIME BC), used by British Columbia police forces
- Niche Records Management System, used by the OPP and the forty-three Ontario municipal police services.

If a charging police service transfers a local criminal record to the RCMP, they must do so using the RCMP's forms and guidelines. Currently, the RCMP data banks are the only ones that every Canadian police service can access from anywhere across the country.

All Canadian provinces have their own court case tracking systems.[5] Each court has a paper record as well as some type of computer record of each case. The information stored in the court computer database systems tends to be limited to name and date of birth, offence information, the date and outcomes of court appearances, the final decision of the judge, and whether fines have been paid; whereas the hard-copy records are more robust, including specific information on the crime, trial transcripts, and the names of co-accused, victims, witnesses, and so on.

## 7. Problems with multiple and varied criminal records systems

Although most criminal record information is transferred to the RCMP and can be easily accessed by any police service in the country, not all of it is. One needs to know where the criminal record is in order to destroy or remove it.

There is also a growing trend toward making criminal records universally accessible. Alberta, British Columbia, and Ontario police services, for example, are working toward integrating their reporting systems so that all police forces in those provinces can access the same criminal intelligence information. CPIC is an example of a concerted effort at the national level, to share information about crimes and offenders with all Canadian police services. As police record management systems continue to be linked, all criminal records may ultimately be accessible from anywhere in Canada, without the added step of having each record individually transferred to the RCMP.

Not having a single system means that some criminal records may not be accessible to all police services, courts, prospective employers, and others. All local Canadian police services generally have access only to their own records and those held by the RCMP, and there is no guarantee that copies of all records have been transferred to the RCMP. Moreover, records transferred to CPIC may not have been kept current, and there is no legal obligation on police services or the courts to share their criminal record information with others in the criminal justice system, except for files related to youth criminal records. This means that in some cases, a criminal record may never get reported or discovered outside of the charging police service's record management system. Making matters more challenging is that *strictly summary conviction* offences—the least serious types of offences—cannot be included in the RCMP Identification data bank because they are not supported by fingerprints—unless included with another *printable* offence.

## 8.  What are the different criminal record data banks in CPIC?

CPIC includes four criminal record data banks: Investigative, Identification, Intelligence, and Ancillary. It can be confusing to understand what the different data banks are, as their names are similar. For our purposes, the Investigative

The CPIC data banks are often thought to be one data bank, and are commonly referred to simply as CPIC. The RCMP *Identification* data bank is often referred to as the Identification data bank or Ident.

and Identification data banks are the two most relevant. See p. 25 for a sample of a CPIC report showing information being drawn from both of these data banks. Most people have never seen their CPIC reports because the police do not normally allow the public to access them.

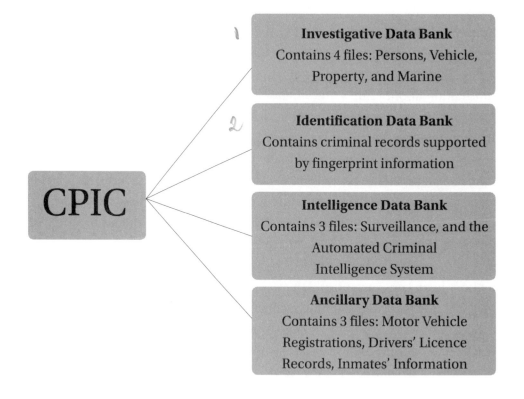

**CPIC**

1  **Investigative Data Bank**
Contains 4 files: Persons, Vehicle, Property, and Marine

2  **Identification Data Bank**
Contains criminal records supported by fingerprint information

**Intelligence Data Bank**
Contains 3 files: Surveillance, and the Automated Criminal Intelligence System

**Ancillary Data Bank**
Contains 3 files: Motor Vehicle Registrations, Drivers' Licence Records, Inmates' Information

.3
**
**

THE CRIMINAL RECORD HELD IN THE CPIC IDENTIFICATION DATA BANKS
AS OF:     MARCH 15, 2004
NAME:
D.O.B:

| DATE & PLACE | CHARGE | DISPOSITION |
|---|---|---|
| JUL 30 1999 OSHAWA | FRAUD UNDER $5000 SEC 380(1)(B) CC | SUSP SENT & PROBATION 12 MOS |
| NOV 05 2002 TORONTO | ASAULT SEC 266 CC | SUSP SENT & PROBATION 3 YRS & (2 DAYS PRE-SENTENCE CUSTODY) & DISCRETIONARY PROHIBITION ORDER SEC 110 CC FOR 5 YRS |

The summary of police information on the criminal record not
intended for sentencing purposes has not been included. This
summary includes withdrawals and dismissals.

ENTRIES ON THE CPIC INVESTIGATIVE DATA BANKS
AS OF:     MARCH 15, 2004
NAME:
D.O.B:

| TYPE OF ENTRY | AGENCY & DATE | PARTICULARS |
|---|---|---|
| PROBATION | TORONTO PS 12-JUN-2003 | SUSPENDED SENTENCE ASSAULT START DATE: 05-NOV-2002 EXPIRY DATE: 04-NOV-2005 CASE: 2003 |
| PROHIBITED | TORONTO PS 11-MAY-2003 | FIREARMS START DATE: 05-NOV-2002 EXPIRY DATE: 04-NOV-2007 CASE: 2003 |

If the person named herein disputes any or all of the
information as it is listed, this report should be considered
null and void. Reliance should then be made solely on
fingerprints. The following should then be applied.

(3 of 4)

CPIC Report

## Investigative Data Bank

The *Investigative* data bank is contained within CPIC itself and includes criminal records broken down into four categories: Persons, Vehicle, Property, and Marine.

| Persons | Vehicle |
|---|---|
| Contains data on individuals who are: charged or wanted by police, parolees, those missing (including children), prohibited from driving, or prohibited from possessing firearms, and others | Contains data on vehicles (including licence plates, motors, and transmissions) that are stolen, abandoned, or wanted in connection with a crime |
| **Property** | **Marine** |
| Contains data on articles, securities, and guns, that are lost, stolen, missing, pawned, or recovered | Contains data on boats that are stolen, missing, abandoned, or wanted in connection with a crime |

There are about seven million records in these four categories. For our purposes, the Persons category is the most relevant. It contains twelve separate classifications.[6] Criminal records in the Investigative data bank are created by authorized CPIC network users. It is important to understand that not all network users are authorized to create criminal records in that data bank. For the most part, authorized network users means all of the police agencies across Canada.

Authorized CPIC network users have discretion over what information to include in the Investigative data bank. They retain responsibility for its accuracy and immediacy, and are the only ones entitled or enabled to alter their records. All records in this data bank must be supported by a *hard-copy operational case-management file*, which must be maintained by the police agency that created the record in CPIC. Police agencies must be able to confirm their CPIC records promptly, 24/7. They must also validate their records six months after entry into CPIC and at least once a year after that.

As the name suggests, the CPIC Investigative data bank is used for investigative purposes only, and, therefore, a specific *hit* should not be used or relied upon without confirmation from the police agency that created the record. An example of a hit would be an indication that a person has been charged with a crime (for which there is no outcome) or is subject to an outstanding criminal warrant. Over the past year, CPIC network users searched the Investigative data bank about twelve million times and created forty-three million transactions

(‹
n

, and deleting records, and messaging other CPIC

divided into three categories of agencies, each with
...ss (based on approval from CPIC's Advisory Com-

These agencies have full peace officer authority
federal or provincial police act. The primary role of
law-enforcement. Police agencies include municipal
l or territorial police, and the RCMP. All of these police
agencies are authorized CPIC network users and, therefore, can *create*, *edit*, and *remove* criminal records in the Investigative data bank.

- **Government agencies with limited law-enforcement roles**:
These agencies have limited law-enforcement responsibilities designated under specific federal and/or provincial legislation. Such responsibilities may include responding to complaints, patrol, and investigating suspected offences, which could lead to a prosecution under the *Criminal Code* or other federal or provincial statutes. The primary role of these agencies is *not* law-enforcement. Examples of these types of agencies include:

◊ Canadian Pacific Railway Police    ◊ Provincial Securities
◊ Canadian National Railway Police       Commission
◊ Canada Border Services Agency    ◊ Environment Canada
◊ Citizenship and Immigration    ◊ Fisheries and Oceans Canada
◊ Canada Revenue Agency    ◊ Provincial Sheriff Services
◊ Canadian Pacific Police    ◊ Federal/Provincial
◊ Ports Canada Police       Correctional Services
◊ Parks Canada    ◊ Via Rail Canada Inc.

These agencies *cannot* usually create, update, or remove criminal records in the Investigative data bank. Sometimes, however, the CPIC Advisory Committee may give them access to create and manage criminal records pursuant to an application for access.

- **Government agencies with a complementary role to law-enforcement**: These agencies have no direct law-enforcement authority but provide assistance to law-enforcement agencies. Examples of these agencies include: the Canadian Security Intelligence Services, provincial Chief Firearms Officers, the Canadian Auto Theft Bureau, Société de l'assurance Automobile du Québec, and Public Works and Government Services Canada (Seized Property and Management Directorate). None of these agencies can create, edit, or remove criminal records from the Investigative data bank.

## Identification Data Bank

The *Identification* data bank is external to, but accessible through CPIC. It contains criminal records *supported by fingerprint information.* That information could include:

- Personal information (names, aliases, date and place of birth)
- Physical characteristics (e.g., sex, height, weight, racial group, eye colour, fingerprints, distinguishing marks, etc.)
- Whether a DNA sample (e.g., hair and blood) has been collected
- An indication of conviction of a sexual offence that has been pardoned or suspended
- A youth criminal record
- Cautionary codes & warnings (e.g., violence, escape custody, mental instability, attempted suicide)
- Detailed charging information (including a classification of the offence, such as violence, theft, fraud, drugs, sex, driving, arson, etc.)
- Detailed disposition information (e.g., dates and jurisdictions of convictions, sentences, discharges, and non-convictions)

As with the Investigative data bank, information from the *Identification* data bank should not be relied upon until the person has been positively identified through fingerprint information.

Unlike CPIC's Investigative data bank, where authorized CPIC network users create, edit, and remove records, *only RCMP staff creates records* in the *Iden-*

*tification* data bank. The records are created based on information submitted by the charging police service. No entry into the Identification data bank is accepted by the RCMP unless it is supported by a set of current and certified fingerprints.

Over the last fifteen years, the number of criminal records in the Identification data bank has remained fairly consistent: in 1997 there were about 2.5 million records; in 2005 there were about 2.9 million records; and in 2012 there were over 3.2 million records. RCMP staff take a number of steps to reduce the possibility of incorrect information being entered into the Identification data bank, including: positively identifying people through their fingerprints, reviewing input forms to ensure the accuracy of charges and dispositions, refusing to make entries until all discrepancies have been resolved, and verifying input before and after releasing it to authorized CPIC network users.

## 9. Are criminal records always created and stored in the RCMP data banks?

With the exception of youth criminal records, there is no legal obligation on police services to report criminal charges and outcomes to the RCMP for inclusion in the Identification data bank.

Further, criminal records relating to strictly summary conviction offences *cannot* be included in the Identification data bank because police cannot legally fingerprint for these offences, and fingerprints are required for records to be included in the Identification data bank.

In 1996, a report by the Privacy Commissioner of Canada stated that:

> "Although the RCMP has never done a study to determine what percentage of all charges are reported and what percentage are not reported, the feeling . . . is that a significant number are not reported to them."

In recent years, technological advancements and the desire of police services to share information has seen most of the criminal record information (for which fingerprints were taken) transferred to the RCMP and included in the Identification data bank. When individuals submit to an RCMP criminal records check and have their fingerprints taken, the data bank from which the report is derived is the Identification data bank.

## 10. What steps are involved in creating a criminal record?

### Charged by the Police

Being charged by the police is the first step in creating a criminal record. Each year, more than half a million people in Canada are charged with a federal offence; almost all of these offences fall under the *Criminal Code*. Other federal laws under which someone may be charged include the *Controlled Drugs and Substances Act*, the *Income Tax Act*, the *Excise Act*, the *Food and Drugs Act*, the *Customs Act*, and the *Immigration and Refugee Protection Act* (to name a few).[7]

### Incident Records and Occurrence Reports

After a charge is laid, the charging police service will create *incident records* and generate an *occurrence report*, using their record management system. Among other things, an incident record could include a host of fragmented information about the accused, such as police notes, newspaper clippings, letters, as well as information about the complainant, the victim, and any witnesses. An occurrence report is a formal report based on incident records. Each year, Canadian police services create an average of about 2.5 million occurrence reports. See pp. 31-33 for a sample Police Occurence Report.

### Fingerprinted and Photographed

After the individual is charged, police will take photographs and fingerprints, pursuant to the *Identification of Criminals Act*. The exemption to this procedure is if the person is charged with a less serious *strictly summary* offence for which fingerprints cannot be taken. Examples of strictly summary offences set out in the *Criminal Code* include: committing an indecent act, being found in a common bawdy house, and loitering.

Practically speaking, the police often charge individuals with more than one offence. Since fingerprints can be taken for most offences, laying more than one charge means the police will be able to take fingerprints for at least one of them.

Consequently, where the person was charged with more than one offence, even strictly summary offence records will be included in the RCMP Identification data bank.

## Court Record

The court is generally notified of criminal charges in one of two ways: an *Information* or *Indictment* is filed with the court for consideration by a judicial official, or a person is arrested and brought before the court for a bail hearing (judicial interim release). The police provide a hard copy of the record to the court. Court staff use the person's name, date of birth, and the police detailed *charging information* to create a criminal record of their own. After that, the charging police and the courts will request information from each other and update one another as the case proceeds towards a final outcome. The police often have access to the court computer system in order to keep apprised of upcoming court appearances, but they do not have the ability to alter the data. See p. 33 for an example of one type of court record, referred to as *an Information*.

| Example of a Police Occurrence Report | | |
|---|---|---|
| **Occurence** | 01-23456789 | |
| **Involvement(s):** | Charged | Male, Age 29 |
| **Name Used:** | John Smith | |
| **Alias(es):** | James Smith | |
| **Address:** | 123 Evergreen Terrace | |
| **D.O.B.:** | 1975-05-02 | |
| **Home Phone:** | 416-123-4567 | |
| | | |
| **Employer:** | Wal-Mart | |
| **Occupation:** | Cashier | |
| **Next of Kin:** | Jane Smith | |
| **Relationship:** | Wife | |
| **Address:** | 123 Evergreen Terrace | |
| **DOB:** | 1976-06-20 | |
| **Home Phone:** | 416-123-4567 | |

## Example of a Police Occurrence Report

| Description: | | |
|---|---|---|
| | | |
| **Height:** 177 cm (5'10") | Mass: 127 kg (279 lbs) | **Build:** Heavy |
| **Complexion:** Light | **Eye Colour:** Brown | **Corrective Lens:** Yes |
| **Hair Colour:** Brown | **Style:** Straight | **Length:** Above ear |
| **Facial Hair:** Yes | **Facial Hair Colour:** Brown | |
| **Speech:** Normal | **Speech Accent:** No | |
| **Racial Origin:** White | | |
| **Driver License:** S-0123456789 | **Place of Issue:** Ontario | |
| **Citizenship:** Canadian | **Place of Birth:** Canada | |
| **Port of Entry:** | **Date of Entry:** | |
| **Deformities:** Tattoo on right arm in Japanese writing | | |
| **Charges:** | 361(1)(b) CCC Fraudulent Use of Credit Card | |
| **Charge Date:** | 2004-02-20 | |
| **Badge Number:** | #01234 DOE | |
| **Arrest Date:** | 2004-02-20          19:40 | |
| **Badge Number:** | #01234 DOE | |
| **Warrant Type:** | | |
| **Release Form:** | Promise to Appear | |
| **Court Location:** | Brampton | |
| **Type:** | Provincial | |
| **Next Court Date:** | 2004-05-15 | |
| **Detained Location:** | | |
| | | |
| **Court Synopsis:** | | |
| **Incident #:** | 01-23456789 | |
| **Date:** | 2004-05-15 | |
| **Badge:** | #01234 DOE | |
| **CPIC Verified:** | Yes | |
| **Queries:** | Yes | |
| **Accused:** | John Smith | |

## Example of a Police Occurrence Report

COUNT 1 FRAUDULENT USE OF CREDIT CARD S. 362(1)(B) CCC

On February 20, 2004, at approximately 1:00 p.m., the accused attended the Sony Store located at 123 East Beaver Drive in Brampton, Ontario. The accused attempted to purchase a 53-inch television and a DVD player. The total value of the items was $4,150.00. The accused used a Capital One Platinum MasterCard with serial number 0123456789, made out in the name of Michael Brown. When the Capital One Platinum MasterCard was swiped through the point-of-sale terminal, the machine stated, "Card not Authorized." The police were then contacted. The police arrived, arrested the accused, and read him his rights. The accused indicated that he understood. The accused was transported to 10 Division where he was released on a promise to appear with a court date of May 15, 2004. Both items were recovered and retained by the store.

PROVINCE OF ONTARIO
PROVINCE DE L'ONTARIO

TORONTO REGION
RÉGION DE TORONTO

Information of
Dénonciation de: James Smith Badge No. 12345

of/de Toronto Police Service

Peace Officer
(occupation/profession)

The informant says
Le dénonciateur

that he/she believes on reasonable grounds that
déclare qu'il a des motifs raisonnables de croire que

John Doe on or about the 29th day of July in the year 2004 in the City of Toronto, in the Toronto Region, did commit Mischief contrary to the Criminal Code

CERTIFIED TO BE A TRUE AND CORRECT COPY OF THE ORIGINAL
COPIE AUTHENTIQUE CERTIFIÉE ET CONFORME A L'ORIGINAL

APR 9 2010

CLERK OF THE COURT
ONTARIO COURT OF JUSTICE
GREFFIER DE LA COUR
COUR DE JUSTICE DE L'ONTARIO

DISCLOSURE

SEP 0 9 2004

**GIVEN**

Sworn before me at the City of Toronto, in the Toronto Region,
Déclaré sous serment devant moi dans la ville de Toronto, dans la région de Toronto,

this
le 29

day of
jour de July 2004
YYYY

A Justice of the Peace in and for the Province of Ontario/Juge de paix dans et pour la Province de l'Ontario

Informant/Dénonciateur

| ☐ Appearance Notice / Citation à comparaître | ☐ Promise to Appear / Promesse de comparaître | ☐ Recognizance for / Engagement pour le | | ☐ Confirmed on / Confirmé (e) le | |

| Date APR 1 8 2005 | ☐ Crown Elects to Proceed / Choix du poursuivant | ☑ Summarily / Procédure sommaire | ☐ By Indictment / Acte d'accusation | ☐ Summary Conviction Offence(s) / Infraction(s) punissable(s) sur déclaration de culpabilité par procédure sommaire |
| | ☐ Accused Elects Trial by / Choix de l'accusé(e) | ☐ Judge (General Division) / Juge seul (Division générale) | ☐ Judge and Jury / Juge et jury | |
| | ☐ Discharged / Libéré | ☐ Committed - / Renvoyé à procès - | ☐ Ordered to Stand Trial - / Astreint en jugement - | ☐ With Consent of Accused and Prosecutor, / Avec le consentement du prévenu et du poursuivant |
| | ☐ Without Taking or Recording - / Sans recueillir ou consigner - | ☐ Any Evidence (or) / de preuve (ou) | ☐ Further Evidence / de preuve supplémentaire | Bail $ / Cautionnement $ |
| | ☐ Accused Elects Trial by a Judge (Provincial Division) / L'accusé(e) choisit d'être jugé(e) (Division provinciale) | | ☐ Absolute Jurisdiction / Juridiction absolue | |
| APR 1 8 2005 | Pleads / Plaidoyer | ☑ Guilty / Coupable | ☐ Not Guilty / Non Coupable | ☐ Withdrawn / Accusation(s) retirée(s) |
| | Found / Décision | ☑ Guilty / Coupable | ☐ Not Guilty / Non Coupable | ☐ In Absentia / Défaut de comparution |
| | | ☐ Absolute Discharge / Absolution inconditionnelle | ☐ Conditional Discharge / Absolution sous condition | |
| | Fined $ / Amende de | & $ s/c waived / $ et de | costs. Time to Pay / $ pour les dépenses. Délai de paiement | |
| | Or / ou | | Date of Birth / Date de naissance | Day/Jour | Mo./Mois | Yr./Année |
| APR 1 1 2005 | Probation for 18 mths. - Suspended Sentence / Période de probation de | | | |
| | Sentenced to Imprisonment for / Peine d'emprisonnement | | | |

(Single Accused - Not more than Two Charges)
(Un seul prévenu - maximum deux accusations)

YC 0924 (rev. 07/93)

OFFICE FOR DISABILITY ISSUES    OFFICE DES AFFAIRES DES PERSONNES HANDICAPÉES
INFORMATION SERVICES FOR BARRIER FREE COURTS    SERVICE D'INFORMATION SUR LES TRIBUNAUX À ACCÈS FACILE
1-800-387-4456    1-800-387-4456
TORONTO AREA 326-0111    RÉGION DE TORONTO 326-0111

Court "Information" Record

### File created in CPIC and in the RCMP Identification data bank

The charging police service may then create a file in the CPIC Investigative data bank and also report the information to the RCMP for inclusion in the Identification data bank. The CPIC file is maintained by the charging police, and ultimately is supposed to be removed once a disposition is made, unless, of course, there is an ongoing prohibition or probation order, or the individual is released on parole.

In reporting the information to the RCMP, the police service must include the person's fingerprint information (taken with ink or digitally). The RCMP assigns a *Fingerprint Section Number (FPS Number)* to the individual's name and date of birth, and a temporary file is opened in the Identification data bank. This temporary file is only accessible to the charging police service or can be disclosed if the individual submits to a criminal record search and provides fingerprints on an RCMP C-216C form (see samples on pp. 35-36). If there is no outcome in the case, the file is supposed to be removed from the Identification data bank after five years, unless there are outstanding warrants related to the charge. In most cases, there is a final outcome in court prior to the five-year period, and the information is then updated in the Identification data bank.

### Final Outcome: Non-Conviction

After an individual is charged, he or she often will appear in court more than once. Court records will be updated to include all these appearances. During the final court appearance, the judge will make a decision. The person will be either convicted or not.

Although the charge may not result in a conviction, in any of the following cases of non-convictions, a criminal file is created at both the local police level and in the federal RCMP Identification data bank.

*Non-convictions* can be one of the following:

- The accused person is *acquitted* or found *not-guilty*.
- The charges are *dismissed* or *withdrawn*.
- The accused person enters into a *peace bond*, which is a legally enforceable promise to keep the peace, to be of good behaviour, and to obey all other terms and conditions ordered by the court for the time period stated (usually one year).

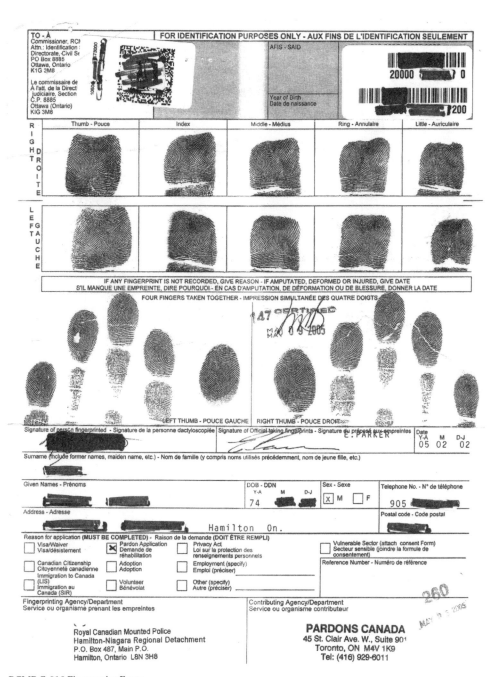

RCMP C-216 Fingerprint Form

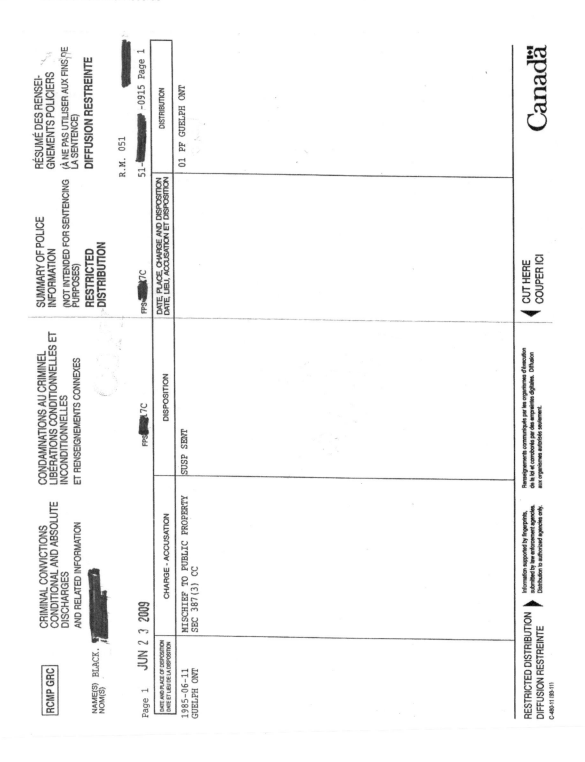

- There is a *stay of proceedings.* This means the court action has been suspended indefinitely or until the occurrence of a condition imposed by the court.
- The accused person is *discharged,* either *absolutely* or *conditionally.* This means that the individual has been *found guilty* but there is *no* conviction. In the case of an absolute discharge there is no punishment. Conditional discharges, however, do carry a punishment, usually a fine payable to the court, and/or probation.

All of the above non-conviction records are accessible to CPIC network users and also will be disclosed in an RCMP criminal record search (submitted with fingerprints). This is a very important point, as most people—criminal justice professionals included—often believe that a non-conviction means there is no criminal record or that all files relating to the charges are automatically destroyed. The individual charged must take steps to ensure that his or her record is removed at all levels.[8]

### Final Outcome: Conviction

If a charge results in a conviction (the person is *found guilty* and *convicted*), the temporary file is updated in the Identification data bank. As with non-convictions, the temporary file of the conviction becomes permanent and accessible to CPIC network users and also will be disclosed in an RCMP criminal record search.

Examples of the types of punishments that can result from a *conviction* and are recorded in the criminal record include:

- **Probation:** This is an order whereby the convicted offender must report to a probation officer for a set period of time, usually one year. The individual is generally required to report on a monthly basis.
- **Fines and Surcharges:** Fines can be ordered on their own or in addition to a probation period. Fines and surcharges are payable to the court.
- **Restitution / Compensation:** These payments are awarded to compensate victims for their injuries. The judge may order these

payments to be paid directly to the injured party or to the court, which will then forward the money to the injured party.

- **Prohibition:** This means that the individual is not permitted to do something. The most common types of prohibitions are driving suspensions and weapons bans. Prohibition orders are often ordered together with a fine.
- **Suspended Sentence:** This means that the judge suspended the jail sentence. Generally, a suspended sentence is accompanied by a fine and/or probation.
- **Conditional Sentence:** This is a more serious form of punishment (approaching imprisonment) and usually means house arrest, with the convicted person being required to wear an electronic bracelet or having a strict schedule for leaving and returning home.
- **Imprisonment:** This is the most serious outcome of all and may include fines, longer probation periods, prohibitions, and lifetime bans.

### Appeal

If the accused person or the prosecutor appeals a court decision, this new information is supposed to be recorded in the Identification data bank, along with the previous information. Since most information inputted into the RCMP Identification data bank originates from the charging police service, and given that those services are not involved in appeals in most cases, changes to dispositions resulting from appeals are not always reported to the RCMP. It is up to the individual wishing to remove his or her record, therefore, to ensure that the criminal record information being removed is complete.

## 11. Are provincial or municipal offences included in criminal record files?

Provincial offences—such as the driving offence of failing to stop at a stop sign—are not criminal and do not form part of a criminal record in a true sense. The same goes for municipal offences, such as making excessive noise.

No legal authority exists for police to fingerprint or photograph someone charged with a provincial or municipal offence. Without that fingerprint information, these charges cannot be submitted to the RCMP for inclusion into the Identification data bank.

That said, the charging police service can create a criminal record in their own data bank as

Having provincial or municipal offences included on a police records check can affect many applications, such as for an RS, employment, career licensing, and so on.

well as in CPIC's Investigative data bank related to provincial and municipal offences. In practice, however, the police will not waste their time doing so unless there is a compelling reason.

If the charging police service includes information about provincial and municipal offences in their own record management system, it could then be disclosed as part of a local police records check. The Parole Board of Canada[9] Local Police Records Check form, needed in Record Suspension (RS) applications, requires the police to include any provincial charges and outcomes stored in the local police system. Therefore, although provincial and municipal offences are not technically criminal, they can be included as part of a criminal record and may be disclosed to important decision-makers.

It is important to note that in some situations, the same conduct could be considered as either a *provincial* or a *criminal* offence. Depending on what the charging police decide, there will be different legal tests and consequences.

For example, if an individual is driving in an unsafe manner, the police can choose to lay a charge of dangerous rather than careless driving. The following chart shows how different the impact can be.

| | Provincial Offence | Criminal Offence | |
|---|---|---|---|
| **Offence** | Careless Driving | Dangerous Driving | |
| **Legislation** | s. 130 *Ontario Highway Traffic Act* | s. 249 *Criminal Code* | |
| **Legal Test** | Driving without due care and attention without resonable consideration for others | Driving in a manner dangerous to the public | |
| **Maximum Sentence** | $1, 000 fine | **Summary** | **Indictment** |
| | 6 months jail | $2,000 fine | 5 years jail |
| | Licence or permit suspended for 2 years | 6 months jail | |
| **Are fingerprints and photographs taken?** | No | Yes | Yes |

|  | Provincial Offence | Criminal Offence | |
|---|---|---|---|
| Can incident or occurrence report be created? | Yes | Yes | Yes |
| Are charges and convictions entered into the RCMP "Investigative" Data Bank? | No | Yes | Yes |
| Are charges and convictions entered into the RCMP "Identification" Data Bank? | No | Yes | Yes |

A similar result can occur in the case of a municipal versus a criminal offence. Take the example of spraying graffiti on property within the City of Toronto:

| | Municipal Offence | Criminal Offence | |
|---|---|---|---|
| Offence: | Spraying Graffiti on Property | Mischief in Relation to Property | |
| Legislation | By-law. 485 City of Toronto, *Municipal Code* | s. 430 *Criminal Code* | |
| Legal Test | Placing, causing or permitting graffiti to be placed on property | Willfully damaging property | |
| Maximum Sentence: | $5, 000 fine | **Summary** | **Indictment** |
| | | $2,000 fine | 2 years jail |
| | | 6 months jail | |
| Are fingerprints and photographs taken? | No | Yes | Yes |
| Can incident or occurrence report be created? | Yes | Yes | Yes |
| Are charges and convictions entered into the RCMP "Investigative" Data Bank? | No | Yes | Yes |
| Are charges and convictions entered into the RCMP "Identification" Data Bank? | No | Yes | Yes |

If, for the same behaviour, someone is charged with a criminal offence instead of a provincial or municipal offence, the consequences are much more severe, both in terms of the record created and the punishment given. In addition, if charged criminally, the individual will need to apply to remove the criminal record from both the local and federal police files.

## 12. How long are criminal records kept?

Criminal records are created and stored by various government bodies, each of which has its own policies and retention schedules. The RCMP, in most cases, retains records in its Identification data bank until the person reaches eighty years of age and has had no criminal activity reported in the past ten years, whereas the retention schedules of other police services vary, and can be anywhere from twenty-five to forty years to permanently.

The courts also have their own record retention time frames, usually from one to forty years (see court letter on p. 43). The criteria used to determine which time frame applies include: type of offence, disposition (outcome in court), age of the individual, continued involvement in criminal activity, and so on. In cases of convictions for serious offences, the records can be kept indefinitely.

Even when the retention time frame has been met, more often than not the record is not automatically removed. People don't want to wait until they are eighty years old (or dead) before their criminal record is removed. It is necessary, therefore, for the individual to take action to ensure that the criminal record is removed as soon as possible.

## 13. Are criminal records removed automatically?

In most cases, criminal records will not be removed automatically. Even in the two following exceptions, the record may not be removed completely:

**Youth Criminal Records.** Generally, youth criminal records are purged from the RCMP's Identification data bank when the non-disclosure date has been reached. However, the individual should take steps to ensure that records have in fact been removed from both the charging police files and the RCMP data bank.

In some cases, where the youth record has been locked in to their adult record,[10] it is not automatically removed and the individual will have to apply for a Record Suspension to remove it. If the youth record was created prior to the *Youth Criminal Justice Act*, 2002, there is a greater chance that the record may have been recorded as an adult record, or that the youth record was created under one of the prior laws that did not provide non-disclosure dates. The result is the same: the youth record may not have been removed, and the individual should double check to make sure it is gone.

**Absolute and Conditional Discharges registered after July 24, 1992**. After one year (for absolute discharges) or three years (for conditional discharges) from the final court date, these records are supposed to be purged from the RCMP Identification data bank. In almost every case, this is done. It is prudent, however, to double check. The file may contain an error showing a conviction or a not-guilty result, in which case it will not fall within the parameters of this removal process and the individual will have to apply to have the record removed.

Absolute and conditional discharges prior to 1992 are sometimes included in this automatic removal process, and the RCMP do readily remove those files when it is brought to their attention.

Although this purge process is federal law and governs the RCMP, it does not in any way have authority over the remaining police services and the courts throughout Canada. This means that absolute and conditional discharge records will be retained according to the varying schedules and policies of each police service and court.

Ontario

| | | | | |
|---|---|---|---|---|
| Ministry of<br>the Attorney General | Ontario Court<br>of Justice | Toronto Region<br>Old City Hall | 60 Queen Street West<br>Room 277<br>Toronto ON M5H 2M4 | Telephone/Téléphone<br>(416) 327-6297<br>Fax/Télécopieur<br>(416) 327-6813 |
| Ministère<br>du Procureur<br>général | Cour de justice<br>de l'Ontario | Région de Toronto<br>Ancien Hôtel de Ville | 60 rue Queen ouest<br>Bureau 277<br>Toronto ON M5H 2M4 | |

March 26, 2010

ACCUSED: ▪▪▪▪▪▪▪▪▪▪▪▪▪▪
D.O.B: **February** ▪▪
CHARGE: **Assault** ▪▪▪▪▪▪▪▪▪▪   **(2 offences)**
DISPOSITION: **Unable to confirm**
DISPOSITION DATE: **May 29, 1981**

The Government Records Storage Centre, which holds all court records **for Old City Hall cases**, cannot locate the Information based on the disposition date provided.

The court has conducted a thorough search of our database and files, and can find no record of criminal conviction to match the above-named for a certified copy of a conviction based on the information provided.

Please note the retention period for indictable conviction is forty years and a summary conviction is destroyed after seven years.

Sincerely,

S. Mangru
Client Service Representative
Records Department
Old City Hall court

Court Letter stating Records are kept for 7 or 40 years

## Quiz

**1. What information could be included in a criminal record?**
    a.  Fingerprints and Photographs
    b.  Physical characteristics
    c.  Details about the offence
    d.  Cautionary codes (e.g., violent, escape risk, mentally unstable, suicidal)
    e.  All of the above

**2. Who creates criminal records?**
    a.  Police
    b.  Courts
    c.  Prisons
    d.  Parole Officers
    e.  All of the above

**3. The Canadian Police Information Centre (CPIC):**
    a.  Is a communication tool used by police services and government agencies
    b.  Gives network users access to the Investigative data bank
    c.  Is Canada's complete and accurate source of criminal records
    d.  All of the above
    e.  (a) and (b)

**4. What is the difference between a non-conviction and a conviction?**
    a.  Convictions may include fines or imprisonment
    b.  Convictions may include suspended or conditional sentences
    c.  Non-convictions include acquittals, withdrawn and dismissed charges, and stays of proceedings
    d.  Non-convictions include discharges
    e.  All of the above

**5. Strictly summary conviction offences:**
    a.  Are the least serious types of crime
    b.  Include causing a disturbance, communicating for the purposes of prostitution, and being intoxicated in a public place
    c.  Do not give charging police services the right to take someone's fingerprints or photographs
    d.  Are generally not included in the Identification data bank
    e.  All of the above

### 6. True or false?
   a.  The RCMP is Canada's only police service
   b.  CPIC is only used by police services
   c.  The Identification data bank contains information on individuals who are subject to warrants
   d.  Information in the Investigative and Identification data banks should be confirmed by fingerprints before being used or relied upon
   e.  Provincial and municipal offences always form part of someone's criminal record

Answer Key: 1 (e), 2 (e), 3 (e), 4 (e), 5 (e), 6 false, false, false, true, false

## End Notes

1. The *Youth Criminal Justice Act (YCJA)* defines *young persons* as those twelve years of age or older, but less than eighteen years of age.

2. When reference is made to *charging police*, in this book, it means the local police service that charged the individual.

3. Provincial Police Services: Newfoundland and Labrador, *Royal Newfoundland Constabulary (RNC)* | Quebec, Sûreté du Québec (SQ), also commonly referred to as *Quebec Provincial Police (QPP)*| Ontario, *Ontario Provincial Police (OPP)*. The RCMP acts as the provincial and territorial police for 7 provinces and our 3 territories, as well as policing the less populated rural areas throughout the country. This means that the charging police in these areas will be the RCMP even where the charge is for a minor offence.

4. Each province has its own legislation: e.g., B.C. *Police Act, Ontario Police Services Act*, Nova Scotia *Police Act.*

5. Each province has its own court management system(s): e.g., B.C. JUSTIN, and Ontario ICON and FRANK.

6. The twelve classifications are: Wanted Persons, Aliases, Prohibited Persons, Probation, Persons charged with Indictable or *Criminal Code* Offence, Pointer Persons, Observation Persons, Parolees, Persons refused certificates for Firearms, Missing Persons, Elopees from mental institutions, and Known Associates.

7. Percentage of charges per Statute: 94% *Criminal Code*, 6% *Controlled Drugs and Substances Act,* 1% Other Federal Statutes, 1% *Youth Criminal Justice Act*. Police-reported crime statistics in Canada, 2010, by Shannon Brennan and Mia Dauvergne, released July 21, 2011. Component of Statistics Canada catalogue no. 85-002-X Juristat. [Note: total may exceed 100% due to rounding]

8. Some records will be purged automatically from the RCMP Identification data bank after a set period of time (discussed in Chapter 7). Different rules apply to youth criminal records, (discussed in Chapter 3).

9. Previously the *National Parole Board of Canada.*

10. A youth record is *locked* in to an adult record if the person reoffends as an adult, and the non-disclosure date for the youth charge has not been reached.

Chapter Two

# Who Can Access Criminal Records And How?

## Who can Access Criminal Records?

## How to Obtain Criminal Record Information

Ever wonder who can access criminal record files? Well, for starters, every individual can access his or her own police and court records. So, too, can the police services and court offices that created the files. If the record is held at the RCMP (as most are), then CPIC network users—namely, all Canadian police services and other authorized government agencies—can access them, too!

So, how does a person get criminal record information and what kind of information will be revealed? Well, this depends on *where* the information is coming from and *what type* of search is being conducted. As you have probably figured out by now, the number of places maintaining criminal record information and the variety of information in each is quite extensive. To help simplify things, this chapter will provide an overview of each of the processes for obtaining the record information.

## ACCESSING YOUR OWN CRIMINAL RECORDS?

# 1. Can individuals access their own criminal records?

Yes. Everyone has the right to get information about his or her Canadian criminal record. Freedom of information laws allow individuals to make requests to the RCMP, the provincial police, the local police, or to government offices that may hold their criminal record information. Keep in mind however, that law-enforcement agencies may not provide the entire content of the criminal record file, and will usually only give an overview of the charges and their outcomes. Furthermore, names of people co-accused, witnesses, and victims will not usually be disclosed.

# 2. Who else can access criminal records?

Law-enforcement agencies and other authorized government departments can access criminal record information—without the individual's knowledge or consent. Every police service can access its own criminal record data bank as well as that of the RCMP through CPIC. Other government agencies, which have been designated as CPIC *network users*,[1] can also access the RCMP data bank.

But what about third parties such as prospective employers, landlords, neighbours, spouses, or schools? Well, apart from youth records, third parties need the individual's written permission to obtain a criminal record held by the police. If the individual would like the information to be forwarded directly to someone else (such as an employer), both local police services and the RCMP require that the individual give written permission by submitting a *Consent for Disclosure of Criminal Record Information* with the search request. That's good news. But the reality is, if someone is applying for a job or volunteer position where the employer requires a police records check, the applicant will be forced either to let the employer see the search results or to lose the job.

## HOW TO OBTAIN CRIMINAL RECORD INFORMATION

How criminal record information can be obtained depends on *where* it is stored—namely, at the local police, RCMP, court, or other government office.

## 3. What is a Local Police Records Check (LPRC)?

Individuals can request their criminal record information from local police services, through a *Local Police Records Check (LPRC)*. Police services, however, can refuse to disclose some or all of their records if doing so could (among other things) invade the personal privacy of third parties (e.g., victims, witnesses, co-accused, etc.), threaten anyone's health or safety, or harm law-enforcement efforts.

Each police service has its own policies concerning what information they will disclose and how that information will be organized and presented. Generally, police services disclose all records that they determine to be relevant to the purpose for which the check is being requested (e.g., employment, vulnerable sector check, etc.).

The local police service conducts a search of police records held in its own data bank, and usually includes a CPIC check as well. Each local police service uses its own *record management system* to create its police record reports.

An LPRC discloses criminal charges resulting in convictions and usually includes a wide variety of other information—such as information about pending charges, charges that resulted in non-convictions, and information about alleged incidents where no charges were laid. Often, the LPRC will even disclose non-criminal charges such as provincial driving infractions. An LPRC check may also include information from other police services (both in and outside of Canada).[2]

### Example of Local Police Records Check

**Acme Police Service**

| Details of Police Records Check - Conducted for Employment | | | |
|---|---|---|---|
| **Name:** | John Smith | Certified on: 2013-01-24 | |
| **D.O.B.:** | 1978-09-03 | | |
| **The following is a detailed account of police information for the above named:** | | | |
| **Date of Disposition** | **Charge** | **Disposition** | Court |
| 2004-07-20 | Assault | Withdrawn | Acme, ON |
| 2006-01-13 | Theft | 1 yr Probation | Acme, ON |
| 2003-06-06 | Attempted Suicide | Involvement* | O |

V = Victim          W = Witness          C = Complainant          A = Accused
S = Suspect          O = Other

To request an LPRC, an individual will need to take two pieces of government is-sued identification (one of which must have a photo) to a local or regional police service and pay a processing fee. Depending on the policies of the individual police service, the results will either be mailed to the individual or can be picked up. The results will contain an original police stamp (or seal), the date the report was generated, and the signature of the police records manager.

Worth noting is that an LPRC is commonly referred to by many names:

- Criminal Background Check
- Criminal Check
- Criminal History Check
- Criminal Record Search
- Police Clearance Check
- Police Information Check
- Police Record Check
- Police Reference Check
- Police Security Check

These names can be confusing and give an inaccurate impression of what the police are certifying. An LPRC does not certify whether the individual has a criminal record elsewhere, nor is it a background check.

## 4. What is a Parole Board of Canada LPRC?

As part of the Record Suspension (RS) process, applicants must obtain LPRCs in the form prescribed by the Parole Board of Canada (PBC). The PBC requires that an LPRC be obtained from the local police where the individual lives at the time the application is submitted, and for each jurisdiction where the applicant has lived for a period of three months or more within the past five years. Using the PBC's standard form, the local police are required to disclose the existence and details of convictions, if any, which are in addition to those appearing on CPIC. Local police are also required to provide all information related to incidents involving police and all charges regardless of the outcome, including convictions and charges under provincial laws.

The police charge a fee for this type of search. The individual must go to each relevant police service in person and present two pieces of identification, one of which must be government issued (such as a driver's license) containing the person's name and date of birth, photograph, and signature. This type of police records check (see sample on pp. 51-52) is only valid for a period of six months; consequently, individuals should not request this search until they are certain that they are eligible to apply for their RS and that all other documents have been acquired.

## 5. What is a CPIC Check?

A CPIC check involves a search of criminal records held in various RCMP data banks.

**RCMP Investigative Data Bank.** A CPIC check of the Investigative data bank can reveal whether a person has been charged with a crime for which there is no outcome—for example, if a person is subject to an outstanding warrant, or if someone is on probation or parole. These records are created, maintained, and under the authority of the charging police, even though they are held at the federal level. All law-enforcement agencies and other government CPIC network users can access information in this data bank.

Parole Board of Canada    Commission des libérations conditionnelles du Canada

**Protected when completed**

# Local Police Records Check Form

### For the purpose of a Record Suspension Application
### Please print clearly using blue or black ink. You must answer all questions.

## SECTION A: PERSONAL INFORMATION – You must answer all questions.

1. **What is your full legal name?** (You must fill in your name and date of birth at the top of page 2 as well.)

   Last Name: _____ Given Name(s): _____

2. **Have you ever used another name other than your legal name above?**

   NO ☐    YES ☐ → If YES, write these other names below or your application will be returned to you.

| Previous Last Name(s) | Previous Given Name(s) |
|---|---|
|  |  |
|  |  |
|  |  |

3. **What is your gender?** MALE ☐  FEMALE ☐    4. **What is your date of birth?** Y Y Y Y M M D D

5. **Do you have a Driver's Licence?** NO ☐  YES ☐ → If YES, what is your Driver's Licence number?

   Number: _____ Province: _____

## SECTION B: MAILING AND RESIDENCE INFORMATION – You must answer all questions.

6. **What is your mailing address?**

   _____

   Apartment/House Number and Street Address    City/Town    Province    Postal Code    Country

7. **What is your telephone number?** (_____) _____ - _____

8. **What addresses have you lived at in the last 5 years?** Include your current address. **P.O. Boxes will not be accepted.**

| Apartment/House Number and Street Address | City/Town | Province | Country | From Y Y Y Y M M | To Y Y Y Y M M |
|---|---|---|---|---|---|
| Current Address |  |  |  |  | Present |
| Previous Address |  |  |  |  |  |
| Previous Address |  |  |  |  |  |
| Previous Address |  |  |  |  |  |

## SECTION C: APPLICANT AUTHORIZATION – You must sign and date here.

9. **You must write in the name of the Police Service, and then <u>you</u> must sign and date this form.**

   I hereby authorize (write in name of Police Service here) _____
   to release to the Parole Board of Canada information that the Police is allowed to divulge.

   Sign here: _____ Date: Y Y Y Y M M D D
   (Applicant's Signature)

10. **Ask the Police Service to fill in the <u>back</u> of this form.** Include this form in your application with the front side filled in **by you** and the back side filled in by the **Police Service.**

**Please turn this form over. →**

Parole Board of Canada • *Toll-free Info line 1-800-874-2652 – www.recordsuspension.gc.ca*

Canada

■✦■ Parole Board of Canada

Commission des libérations conditionnelles du Canada

**Protected when completed**

# Local Police Records Check Form

**For the purpose of a Record Suspension Application**

**Please print clearly using blue or black ink. You must answer all questions.**

## SECTION D: FOR POLICE USE ONLY. DO NOT WRITE IN THIS SECTION.

Indicate the full legal name and date of birth of the applicant provided on the front of this form:

Full legal name: _____ Date of birth: [ Y Y Y Y M M D D ]

**Are There Convictions in Addition to Those Appearing on CPIC?** ☐ NO ☐ YES

**Conviction(s) in Addition to Those Appearing on CPIC**

| Offence Description | Sentence | Place of Sentence | Arresting Police Service | Date of Sentence Y Y Y Y M M D D |
|---|---|---|---|---|
| | | | | |
| | | | | |
| | | | | |
| | | | | |
| | | | | |
| | | | | |
| | | | | |

**List all Information Related to Incidents Involving Police and All Charges Regardless of Disposition Including Provincial Convictions/Charges.**

| Nature of Occurrence | Outcome | File Number | Date of Occurrence Y Y Y Y M M D D |
|---|---|---|---|
| | | | |
| | | | |
| | | | |
| | | | |

**Police Representative Information:**

Police Service Name: _____

Police Representative Name: _____ Telephone Number: ( _____ ) ___-_____

Signature: _____

Date: [ Y Y Y Y M M D D ]  Internal Use Only [ ]

Please put Police Service seal or stamp here.

PBC/CLCC 0301E (2012)

Individuals who want access to their personal criminal records held in the Investigative data bank cannot make the request directly to the RCMP, rather, they must make an LPRC or Freedom of Information request to the local police service that created the record in CPIC. The extent of the information disclosed will depend on the privacy laws and the internal policies of the local police service that created it.

Here is a sample of a CPIC Check of the Investigative data bank.

## Sample of CPIC Check: Investigative Data Bank

**Entries on the CPIC Investigative Data Banks**

| As of: | 2004-03-15 | |  |
|---|---|---|---|
| **Name:** | John Doe | | |
| **D.O.B.:** | 1978-09-03 | | |
| **Type of Entry** | **Agency & Date** | **Particulars** | |
| **Probation** | **Toronto PS** | **Suspended Sentence** | |
| | 2003-06-06 | Assault | |
| | | Start Date: | 2003-02-20 |
| | | End Date: | 2005-02-19 |
| | | Case: | 2003.123456 |
| **Prohibition** | **Vancouver PD** | **Firearms** | |
| | 2004-03-16 | Start Date: | 2004-02-12 |
| | | End Date: | 2005-02-11 |
| | | Case: | 2005.789101 |

If the person named herein disputes any or all of the information as it is listed, this report should be considered null and void. Reliance should then be made solely on fingerprints.

**Identification Data Bank.** A check of the Identification data bank shows a person's criminal record supported by fingerprint information. Although the information in this data bank originates from the local charging police services, the RCMP uses it to create and maintain its own records. Both individuals and CPIC network users can make a request to the RCMP for information held in the Identification data bank.

Depending on who is requesting access and the level of detail they require, a variety of information can be obtained from this data bank:

- **Criminal Name Index.** Only shows if a criminal record (which has not been pardoned or suspended) exists in the Identification data bank for a given name.

- **Criminal Records II.** If a record exists, this output will only provide the name, date of birth, and criminal convictions.
- **Criminal Record Synopsis.** This level of output is the most robust and contains personal information, physical characteristics, detailed charging and disposition information (including non-convictions), cautionary codes warning others about the person, and an indication of whether a sample of the person's DNA has been taken.

## 6. What is a Certified RCMP Criminal Record Report?

The RCMP Identification Data Bank contains criminal records supported by the submission of fingerprints. Both CPIC network users and individuals can access information in this data bank. Individuals can make an application directly to the RCMP either under the federal *Access to Information Act* and the *Privacy Act* (while this report may provide valuable information, it will not be acceptable for most applications requiring a certified criminal record report) or by requesting a certified RCMP report. For a certified report, fingerprints must be submitted to the RCMP using form C-216C together with a small processing fee. Individuals commonly request this type of report because it is required for many applications, including the following:

- Adoptions
- Foreign Travel
- Employment or Volunteer Work

- Immigration or Citizenship
- Name Change
- RS Application

The RCMP will search the Identification data bank to determine if the fingerprints match a record in their system. In addition to detailed charging information, this data bank also contains information about the outcome of the case and whether the information has been distributed elsewhere (such as to Citizenship and Immigration Canada or the FBI, etc.).

If the individual wishes to have the search results sent directly to a third party, as mentioned previously, the individual must give the RCMP permission to do this through a Consent for Disclosure of Criminal Record Information form.

If no criminal record exists, then a certified result stating this fact will be provided. (See p. 56.)

If, however, a criminal record *does* exist, then a certified report, similar to the following, will be provided. (See p. 57-58.)

Certified RCMP reports, from the Identification data bank, are divided into two sections:

- **Criminal Convictions, Conditional and Absolute Discharges, and Related Information** (the first three columns on the left side). The first column shows the final court date and the location of the court. The second column shows the charge and may include the relevant legislation. The third column shows details about the final disposition (outcome) and any punishment, such as whether there was a fine, jail time, probation, and so on. The information on this left side of the report shows charges that resulted in a finding of guilt and is more readily accessible than the information on the right side of the page.

  In the past, fingerprints were taken by using ink and rolling out the fingers onto the C-216C form—commonly referred to as the dirty method. Over time, this method is being replaced by digital fingerprinting.

- **Restricted Distribution—Summary of Police Information** (the two columns on the right side). The first column in this restricted section shows only information related to charges that did not result in a finding of guilt—such as withdrawn and dismissed charges. This information is *not supposed to be* as readily accessible because it deals with charges where there was no finding of guilt. Whether an RCMP report provided to a third party will include the Restricted Distribution information depends on why the information is requested, the purpose for which the information will be used, and who made the request. However, as long as there is anything on this side of the page, the individual still has an RCMP Fingerprint Section number (FPS) associated with his or her name and, therefore, runs the risk of having the record discovered.

  The final column in this report shows where the RCMP has distributed

Royal Canadian Gendarmerie royale
Mounted Police du Canada

1200 Vanier Parkway 1200 promenade Vanier
Ottawa, Ontario Ottawa (Ontario)
K1A 0R2 K1A 0R2

Our File Notre référence

Reference Number Numéro de référence

Dear Sir/Madame:

This certifies that a search of the National Criminal Records repository maintained by the RCMP concerning the person whose fingerprints, name, and date of birth appear below could not be associated to any existing Criminal Record of conviction which may be disclosed in accordance with Federal Laws.

Madame, Monsieur,

La présente atteste que la recherche effectuée au répertoire national des casiers judiciaires tenu à jour par la Gendarmerie royale du Canada (GRC) concernant la personne dont les empreintes digitales, le nom et date de naissance apparaissent ci-dessous n'a révélé l'existence d'aucun dossier ou relevé de condamnation qui peut être divulgué en vertu des lois fédérales.

Application Type/Genre de demande:
Application Specifics/Détails sur la demande:
Date Fingerprinted/Date de prélèvement des empreintes:

Applicant Full Name/
Nom complet du
demandeur :

Date of Birth/
Date de naissance :

Sex/
Sexe :

Address/Adresse :

Date Criminal Record Search Completed / Date de la recherche du casier judiciaire :

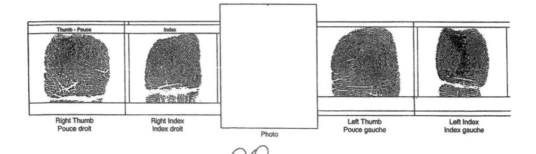

| Thumb - Pouce | Index | | Left Thumb | Left Index |

Right Thumb
Pouce droit

Right Index
Index droit

Photo

Left Thumb
Pouce gauche

Left Index
Index gauche

Guylaine A. Dansereau
Director / Directrice
Canadian Criminal Real Time / Services canadiens d'identification
Identification Services  criminelle en temps réel

(2006-05) RTID/ITR 100.01  v1.0.4.1.2312
Note: The fingerprint form originally submitted to process this application has been destroyed. The provisions of the Privacy Act pertaining to access, collection, accuracy, completeness and amending incorrect data apply. This information is retained in PIB CMP/P-PU-030, P-PU-065, P-PE-810 and P-PE-811.

Remarque : La formule dactyloscopique originale transmise aux fins du traitement de cette demande a été détruite. Les dispositions de la Loi sur la protection des renseignements personnels régissant l'accès aux renseignements, la collecte, l'exactitude, l'exhaustivité et la modification des données s'appliquent. Cette information se trouve dans les dossiers PIB CMP/P-PU-030, P-PU-065, P-PE-810 et P-PE-811.

Canada

RCMP Report stating "No Criminal Record"

Royal Canadian Gendarmerie royale
Mounted Police du Canada

1200 Vanier Parkway  1200 promenade Vanier
Ottawa, Ontario  Ottawa (Ontario)
K1A 0R2  K1A 0R2

Our File  Notre référence

Reference Number  Numéro de référence

Dear Sir/Madame:

This certifies that a search of the National Criminal Records repository maintained by the RCMP using the fingerprints dated submitted under the name and date of birth of the subject indicated below has resulted in a **POSITIVE IDENTIFICATION** to fingerprints registered under the criminal FPS Number

The attached contains criminal record information that is releasable in accordance with Federal Laws.

Application Type/Genre de demande:
Date Fingerprinted/Date de prélèvement des empreintes:
Application Specifics/Détails sur la demande:

Applicant Full Name/
Nom complet du
demandeur :
Address/Adresse :

Madame, Monsieur,

La présente certifie qu'une recherche dans le répertoire national des casiers judiciaires tenu par la GRC à partir des empreintes digitales prélevées le 2009-08-11 sur la personne dont le nom et la date de naissance figurent ci-dessous a produit une **IDENTIFICATION POSITIVE** avec le dossier dactyloscopique enregistré sous le numéro FPS 101422C.

Le document ci-joint fourni les renseignements contenus dans le casier judiciaire pouvant être divulgués en vertu des lois fédérales.

Date of Birth/
Date de naissance :

Sex/
Sexe :

Date Criminal Record Verified / *Date de la vérification du casier judiciaire*

Certified By/Certifié par:  Date:  FPS:

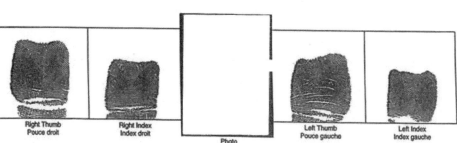

Right Thumb  Right Index    Left Thumb  Left Index
Pouce droit  Index droit    Pouce gauche  Index gauche
  Photo

Guylaine A. Dansereau
Director / Directrice
Canadian Criminal Real Time / Services canadiens d'identification
Identification Services  criminelle en temps réel

FPS Barcode / Code à barres FPS

(2006-08) RTID/ITR 102.01  v1.0.5.0021

Note: The fingerprint form originally submitted to process this application has been destroyed. The provisions of the Privacy Act pertaining to access, collection, accuracy, completeness and amending incorrect data apply. This information is retained in PIB CMP/P-PU-030, P-PU-065, P-PE-610 and P-PE-611.

Remarque : La formule dactyloscopique originale transmise aux fins de traitement de cette demande a été détruite. Les dispositions de la *Loi sur la protection des renseignements personnels* régissant l'accès aux renseignements, la collecte, l'exactitude, l'exhaustivité et la modification des données s'appliquent. Cette information se trouve dans les dossiers PIB CMP/P-PU-030, P-PU-065, P-PE-610 et P-PE-611.

RCMP Report stating a Criminal Record Does Exist

| RCMP GRC | CRIMINAL CONVICTIONS CONDITIONAL AND ABSOLUTE DISCHARGES AND RELATED INFORMATION | CONDAMNATIONS AU CRIMINEL LIBERATIONS CONDITIONNELLES ET INCONDITIONNELLES ET RENSEIGNEMENTS CONNEXES |
|---|---|---|

Names(s) / Nom(s)  John Doe

Page 1  2009-17-08  FPS 123456A

| DATE AND PLACE OF DISPOSITION / DATE ET LIEU DE LA DISPOSITION | CHARGE - ACCUSATION | DISPOSITION |
|---|---|---|
| 1998-02-03 TORONT ONT | THEFT UNDER $5,000 SEC 332(1) CC | $500 1-D 20 days |
| 2000-02-20 OSHAWA ONT | DRIVING WITH MORE THAN 80 MGS OF ALCOHOL IN BLOOD SEC 253(B) CC | $600 1-D 25 DAYS & PROHIBITED FROM DRIVING FOR 1 YEAR |
| 2001-05-10 EXETER ONT | OBSTRUCT PEACE OFFICER SEC 129(A) CC | $400 |
| 2004-07-01 OTTAWA ONT | POSSESSION OF A SCHEDULE SUBSTANCE SEC 4(I) CDS ACT | $100 |

RESTRICTED DISTRIBUTION / DIFFUSION RESTREINTE

Information supported by fingerprints, submitted by law enforcement agencies. Distribution to authorized agencies only.

---

| SUMMARY OF POLICE INFORMATION (NOT INTENDED FOR SENTENCING PURPOSES) RESTRICTED DISTRIBUTION | RESUME DES RENSEIGNEMENTS POLICIERS (A NE PAS UTILISER AUX FINS DE LA SENTENCE) DIFFUSION RESTREINTE |
|---|---|

FPS 123456A  Page 1

| DATE, PLACE, CHARGE AND DISPOSITION / DATE, LIEU, ACCUSATION ET DISPOSITION | DISTRIBUTION |
|---|---|
| 1991-07-11 ASSAULT SEC. 266 CC - WITHDRAWN (METRO TORONTO PF 340-91) | FBI WASH DC USA 741 763 K1 |
| 1995-11-27 DRIVING WHILE ABILITY IMPAIRED SEC 253(A) CC - ACQUITTED (WHITBY OPP 0176-95) | X01 0PP EXETER ONT 06-17-82 |

CUT HERE / COUPER ICI

Renseignements communiqués par les organismes d'execution de la loi et corrobores par des empreintes digitales. Diffusion aux organismes autorises seulement.

Canada

Sample Certified RCMP Criminal Record Report

the information. Common places of distribution include other law-enforcement agencies and other government agencies, both domestic and foreign.

## 7. What is a Freedom of Information request?

Any individual can make a *Freedom of Information (FOI)* request to any organization covered by federal, provincial, or municipal privacy laws. The type of information available in an FOI search includes medical information, social insurance number information, criminal record information, and so on. This type of request also can be known by different names—*Personal Information*, or *Access to Information*—depending on the jurisdiction and the individual police service.

The person must first decide what type of information is sought and which organization is most likely to have the information. Otherwise, it is too cumbersome for the authorities to check all possible data banks. The application process and the way the information is presented vary depending on which government office is providing it.

Criminal records are most commonly held by local or regional police services and the RCMP. Privacy laws at every level give everyone the right to request access to their own criminal record information. A standard form is submitted to the relevant police service, along with a small processing fee.

Records must be disclosed unless they fall within an exemption. If disclosing some or all of a record would invade the personal privacy of third parties, threaten anyone's health or safety, or harm law-enforcement efforts, then an institution may refuse to disclose it. This could be the case, for example, if the police want to keep a suspect's identity secret for an ongoing investigation. In these situations, the police service could provide partial disclosure with a letter explaining the reasons for non-disclosure of the rest of the information.

If a police service refuses to disclose all or part of an individual's criminal record, an appeal can be made to the appropriate information and privacy commissioner. Depending on the jurisdiction, the appeal process may include mediation. If there is no settlement at the mediation stage, an adjudicator will review the application and may investigate it, which could lead to a formal hearing and decision. A decision of the privacy commission can also be appealed to the court and ultimately decided there.

The Personal Information Request form on p. 61 is used to obtain information from a federal government institution under the *Access to Information Act* and the *Privacy Act.*

## 8.   What is a Vulnerable Sector Check?

Police Records checks are mandated by law for employees and volunteers of organizations dealing with *vulnerable people*. Vulnerable people are those who because of age, disability, or other circumstances are less able to protect themselves from harm—such as children or the disabled.

When the police conduct a Vulnerable Sector Check (VSC), they provide a more comprehensive report. For example, a VSC will disclose whether the individual is a pardoned sex offender, whereas the *Criminal Records Act* ordinarily prohibits the disclosure of criminal records that have been pardoned or suspended. It may also disclose other types of information if the police believe it to be pertinent. The VSC must be requested from the local police service and must include the person's written consent. The police usually charge a small processing fee for this service. For the consent to be considered legal, the person must provide:

- Personal information (e.g., name, sex, date and place of birth, and address)
- Two pieces of identification, one of which must be government-issued and includes name, date of birth, signature, and photograph
- The name of the organization (or person) for which the job or volunteer position is sought
- A description of the position being applied for, and
- A statement that the applicant understands what type of information could be disclosed to the organization.

The police will generally release the *initial* results only to the individual. Those results will indicate if a criminal record matches the information submitted. If it

Government    Gouvernement
of Canada    du Canada

# Info Source

**Privacy Act**

# Personal Information Request Form

*Protected when completed*

For official use only

---

**Step 1**
Determine which federal government institution is most likely to hold personal information about you. Decide whether you wish to submit an informal request for the information or a formal request under the *Privacy Act*. If you wish to make an informal request, contact the appropriate institution. The address can likely be found in *Info Source* publications which are available across Canada, generally in major public and academic libraries, constituency offices of federal Members of Parliament and most federal government public enquiry and service offices.

**Step 2**
To apply for personal information about you under the *Privacy Act*, complete this form. Describe the information being sought and provide any relevant details necessary to help the institution find it. If you require assistance, refer to *Info Source (Sources of Federal Government Information)* for a description of personal information banks held by the institution or contact its Privacy Coordinator.

**Step 3**
Forward the personal information request form to the Privacy Coordinator of the institution holding the information. The address is listed in the "Introduction" to *Info Source*.

**Step 4**
When you receive an answer to your request, review the information to determine whether you wish to make a further request under the Act. You also have the right to complain to the Privacy Commissioner should you believe that you have been denied any of your rights under the Act.

---

**Federal Government Institution**

---

**I wish to examine the information**

☐ As it is          ☐ All in English          ☐ All in French

**Provide details regarding the information being sought**

---

**Method of access preferred**

☐ Receive copies of originals          ☐ Examine originals in government offices

**Name of applicant**

---

Street, address, apartment                    City or town

---

Province                    Postal Code                    Telephone number

---

I request access to personal information about myself under the *Privacy Act* as I am a Canadian citizen, permanent resident or another individual, including an inmate, present in Canada

Signature                    Date

---

The personal information provided on this form is protected under the provisions of the *Access to Information Act* and the *Privacy Act*.

TBC 350-58 (Rev. 2000/06/19)

**Canadä**

does, a criminal record can only be *confirmed* by the *submission* of the person's *fingerprints*. Whether a record is confirmed or there is no record, the police service will first obtain the applicant's consent before disclosing this information to the organization.

## 9.  What is not disclosed in an LPRC?

Additional screening used by those working with vulnerable people includes: in-depth interviews, psychological exams, buddy system work teams, progress reports, and reference checks.

It is important to note that police records checks can only disclose information accessible through the local police service and cannot be taken as an all-inclusive background investigation of an individual. A police report stating that no record exists, therefore, cannot be taken to mean that the individual has not, or will not, commit a crime. When screening individuals for employment or volunteer positions, it is up to the employer to have appropriate interview and screening processes. In the case of those working with vulnerable people, it is advisable that special, comprehensive, and ongoing screening be conducted.

## 10. Obtaining Court Records

While most court records are within the public domain, finding specific court records can be a challenge. Courts normally have access to criminal cases that have been tried at their court, limited access to cases tried at other courts in the same province, but do not have access to local police or RCMP records. In practice, when individuals require a copy of their criminal records (as opposed to a specific court record), the courts usually direct them to the local police service, which has access to its own criminal records (including court outcomes) as well as those records located at the RCMP.

If the correct personal and case information is given to the court, however, the individual will be provided with a copy of specific court information. Such information can be presented in a number of different ways, depending on the policies of the individual court office and the type of request (e.g., for fine payment purposes or for an RS application). If the names of the parties, the final court date, and/or the court file number cannot be provided, the court will not usually be able to find and disclose the records. Furthermore, records that have been sealed or destroyed according to the court's retention policies and other provincial and federal laws will not be available.

Following are samples of the Ontario Court ICON Report (often used for fine payment purposes), the PBC Court Information form required for RS applications, and a Court Letter stating some common reasons why records cannot be provided.

```
IISCD    22/03/10 13:07:19  ICON INQUIRY SUBSYSTEM          TAT
                                  COUNT DISPOSITION
CASE: 481499   OO OFFENDER:
COUNT: 0001      #COUNTS: 0001 DOCKT DT:   LINE: 0000      APPRNC: FA        0.01
JUD: 3                        JM CLERK: PATITUCCI M  REPRT: WATSON        L
CRWN:                         LREP:
STAT: CCC SECT: 253       B   COMPL DT: 18   06   02
ACTLDUR:        PURGE DT:     INTERP:
ACTN: S  CR ELC: S  AC ELC: NE  PLEA: G  FND: G  CONV: 100402 SENT: 100402
NEXT APP:       TM:    RM:   CRT:   DUR:          TYPE:          MT:
BY:    FOR:   PBAN:  ASDL:  NOTE:
                                                        ALTERNT
         SENT    AMOUNT   COST    LTH/UNT        INST    LTH/UNT DETAIL
         FIN     800.00           0.00      6   MTH
         OPD     0.00             0.00      1   YR
         PRO     0.00             0.00      90  DAY
         SUR     120.00           0.00      6   MTH
- - - - - - - - - - - - - - - - - - - - - - - - - - - - - - - - - -
SEL:          CRT: 4814 JUR: 998 YR: 02  INF:            MAJ:           DATE:
                                                          OTHER: 0001
```

4-©            1     SNA-F                                            23/7

Ontario Court "ICON" Report

Parole Board
of Canada

Commission des
libérations conditionnelles
du Canada

Page 1 of 2

**Protected when completed**

# Court Information Form

### For the purpose of a Record Suspension Application
**Please print clearly using blue or black ink. You must answer all questions.**

---

**SECTION A: PERSONAL INFORMATION – You must answer all questions.**

1. **What is your full legal name?** (You must fill in your name and date of birth at the top of page 2 as well.)

   Last Name: _____ Given Name(s): _____

2. **Have you ever used another name other than your legal name above?**

   NO ☐   YES ☐ → If YES, please write the other names that you have used here. If you do not give all of the names that you have used in the past, your application will be returned to you.

   | Previous Last Name(s) | Previous Given Name(s) |
   |---|---|
   |  |  |
   |  |  |
   |  |  |

3. **What is your gender?** MALE ☐ FEMALE ☐   4. **What is your date of birth?** Y Y Y Y M M D D ☐☐☐☐☐☐☐☐

**SECTION B: CONTACT INFORMATION – You must answer all questions.**

5. **What is your mailing address?**

   _____

   _____

   Apartment/House Number and Street Address    City/Town    Province    Postal Code    Country

6. **What is your telephone number?** ( _____ ) - _____

**FOR COURT USE ONLY. DO NOT WRITE IN THIS SECTION.**

Name and Address of Court:                Telephone Number ( ) -

Court Name        Street Address        City/Town        Province        Postal Code

**OFFENCE INFORMATION – FOR COURT USE ONLY. DO NOT WRITE IN THIS SECTION.**

**OFFENCE INFORMATION #1**

| Offence Description | Sentence | Place of Sentence | Date of Sentence Y Y Y Y M M D D |
|---|---|---|---|
|  |  |  |  |

Method of Trial:  ☐ Summary   ☐ Indictable   ☐ Unable to Confirm   Court Reference # _____

If Unable to Confirm Method of Trial, State Reason Why: _____

Have all Fines, Surcharges, Restitutions, Compensation Orders and Other Costs Been Paid in Full? ☐ NO  ☐ YES

If They Have Been Paid in Full, What Was the Date of the **Last** Payment? Y Y Y Y M M D D ☐☐☐☐☐☐☐☐

If No, How Much is Outstanding? $ _____

☐ **Our records have been destroyed;**
however we can confirm there are **no outstanding monies** owed with regard to this case.

**Please turn this form over. →**

*Parole Board of Canada  •  Toll-free Info line 1-800-874-2652 – www.recordsuspension.gc.ca*   Canadä

PBC/CLCC 0301E (2012)

**I+I** Parole Board    Commission des
of Canada    libérations conditionnelles
du Canada

**Page 2 of 2**

**Protected when completed**

# Court Information Form

### For the purpose of a Record Suspension Application
### Please print clearly using blue or black ink. You must answer all questions.

## APPLICANT INFORMATION – YOU MUST FILL IN THIS INFORMATION.

Indicate the full legal name and date of birth of the applicant provided on the front of this form:

Full legal name: _____ Date of birth: |Y|Y|Y|Y|M|M|D|D|

## OFFENCE INFORMATION – FOR COURT USE ONLY. DO NOT WRITE IN THIS SECTION.

### OFFENCE INFORMATION #2

| Offence Description | Sentence | Place of Sentence | Date of Sentence |
|---|---|---|---|
| | | | Y Y Y Y M M D D |

Method of Trial:  ☐ Summary    ☐ Indictable    ☐ Unable to Confirm    Court Reference # _____

If Unable to Confirm Method of Trial, State Reason Why: _____

Have all Fines, Surcharges, Restitutions, Compensation Orders and Other Costs Been Paid in Full?  ☐ NO   ☐ YES

If They Have Been Paid in Full, What Was the Date of the **Last** Payment? |Y|Y|Y|Y|M|M|D|D|

If No, How Much is Outstanding? $ _____

☐ **Our records have been destroyed;**
however we can confirm there are **no outstanding monies** owed with regard to this case.

### OFFENCE INFORMATION #3

| Offence Description | Sentence | Place of Sentence | Date of Sentence |
|---|---|---|---|
| | | | Y Y Y Y M M D D |

Method of Trial:  ☐ Summary    ☐ Indictable    ☐ Unable to Confirm    Court Reference # _____

If Unable to Confirm Method of Trial, State Reason Why: _____

Have all Fines, Surcharges, Restitutions, Compensation Orders and Other Costs Been Paid in Full?  ☐ NO   ☐ YES

If They Have Been Paid in Full, What Was the Date of the **Last** Payment? |Y|Y|Y|Y|M|M|D|D|

If No, How Much is Outstanding? $ _____

☐ **Our records have been destroyed;**
however we can confirm there are **no outstanding monies** owed with regard to this case.

### OFFENCE INFORMATION #4

| Offence Description | Sentence | Place of Sentence | Date of Sentence |
|---|---|---|---|
| | | | Y Y Y Y M M D D |

Method of Trial:  ☐ Summary    ☐ Indictable    ☐ Unable to Confirm    Court Reference # _____

If Unable to Confirm Method of Trial, State Reason Why: _____

Have all Fines, Surcharges, Restitutions, Compensation Orders and Other Costs Been Paid in Full?  ☐ NO   ☐ YES

If They Have Been Paid in Full, What Was the Date of the **Last** Payment? |Y|Y|Y|Y|M|M|D|D|

If No, How Much is Outstanding? $ _____

☐ **Our records have been destroyed;**
however we can confirm there are **no outstanding monies** owed with regard to this case.

## COURT AUTHORIZATION – Please sign, date, and stamp this form.

Name of Authorized Officer of the Court: _____

Signature: _____

Date: |Y|Y|Y|Y|M|M|D|D|

Please put
Court seal or
stamp here.

PBC/CLCC 0301E (2012)

| Ministry of the | Ministère du | |
|---|---|---|
| **Attorney General** | **Procureur général** | |
| Ontario Court of Justice | Cour de l'Ontario de justice | |
| 1000 Finch Ave West | 1000 Avenue Finch Ouest | |
| Toronto, Ontario M3J 2V5 | Toronto (Ontario) M3J 2V5 | |
| Telephone: 416-314-8489 | Téléphone: 416-314-8489 | |
| Facsimile: 416-314-4233 | Télécopieur: 416-314-4233 | |

**DATE: February 11, 2010**

**ACCUSED  James,** ▮▮▮▮▮▮▮▮▮▮
**DOB: February** ▮▮**, 19**▮

☐ The court has conducted a thorough search of our database and can find no record of criminal conviction(s) to match the above-named for a certified copy of a conviction based on the information provided.

☐ The court has conducted a search of the docket for the above-named and the search failed to disclose any information on such person.

☐ Unable to confirm with the information if it is an ☐ indictable or ☐ summary offence.

☐ Please note that although the individual has been charged with an offence, they were not convicted. They were found guilty of the offence; not convicted.

☐ Please note the retention period for indictable offences is forty years and a summary conviction is destroyed after seven years.

☐ We have checked outstanding payments in our computerized system (ICON) and there are no outstanding fines indicated for any criminal convictions for the above- named individual.

☐ We are unable to confirm if the restitution was paid. We have checked the outstanding payments in our computerized system (ICON) and there are no outstanding payments indicated for any criminal convictions for the above-named individual.

☐ We are unable to locate the documents you have requested.  This may be as a result of your application being made at the incorrect courthouse.

☒ The Government Records Storage Centre, which holds all court records, cannot locate the Information based on the information provided.  At this time we cannot provide a certified copy. This also may be as a result of your application being made at the incorrect Courthouse.

☐ We are unable to locate the documents you have requested at this time.  We have endeavoured to supply you with the information available to us from our computerized system (ICON).

**Note: Toronto area Court Locations:** 2201 Finch Ave. W. # 416-314-3963; 1000 Finch Ave. W. #416-314-4208; 1911 Eglinton Ave. E.  #416-325-0982; 444 Yonge St.  #416-325-8950; 60 Queen St. W. #416-327-5614; 361 University Ave. 416-327-5917.

Sincerely,

Client Services Representative

Court Letter showing all the reasons why a court record can't be produced

## Quiz

**1. An LPRC:**
  a. Usually includes information held in CPIC
  b. Involves a local or regional police service searching for an applicant's criminal record within their record management system
  c. Can disclose information about incidents for which no charges were laid
  d. a, b and c
  e. None of the above

**2. A CPIC Check:**
  a. Involves having the police look for a criminal record in various RCMP data banks
  b. Usually refers to information contained in the RCMP Investigative data bank
  c. Can only be relied upon with the submission of fingerprints
  d. All of the above
  e. None of the above

**3. A Vulnerable Sector Check:**
  a. Is mandatory for individuals applying to work or volunteer with vulnerable people (e.g., children, elderly, disabled)
  b. Can reveal whether a Pardon or an RS has been received for an offence of a sexual nature
  c. Is required by the PBC as part of the RS application.
  d. All of the above
  e. a and b

**4. A Parole Board of Canada LPRC:**
  a. Is required as part of an RS application
  b. Is required for every jurisdiction the applicant has lived in for 3 months or more in the past 5 years
  c. Can disclose provincial charges and convictions
  d. All of the above
  e. None of the above

### 5. A Freedom of Information Request:

a.  Is made pursuant to Canadian federal, provincial, or municipal privacy laws
b.  Guarantees everyone a right to request records (including criminal records) that pertain to them and that are held by government institutions
c.  Discloses all records held in a government institution with no exception
d.  All of the above
e.  (a) and (b)

### 6. True or False:

a.  All criminal record checks have the same purpose and show the same results
b.  Everyone has the right to request access to their own criminal record held in government institutions
c.  No one can access someone else's criminal record without his or her knowledge and consent
d.  Criminal records held in the courts can always be accessed
e.  An LPRC typically also includes a CPIC check

Answer Key: 1 (d), 2 (d), 3 (e), 4 (d), 5 (e), 6 false, true, false, false, true

## End Notes

1. CPIC network users include all law-enforcement agencies and a number of other government agencies, such as Canada Border Services Agency, Canada Revenue Agency, and Parks Canada. For a more detailed discussion of CPIC network users and *authorized* CPIC network users, refer to Chapter 1.

2. The Vancouver Police Department conducts police records checks using six records systems, including Vancouver records (Legacy RMS + Versadex), other agency records, provincial court records, CPIC and PIRS (local RCMP records).

Chapter Three

# Youth Criminal Records

Youth criminal records are quite different from adult criminal records because they are created, stored, accessed, removed, and destroyed under a separate Act, called the *Youth Criminal Justice Act (YCJA)*. The *YCJA* came into effect on April 1, 2003, replacing the *Young Offenders Act (YOA)*, which in turn had replaced the *Juvenile Delinquents Act (JDA)*.[1] The *YCJA* was designed to help deal with the young person's criminal behaviour outside of the courts and jail, whenever possible. It strives to balance rehabilitation, reintegration and timely intervention, while ensuring that the young person has meaningful consequences of his or her crime.

Although many feel that the *YCJA* is too lenient on youth crime, the *YCJA* creates more serious results than you might expect when it comes to youth criminal records. Some common beliefs about youth criminal records, such as, they *aren't permanent*, they *can't be accessed*, and they *can't really affect the person's life*, are not true. If young people were aware of how far-reaching and accessible youth criminal records really are, it would be a big deterrent and might prevent many of them from committing a crime.

This chapter will dispel a number of myths about youth criminal records, such as:

- No one can access them other than the young person
- They disappear after the individual turns 18 years old
- They cannot be disclosed even if the person reoffends
- They don't affect employment, and
- The U.S.A. can't find them.

## 1. What is a youth criminal record?

A youth criminal record is anything containing information (regardless of its physical form or characteristics) created or kept for the purpose of dealing with a young person under the *YCJA*, such as sentencing, rehabilitation, or re-integration. In addition to records created by the police and court, the *YCJA*, also allows records to be created for the administration of extrajudicial measures— such as police warnings, community programs, and extrajudicial sanctions.

These records are, therefore, considered part of the youth criminal record.

A young person is defined in the *YCJA* as anyone from twelve up to and including seventeen years of age.[2] Children under the age of twelve are excluded from criminal prosecution because, under the law, they are not considered capable of understanding their actions and the consequences of those actions. Some provinces wanted to include ten- and eleven-year-olds in the criminal justice system, but the federal government disagreed and excluded those age groups from the *YCJA*. Children under the age of twelve, who become involved with crime, are dealt with by the provincial Ministries that govern children and family matters.[3]

The following chart shows that in 2010, youth records only comprised two percent of the criminal records held in the RCMP Identification data bank. Although the percentage of young people involved in crime actually may have been higher, most often they are dealt with outside of the police and courts. Since, in those cases, their fingerprints are not taken, they would not appear in the RCMP Identification data bank and, consequently, are not represented in the chart below.

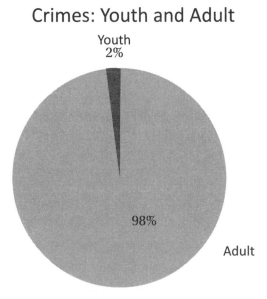

## Crimes: Youth and Adult

Youth
2%

98%

Adult

Based on **RCMP** data, 2010

## 2. Who creates youth criminal records, and where are they stored?

- **Courts.** A youth justice court, review board (e.g., for bail purposes), or any court dealing with matters arising out of the *YCJA* can keep a record of any case that comes before it.
- **Police.** The charging police service can keep records related to any offence alleged to have been committed by a young person. If the young person is found guilty of a hybrid or indictable offence (more serious), then the charging police must also provide these records to the RCMP for inclusion in the Identification data bank.
- **RCMP.** The RCMP stores both the youth records it creates (where the RCMP act as the local police), and those records that have been transferred to them by local charging police services throughout the country. Moreover, the RCMP maintains various types of information related to outstanding warrants, prohibitions, and parole, which are accessible to all authorized CPIC network users.
- **Government.** Any Canadian government department or agency can keep self-created records to investigate an alleged offence, prosecute a young person, administer a youth sentence, or to deal with a young person with respect to using extrajudicial measures.
- **Private.** A private person or organization can keep self-created records as a result of using extrajudicial measures to deal with a young person or to administer (or participate in the administration of) a youth sentence.

Furthermore, youth criminal records can also be transmitted to the Library and Archives of Canada or any provincial archive at any time. The person or body keeping the record has the discretion to do so. Youth criminal records held in the RCMP's Identification data bank could also be transmitted to the Library and Archives of Canada if the Librarian and Archivist of Canada require it.

## 3. What information can be included in a youth criminal record?

- **Youth Court Records.** In addition to personal information (e.g., name, date of birth, address, etc.), these records can include detailed charging information, court orders, transcripts of proceedings, evidence (including DNA evidence), legal arguments and authorities, and reports (e.g., court-ordered medical or psychological assessment, pre-sentence reports).

- **Police Records.** Each local police service uses a record management system to keep detailed reports about incidents, people accused of crimes, victims, witnesses, and complainants. This information can be both very personal and potentially prejudicial (e.g., allegations without charges, pending charges, etc.). The charging police service can also keep the young person's fingerprints and photographs.

- **RCMP Records.** If a young person is charged with an indictable or hybrid offence and he or she is ultimately found guilty, then the charging police service must report the criminal record to the RCMP for inclusion in its Identification data bank. That means the RCMP will have a copy of the charges, the outcome, fingerprints, photographs, and personal information about the individual, and further details of the offence.

  In addition to the Identification data bank, the RCMP Investigative data bank, commonly referred to as CPIC, contains a great deal of youth criminal record information, such as, ongoing investigations, outstanding warrants, and information related to prohibitions. Any youth criminal information entered into this data bank is accessible by all CPIC network users.[4]

- **Government and Private Records.** In addition to court and police reports, records held by those providing services to young people involved with crime can include a variety of other personal information, for example, medical reports, progress reports, information about the completion of the sentence, school reports, information about the young person's family, and so on.

## 4. How long are youth criminal records retained?

Youth criminal records are retained for specific periods of time as determined by the *YCJA*. The time frame for which the records are accessible is called the *period of access*. With certain exceptions, after the expiry of these time limits, often called the *non-disclosure date*, a young person's criminal record *cannot be disclosed* to anyone, and must be removed, and, in the case of records held in the RCMP Identification data bank, *destroyed*. The waiting times that must pass until the *non-disclosure* dates are reached depend on the outcome of the charges:

| Outcome of Charge | Period of Access |
|---|---|
| **Acquittal** (other than by reason of a verdict of not criminally responsible on account of mental disorder) | • two months after the expiry of the time allowed for making an appeal<br>• If an appeal is held, three months after all appeal proceedings are completed |
| **Withdrawn or Dismissed Charges** | two months after withdrawal or dismissal |
| **Stayed Charges** | one year after the charges were stayed |
| **Extrajudicial Sanction** | two years after the young person consents to be subject to the sanction |
| **Absolute Discharge** | one year after the young person is found guilty |
| **Conditional Discharge** | three year after the young person is found guilty |
| **Conviction: Summary** | three years after the youth sentence has been completed |
| **Conviction: Indictment** | five years after the youth sentence has been completed |

After the non-disclosure date has been reached, a person wanting to access youth criminal records can apply to the court. Access can be granted if a judge is satisfied that the person has a valid interest in the record and that disclosure would be in the interest of the proper administration of justice and if disclosure is not prohibited under any other federal or provincial legislation. Alternatively, access can be granted if the judge is satisfied that disclosure is desirable in the public interest for research or statistical purposes. In granting access, the judge must set out the purposes for which the record may be used.

## 5. Who can access youth criminal records?

The *YCJA* stipulates that no one can access a youth criminal record (even *before* the non-disclosure date has been reached) unless they are specifically autho-rized under the *Act* or have obtained the young person's written consent. In ac-tuality, however, the *Act* permits many departments, agencies, and individuals to easily obtain and transfer a copy of the youth criminal record. For example, the *Act* allows the following persons (among others) to access a youth's criminal record upon request:

- The young person
- The youth's parents or guardian
- The youth's legal counsel
- Any judge, court, review board
- Any peace officer for law enforcement purposes
- The victim
- Corrections staff
- Extrajudicial sanctions staff
- The Attorney General of Canada
- Government staff engaged in the supervision or care of the young person
- A government of Canada employee, for statistical purposes
- Any person who carries out criminal record checks that are mandatory for performing services or employment
- American Immigration

Certain authorized persons—including the Attorney General of Canada, youth workers, peace officers, and other persons engaged in the provision of services to young persons—can even disclose the criminal record to the young person's school in the case of reintegration leave (whereby a young person can leave a youth custody facility to be reintegrated into the community), in order to ensure the safety of staff and students (among others), or to facilitate the reha-bilitation of the young person.

The decision as to whether there is a safety issue and whether the disclosure would facilitate the rehabilitation of the young person is left to those depart-ments, agencies, and individuals who have been involved in some way with pro-viding services to the young person while he or she was in the criminal justice system. Since so many government offices and boards participate in the youth criminal justice system, it means that the decision of when and to whom the youth's criminal record will be disclosed can be made by many different individuals, using different criteria.

In addition, those who are not specifically authorized under the *YCJA* can still ask the court for access to a youth criminal record on the basis that they have a valid interest in the record. The judge can grant access to that person if it is desirable in the public interest for research or statistical purposes or desirable in the interest of the proper administration of justice. In such cases, having the request reviewed by a judge guarantees that the young person has an opportunity to oppose the request, and that the information-seeker must present a valid reason as to why they need the record, and give assurances as to safeguarding the information if the request is granted.

A Government of Canada employee who has accessed a youth criminal record for statistical purposes may disclose information contained in the record so long as the identity of the young person—or information that could reasonably be expected to identify the person—is not disclosed.

So much for the belief that youth criminal records are under lock and key. Although there are rules about how these records are to be maintained and provisions to help protect the young person's privacy, the records are still accessible to many people and can be a significant obstacle in the young person's future.

## 6.  What youth criminal record information can be disclosed?

What records can be disclosed, by whom, according to what criteria, and to whom is quite complicated. The chart on p. 77 outlines the general rules as set out in the *YCJA*.

## 7.  How are youth criminal records sealed or destroyed?

Contrary to popular belief, a youth criminal record does not simply cease to exist when a young person turns eighteen years old. With the exception of records kept in the RCMP's Identification data bank, which must be destroyed when the non-disclosure date is reached,[5] a person, agency, or government office may, at

| Who can disclose? | What can be disclosed? | Criteria for disclosure: | Who can receive? |
|---|---|---|---|
| **Peace Officer** | Court and police records | Necessary for investigating an offence | Any Person |
| | | Necessary to deal with a request to or by a foreign state (e.g., for extradition) | Minister of Justice of Canada |
| | | Necessary to investigate a claim arising out of an offence (allegedly) committed by the young person | Insurance Company |
| | Court, police, government, private records | Necessary to ensure compliance by the young person with reintegration leave (from a youth custody facility) or a youth justice court order | Any professional or other person engaged in the supervision or care of a young person (includes school boards, schools, and other educational or training facility). |
| | | Necessary to ensure the safety of staff, students, or other person | |
| | | Necessary to facilitate the rehabilitation of the young person | |
| **Attorney General of Canada** | Court and police records | Is in respect of the offence for which the record is kept | A person who is a co-accused with the young person |
| | | Necessary to deal with a request to or by a foreign state (e.g., for extradition) | Minister of Justice of Canada |
| | Any information in a court or police record that identifies a witness | Is in respect of a witness in the proceeding | An accused in a proceeding |
| | Court, police, government, and private records | Necessary to ensure compliance by the young person with reintegration leave (from a youth custody facility) or a youth justice court order | Any professional or other person engaged in the supervision or care of a young person (includes school boards, schools, and other educational or training facility). |
| | | Necessary to ensure the safety of staff, students, or other person | |
| | | Necessary to facilitate the rehabilitation of the young person | |
| **Provincial Director or Youth Worker** | Self-created records | Necessary for procuring information that relates to the preparation of a report (e.g. medical and psychological assessment reports) | Any person |
| | Court, police, government, and private records | Necessary to ensure compliance by the young person with reintegration leave (from a youth custody facility) or a youth justice court order | Any professional or other person engaged in the supervision or care of a young person (includes school boards, schools, and other educational or training facility). |
| | | Necessary to ensure the safety of staff, students, or other person | |
| | | Necessary to facilitate the rehabilitation of the young person | |
| **Any person engaged in the provision of services to young persons** | Court, police, government, and private records | Necessary to ensure compliance by the young person with reintegration leave (from a youth custody facility) or a youth justice court order | Any professional or other person engaged in the supervision or care of a young person (includes school boards, schools, and other educational or training facility). |
| | | Necessary to ensure the safety of staff, students, or other person | |
| | | Necessary to facilitate the rehabilitation of the young person | |
| **Librarian and Archivist of Canada and provincial archivists** | Court, police, government, and private records | A youth justice court judge must be satisfied that disclosure is desirable in the public interest for research or statistical purposes and the recipient undertakes not to disclose the identity of the young person | Any person |

their discretion, destroy these records at any time. Each partner within the criminal justice system who creates youth records can either keep them for as long as they wish, or remove or destroy them pursuant to an internal policy.

> The physical records held in the RCMP Identification data bank must be destroyed by shredding, burning, or otherwise physically destroying them. The Electronic records are deleted, written over, or otherwise rendered inaccessible.

Although they are not under a legal obligation to do so, most police services destroy (or at least seal) youth criminal records once the non-disclosure period, as set out in the *YCJA*, has been reached. In addition, when the non-disclosure period has been reached, individuals, agencies, or government offices will also usually destroy their records upon request from the young person.

Notwithstanding this removal and destruction process, youth criminal record information relating to an ongoing investigation or outstanding orders (e.g., prohibition order, or parole) must only be removed from the RCMP *Investigative* data bank (commonly referred to as CPIC) at the end of the period for which the order is in force. Often, prohibition or parole orders are still in existence after the non-disclosure date for the conviction has been reached. Consequently, a youth record may still be found on a CPIC search even though the records in the RCMP Identification data bank have been destroyed.

Furthermore, the *YCJA* states that if the information in the RCMP data bank is "maintained . . . to match crime-scene information and that relates to an offence committed or alleged to have been committed by a young person," this information shall be removed from the main data bank and sealed in the same manner as adult records where a pardon has been granted.[6] This means that many of the youth records held by the RCMP are never destroyed, but are kept in a separate data bank accessible to the RCMP for investigative purposes. Given the numerous places a youth record may be created, maintained, and transferred to, it is in the young person's best interest to contact all the known places where the record may exist and request that it be destroyed (see OPP letter p. 79).

## 8.   What happens to the records if a young person reoffends?

When a young person reoffends, the impact their previous criminal record will

| Ontario Provincial Police | Police provinciale de l'Ontario | | Grenville County Detachment Prescott Office |
|---|---|---|---|

| | 200 Development Dr., P.O. Box 399, Prescott, (ON), K0E 1T0 Tel: (613) 925-4221 V-Net 5 10 3400 | 200 development dr. C.P. 399, Prescott, (ON), K0E 1T0. Fax: (613) 925-1115 |
|---|---|---|

File Reference:
Reference: ▓▓▓▓▓

July 10, 2007

**MEMORANDUM TO:**

**Pardons Canada**
**45 St. Clair Ave., W. Ste 901**
**Toronto, Ontario**
**M4V 1K9**

**Attention:** ▓▓▓▓▓▓▓▓▓▓▓▓**olice Records Liaison**

**RE:** ▓▓▓▓▓▓▓▓▓▓▓▓▓▓▓▓▓- **Destruction Fingerprints & Photos**

Please be advised that all photographs and fingerprints taken with relation to the charges under Section 430(4) of the Criminal Code, involving the above named accused were destroyed on July 10th 2007 as per your request dated June 4th 2007.

As far as our local files associated with ▓▓▓▓▓▓▓▓▓▓ these **cannot** be purged or destroyed but are sealed under the **YCJA** and will not be released as per policy of the OPP.

If you have and questions with relation to this request then please contact The Ontario Provincial Police, Security EnquiryOffice, 2nd Floor, 777 Memorial Avenue, Orillia, ON L3V 7V3 or General Inquiry at (705) 329-7637.

Sincerely

Angie Wyatt #1698
Office Administration
Grenville County OPP

/aw

Ontario Provincial Police Letter confirming destruction of Photographs and Fingerprints

have in a subsequent criminal trial depends on whether the non-disclosure date for the previous offence has been reached.

If a young person with a criminal record is found guilty of a new offence before the non-disclosure date for the original offence has been reached, then the original crime will remain on record until the latest of the non-disclosure dates for it or the new offence is reached. In other words, when determining the non-disclosure date for the entire criminal record, the time period for the crime with the latest non-disclosure date, must have passed before the information relating to any of the crimes is no longer accessible. [7]

In these situations, information about the original offence will be given to a parent or adult assisting the young person at a trial, hearing, or review. Access will also be given to a judge, court or review board dealing with the young person (either as a young person or as an adult) in proceedings under the *YCJA* or any other federal legislation. Finally, access will be given to government staff (or an organization that is an agent of, or under contract with a government department or agency) for the purpose of:

- preparing a report about the young person (e.g., a medical and psychological report, or pre-sentence report, etc.)
- assisting a court in sentencing the young person after the young person becomes an adult
- supervising or caring for the young person
- administering a youth sentence
- considering an application for conditional release or Record Suspension made by the young person after he or she becomes an adult.

## 9. Is a Record Suspension (RS) required for a youth record?

Almost never. The only exception is if a young person receives an adult sentence, for a very serious crime. This youth criminal conviction will then be treated as an adult record, and an RS will be required.

## 10. What happens to a youth record if the person commits a crime after becoming an adult?

That depends.

- If an adult with a youth criminal record is convicted of a new offence *before* the non-disclosure date for the youth record has been reached, then the youth criminal record will be locked in with the adult record and considered to be part of the adult criminal record.[8] This means that the youth record can be used as evidence in an adult court, stored in the RCMP's Identification data bank, and must be removed in the same way as an adult criminal record. In such circumstances, the individual will need an RS for all convictions contained in the criminal record, regardless of whether some are youth convictions. Any charges on the record not resulting in a conviction will be sealed together with the convictions when an RS is ordered.
- If an adult with a youth criminal record is convicted of a new offence *after* the non-disclosure date of the original youth offence has been reached, then the criminal record for the original youth offence cannot be disclosed. This means that the person will be considered to have no prior criminal record when prosecuted in adult court. Consequently, the youth record does not need to be sealed with the adult record.

## 11. How does a youth record affect employment?

This depends on a number of factors, such as: (1) if the job requires a police records search, (2) if the non-disclosure date for the youth criminal record has been reached, (3) the nature of the job, (4) who the employer is, (5) whether there is an outstanding prohibition order on CPIC, and so on.

It is now quite common for employers to ask potential employees to verify that they do not have a criminal record through mandatory police records checks. In such cases, if the non-disclosure date has not been reached, the police may release this information to the employer. In other cases, someone working with the young person (such as a social worker) may disclose the information. Furthermore, the employer may be a government department or agency that already has access to this information.

Once the non-disclosure date has been reached, however, the youth criminal record should be sealed or destroyed by all those who have a record of it. It is in the best interests of the young person to verify that the records are in fact sealed or destroyed and to find out what will be shown on a *Local Police Records Check (LPRC)* and in a search of both the RCMP Investigative and Identification data banks.

## 12. Can a youth criminal record affect college or university opportunities?

Yes, depending on the school and the program. Many programs will not enroll people with criminal records, and will require a police records check before admission. In some cases, the person may be able to become a student and take the necessary courses, but will be precluded from being licensed, (e.g., personal support worker, nurse). It is best to determine what the school and program requirements are before submitting an application. In some cases, if the offence was minor, the school or licensing board may permit the person to be enrolled or licensed. Otherwise, the young person will have to wait until the non-disclosure date has been reached before applying.

## 13. Can a youth record prevent someone from travelling to the U.S.A.?

Yes. If the youth criminal record is in either the RCMP *Identification* or *Investigative* data banks, it will appear at the border if the American Immigration officer conducts a CPIC search. When a person attempts to enter the U.S.A., the American Customs and Border Patrol (CBP) officers have the authority to conduct a search using their National Crime Information Centre (NCIC) system, which accesses CPIC. In such cases, the RCMP's *Investigative* and the *Identification* data banks are accessible to the CBP officers.

If a criminal record exists in one of these data banks, the CBP officer will see it. Even in cases that did not result in a finding of guilt (e.g., cases that were thrown out of court or where the person was found to be innocent) and which are *supposed to be restricted*, the fact that a criminal record exists will be revealed because the person's name and date of birth are associated with an RCMP fingerprint section number (FPS number). Even if the details of the crime and the outcome are not instantly available, the simple fact that an FPS number exists is sufficient to have the file downloaded into the American data banks and for the person to be turned away at the border.

Once the non-disclosure date has been reached, however, the youth record information will be removed from the RCMP *Identification* data bank and is no longer accessible to American border officers. Provided there is no outstanding order or ongoing investigation that could be found on CPIC, the youth record will no longer be accessible.

Some would argue that youth records do not constitute grounds for inadmissibility to the U.S.A. and would not prevent them from entering. Although this might be technically true, in practice, CBP officers have the discretion to turn anyone away at the border if they feel the person is a threat to the safety of their country. They err on the side of safety when they are not sure of the laws. This means that people with youth criminal records could be easily turned away at the border and have their information downloaded into the American data banks, where it will remain forever. At that point, the person with the youth record would need to apply for a U.S.A. Entry Waiver to legally enter the U.S.A. In the end, the individual could be issued either a Waiver document (which needs to be renewed), or an official letter from the American Immigration Department stating that a Waiver is not required (this letter does not expire, but must be shown when travelling to the U.S.A.). For a more detailed discussion on travelling to the U.S.A. with a criminal record, refer to Chapter 6.

## 14. How does a youth record affect Canadian Immigration?

A youth criminal record can negatively affect every type of Canadian immigration application. A youth record will not only impact the individual, but will also affect the entire family's application. Although it may not necessarily mean that the applications will be denied, a record will definitely slow down and compli-cate the process. For a more detailed discussion on how criminal records affect Canadian immigration applications, refer to Chapter 5.

## 15. Do youth records created under previous laws still exist?

Maybe. Laws relating to the disclosure, removal, and destruction of youth crimi-nal records have changed with each new *Act*. Records created under prior legis-lation—the *YOA*, and the *JDA*—may still exist. Although in many cases the files have been removed, either because the *retention period* has been reached or be-cause the individual has taken steps to remove it, having a past criminal record resurface when seeking employment or trying to cross the American border can be devastating.

It is up to the individual to conduct various checks to determine what is still on file. The most common searches are: (1) an LPRC, and (2) an RCMP search supported by fingerprints. The individual may also want to see if the court where the case was heard still has any records on file.

## Quiz

**1. Who can create youth criminal records?**
- a. Youth justice courts
- b. Charging police services
- c. Certain government departments and agencies
- d. Certain authorized private persons or organizations
- e. All of the above

**2. What information can be included in a youth criminal record?**
- a. Personal information
- b. Detailed charging and outcome information
- c. Reports (e.g., court-ordered medical or psychological assessment reports)
- d. The charging police service's incident records and occurrence reports
- e. All of the above

**3. What is the non-disclosure date for a charge that has been withdrawn?**
- a. 3 years after the youth was charged
- b. 5 years after the withdrawal
- c. 1 year after the withdrawal
- d. 2 months after the withdrawal
- e. Never

**4. Police can disclose their records to a young person's school if doing so is:**
- a. Necessary to ensure compliance by the young person with reintegration leave or a youth justice court order
- b. Necessary to ensure the safety of staff, students, or other person
- c. Necessary to facilitate the rehabilitation of the young person
- d. (a), (b), and (c)
- e. None of the above

**5. The following people have the right to access youth criminal records on request:**
- a. The young person and his or her parents or guardian
- b. The young person's legal counsel
- c. Any peace officer for law-enforcement purposes
- d. Any judge, court, review board
- e. All of the above

## 6. True or False:

a.   Youth criminal records can often be accessed through a CPIC search

b.   Youth criminal records held in the RCMP's Identification data bank are destroyed before the non-disclosure date has been reached

c.   Youth criminal records are automatically purged from wherever they are stored after the youth turns 18 years old

d.   After the non-disclosure date has been reached, a person can apply to the court for access to a youth criminal record

e.   A youth with a criminal record always needs a Record Suspension

Answer Key: 1 (e), 2 (e), 3 (d), 4 (d), 5 (e), 6 true, false, false, true, false

## End Notes

1. *Juvenile Delinquents Act*, (1908-1984); *Young Offenders Act*, (1984-2003); *Youth Criminal Justice Act*, (2003-present).

2. The definition of young person in the prior *Acts* is as follows:
*Young Offenders Act (YOA)*—twelve years was the minimum age for charging a child with a criminal offence. Seventeen was the maximum age to be considered a young person.
*Juvenile Delinquent Act (JDA)*—seven years was the minimum age for charging a child with a criminal offence, while children under twelve years of age only could be committed to an institution if no other option was available. A provision that allowed the provinces to set the maximum legal age for defining youth led to variations. For example, Quebec and Manitoba set the age at eighteen, while Prince Edward Island, Nova Scotia, New Brunswick, Ontario, and Saskatchewan set the age at sixteen, and Alberta set the maximum age at sixteen for boys and eighteen for girls.

3. For example: in British Columbia, the *Ministry of Children and Family Development*, in Ontario, the *Ministry of Children and Social Services.*

4. As stated in Chapter 2 CPIC network users include all law-enforcement agencies and a number of other government agencies, such as Canada Border Services Agency, Canada Revenue Agency, and Parks Canada. For a more detailed discussion of CPIC network users and *authorized* CPIC network users, refer to Chapter 1.

5. *YCJA* s. 128 (3).

6. *YCJA* s. 128 (5).

7. *YCJA* s. 119 (2).

8. *YCJA* s. 119 (9).

Chapter Four

# How Criminal Records Affect People's Lives

– Obstacles Created by Criminal Records –

Employment and Education

## Volunteering

## Family Matters

## Housing

## Discrimination and Peace of Mind

The Canadian Charter of Rights and Freedoms[1] guarantees everyone charged with an offence the right, if they are found guilty and punished for the offence, not to be tried or punished for it again. But when it comes to having a criminal record, the negative effects can be everlasting. Until their criminal records are removed, people will continue to be tried and punished in everyday life.

Most people who have a criminal record—and there are about 4 million in Canada who do—live in fear of it's being discovered. They seldom speak of it because of shame, the fear of prejudice, and because they don't want to jeopardize their future. In recent years, it has become much easier for criminal records to be discovered due to technological advancements and the increased sharing of information between police services. The result is that criminal records will almost always hinder individuals in many of the important aspects of their lives unless and until the records are removed.

## EMPLOYMENT AND EDUCATION

# 1. Can employers find an applicant's criminal record?

Yes, with the individual's consent. In 2001, Statistics Canada reported that one in every eight new hires said they were subject to a security check during the hiring process (compared with only one in every twenty new hires before 1980).[2] Since the fallout of the terrorist attacks of September 11, 2001 (9/11), the frequency of security checks has increased dramatically. I expect that now, one in three new hires must undergo a security check.

Standard job applications almost always ask such questions as: Do you have a criminal record for which a Pardon or Record Suspension has not been granted? Have you ever been convicted of a crime for which a Pardon or Record Suspension has not been granted? Or, Are you bondable? Near the bottom of the application, it will state that the person signing gives permission to the employer to verify all statements. Often, they also will include a requirement that the applicant provide or consent to a *Local Police Records Check (LPRC)*. Regardless of whether a name and date of birth records check or a police records check supported by fingerprints is requested, the employer must have the applicant's permission to access the information. Once such an application is signed, the employer has permission to check police files.

Many employers, especially government departments and larger corporations, routinely conduct *name and date of birth* LPRCs. The employer will submit the applicant's name and date of birth to the local police, who then compare this information with the names and dates of birth of people in their database, and at the RCMP. If the name and date of birth check comes back clear, then the individual may never know that a preliminary police records check was even conducted.

If there is a *match* to a criminal record, the employer might ask the applicant for further information and even to submit to fingerprinting to verify the record. In some cases, however, the employer simply might not call the applicant back and will dismiss the application altogether.

Many times those who do not pass a security clearance are not aware of the reason because they are under the mistaken belief that they do not have a criminal record. This if often the case where the person was discharged or their charges were thrown out of court (e.g., dismissed or withdrawn). These people go on looking for work not understanding why they don't get hired.

In the past, LPRCs were most common for those seeking professional jobs at large workplaces in the technology, utility, education, health, finance, police, and insurance industries. Since the Statistics Canada 2001 survey was conducted, they have become much more common. In the wake of 9/11 and prominent corporate failures, many businesses and organizations are reluctant to hire those with a criminal past.

Another important change is that more types of jobs where record checks were not previously required now include them as part of their hiring process, either because the *law* now *requires it*, or because it has become an *industry standard*. Even *long-time employees*, who were once immune to security checks, may have to undergo a police records check if the company has new policies, or if there are new laws, such as mandatory police records checks for teachers.

## 2.  Which careers and licences require a local police records check (LPRC)?

Almost all employment applications give the employer the right to make enquiries about the applicant's criminal past, or require the applicant to obtain an *LPRC*. Further, there are numerous career categories where the *law requires* police records checks, such as:

- Airport workers
- Bank employees
- Bus drivers
- Canada Post
- Car dealers
- Casino employees
- Coaches
- Collection agents
- Couriers
- Day care workers
- Funeral directors
- Firefighters
- Government offices
- Health professionals (e.g., PSW, dentists, doctors, nurses, chiropractors, etc.)
- Insurance agents and brokers
- Investment advisors
- Limousine and taxicab drivers
- Machine operators
- Manufacturing
- Movers
- Members of governing bodies (e.g., teachers, doctors, nurses, etc.)
- Owners of restaurants requiring liquor licences
- Police officers
- Private Investigators
- Probation officers
- Real estate brokers + agents
- Retail workers (cashiers, clerks, stockroom)
- Salon owners
- School staff (teachers, counsellors, etc.)
- Security guards
- Stockbrokers
- Temporary agency workers
- Truck drivers
- Volunteers (e.g., those working with children, seniors etc.)
- Vulnerable sector workers

In addition to these examples, there are also many employers whose internal policies require police records checks. Practically speaking, those with a criminal record are almost unemployable. Consequently, many resort to low-paying, casual-labour jobs or they try to be self-employed in jobs such as lawn main-tenance or snow removal—where there is little security risk and where LPRCs usually are not required. The best approach for the applicant is to have the record removed so it will no longer be a barrier to employment.

## 3. How can a criminal record affect educational opportunities?

Many school programs throughout Canada require that students provide or consent to a police records check before being enrolled. For example, the University of Ottawa requires LPRCs for its Human Kinetics, Nursing, Rehabilitation, Nutrition, and Medicine programs. The University of Manitoba requires LPRCs for its Teaching and Pharmacy programs. All post-secondary education institutions in B.C. ensure that every registered student who will work with children has undergone an LPRC before being admitted. Finally, admission into a professional school program or a program requiring licencing after graduation (e.g., law, medicine, dentistry, engineering), generally requires an LPRC.

The above examples are by no means an exhaustive list. There are numerous municipal, provincial, and federal programs that require LPRCs. The question should really be: Is there any school program or licence that does not require a police check? For the most part, any school program worth taking or any licence worth having requires a check. Obviously, removing the criminal record first is best. If this is not possible, the applicant should be prepared to answer questions about it.

## 4. How can a record affect current employment and job promotions?

Even a person employed by the same employer for several years is not protected against future criminal record search requests. Many organizations that have implemented LPRCs for new employees are now requiring existing employees to undergo the search (e.g., when applying for a job promotion, or because of new policies or laws).

Further, someone who *initially* might have passed a criminal record check when first hired, may have subsequently been charged with a crime (e.g., impaired driving), which is later discovered during a routine security screening or a licence renewal process. Not only can discovery of a criminal record hinder the opportunity for career advancement, it could even lead to the employee being fired—for example, if the employee is not legally permitted to do the job without a licence.

## 5. Can an employer find pardoned or suspended records?

No. After a *Pardon* or *Record Suspension (RS)* is obtained, the criminal record is sealed and an LPRC or RCMP search will state that *no criminal record* was found.

The only exception is in the case of checks done for the purpose of working with vulnerable people (e.g., children, the elderly, people with disabilities). In those circumstances, the police will disclose whether the individual is a pardoned sex offender.

## 6. Can employers find charges that were withdrawn, dismissed, or stayed?

Yes. *Non-convictions*—that is, stayed, withdrawn or dismissed charges, absolute or conditional discharges and acquittals—show up on most LPRCs and RCMP reports. Ironically, having non-convictions can often lead to serious problems because the removal or destruction of non-conviction charges is decided at the discretion of the individual charging police service. If the police decide not to destroy the person's photographs and fingerprints, the individual will have a criminal record for life!

It is unclear under what circumstance the police services have the legal right to keep, use or disclose information pertaining to non-conviction, and especially not-guilty outcomes. There are strong Privacy Law and Charter arguments against the maintenance and use of such information. There have been cases where the court has ruled against the policy to retain non-conviction records and has awarded damages be paid to the individual.

In fact, LPRCs may also reveal information about incidents where the individual was not the one charged (e.g., in cases where the person was the one making the complaint, was the victim or a witness). Although this type of file might not be what people commonly think of as a criminal record, a prospective employer might feel that someone is living an *unstable* life if they are in any way involved with a criminal occurrence (even if they were simply the witness), or the employer might misread the police report and mistakenly believe the applicant was the accused.

Often, the police records check results will be given to the individual to forward to the employer. In such a case, the individual can review the report and have an opportunity to explain the circumstances to the prospective employer. If the report is to go directly from the police to the employer, the individual may find it prudent to inform the employer of what to expect before the report is received.

Whether an LPRC showing a non-conviction will preclude the individual from getting the job depends on many factors—such as the nature of the offence, the outcome, the type of job applied for, the employer's perspective, and the applicant's explanation of the events.

In many cases, the employer may not be able to, or even care to differentiate between a conviction and a non-conviction. Most employers simply choose not to hire anyone who has been involved with the police.

Ironically, although people with Pardons or Record Suspensions for convictions will receive a police report saying that *no criminal record exists*, those who received a less serious disposition by way of a discharge and those who were actually found *not-guilty* will, in most cases, have that information disclosed.

## 7.   Does a criminal record affect people who are self-employed?

Yes. People who are self-employed are not immune to criminal record search requirements. Many companies and government departments that sub-contract to self-employed individuals (or to small businesses), require LPRCs to be conducted on the owners and employees of the business. This is especially true in situations where the sub-contractor will have access to confidential information (e.g., financial or health information) or will be working with vulnerable people—children, the elderly, or the disabled.

Additionally, many companies require the sub-contractor to have appropriate insurance before they will award them the contract. Depending on the type of insurance sought, insurers often require the owner and employees of the business to have clear criminal records checks.

## 8. Can employees be bonded if they have a criminal record?

It depends. Being bonded means that the employer has insurance against the risk of employees committing crimes, such as theft. Many people are insurable even if they have a criminal record; however, it will cost the employer more to insure an employee who has a criminal record.

How much it will cost depends on various factors, such as: how serious the charge was, the nature of the offence, the type of insurance required, the maximum liability being assumed by the insurer, and the insurer's internal policies. If having the employee bonded is too expensive for the employer, that person will not get the job.

## 9. Can employees with criminal records travel to the U.S.A. for employment?

Not usually. Individuals who are not Americans or who do not hold valid American immigration status are not usually permitted to enter the U.S.A. if they have a criminal record. In order to *waive* this *inadmissibility*, the individual must obtain a *U.S.A. Entry Waiver* from the U.S.A. Department of Homeland Security. Although a Waiver does not guarantee entry into the U.S.A., it does remove the problems associated with the criminal record. (For a detailed discussion about travelling to the U.S.A. with a criminal record, please refer to Chapter 6.)

## 10. How does a record affect FAST and NEXUS Card applications?

As part of their Western Hemisphere Travel Initiative[3] the American government has been promoting their Trusted Traveler Programs. For Canadians who travel frequently to the U.S.A. for employment, the NEXUS and FAST Card applications are the most popular. The FAST Card is for truckers, while the NEXUS Card is for others who travel frequently across the border. The purpose of these programs is to allow frequent travellers to cross the border faster. For example, truckers with a FAST Card are permitted to use a specially designated lane when driving their load across the border; and at major airports, those with a NEXUS Card use special expedited lines. In order to gain such privileges, these programs require the individual to complete an application and undergo a security screening. The applicants must become members by completing an online application,[4] after which they will be interviewed and their relevant documents will be reviewed. The applications all contain questions about criminal records. Those with records will be required to produce further documentation and their application will usually be denied.

## 11. Can someone with a record work with vulnerable people?

Not usually. The law requires that those wishing to work with or volunteer with vulnerable people—those who are less able to protect themselves from harm, such as children, the elderly, those with mental or physical disabilities—submit an LPRC, often referred to as a *Vulnerable Sector Check*. A vulnerable sector check is a more comprehensive report than a regular LPRC. For example, they will disclose whether the individual is a pardoned sex offender, and may also disclose other types of information not normally disclosed, such as incident reports.

Whether the employer will allow the individual to have the position will depend on the nature and severity of the charges and the organization's screening policies. In most cases, those responsible for the welfare of vulnerable people are extremely cautious and will not accept anyone who has a criminal record.

VOLUNTEERING

## 12. Is an LPRC required in order to be a volunteer?

Yes. It is a legal requirement that volunteers undergo a police records check. If a criminal record exists, the individual may have an opportunity to explain the circumstances surrounding the event, but often will not be accepted as a volunteer.

## 13. Are applicants required to disclose their records to the organization?

It depends. If the criminal record has been pardoned or suspended, the applicant is not legally required to disclose it. The Pardon or RS "removes any disqualification or obligation to which the person so convicted is, by reason of the conviction, subject by virtue of the provisions of any Act of Parliament."[5] If the record has been otherwise removed from public record (e.g., purged) or if the person's fingerprints and photographs have been destroyed, likewise, the record will no longer be disclosed in an LPRC.

If the criminal record has not been pardoned or suspended (or otherwise sealed or destroyed), however, the applicant is under a legal obligation to disclose it. Failure to do so will most likely lead to the person not being hired once the criminal record is discovered.

Practically speaking, for criminal records that have not been properly sealed or destroyed, it is best to disclose the information to the prospective employer. This gives the applicant the opportunity to discuss the circumstance of the situation; it is not only the most ethical approach, but also the one proven to give the applicant the best chance of being hired. Writing a letter explaining what happened and showing remorse and rehabilitation can help. If an application has been made to have the record removed, this should be stated, as taking steps to remove a record shows that the person intends to lead a crime-free life.

## 14. Where do volunteers go to complete an LPRC?

The volunteer organization will often give the applicant a form to take to the local police service. In some jurisdictions, the local police service will be the municipal police, while in others it may be the provincial police or the RCMP.

If the organization deals with children, the elderly, or the disabled, then the applicant will be asked to consent to a police check specific for the vulnerable sector, which will include additional information. The police will conduct the search and, depending on the jurisdiction, will either mail the result to the individual or require them to go to the police station to pick it up.

In some cases, the applicant will simply be asked to sign a consent allowing the organization to request an LPRC, using the applicant's name and date of birth. In such cases, the organization will normally bundle all of the consents together and submit them to the police at one time. The police will then conduct their searches and provide the results directly to the organization.

## 15. What will the organization look for when reviewing a criminal record report?

Each organization will have set guidelines to follow. The criteria considered will usually include: the nature of the volunteer position, the number and type of offences in the criminal record, when the offences took place, the character of the applicant, and whether the applicant is applying to have the record removed.

> Some police services disclose charges under provinicial laws, such as the non-payment of child support.

Ironically, what makes people ideal for many volunteer positions is also the reason they have criminal records, which can prevent them from being accepted as volunteers. For example, many of the volunteers on substance-abuse-support help lines have wrestled with drug or alcohol addiction and have acquired a criminal record as a result of the addiction. This obstacle will disappear once the criminal record is cleared and they are able to pass a security check.

## 16. What will be disclosed on an LPRC for volunteer purposes?

This depends on what type of check is being conducted (e.g., if the check is for the vulnerable sector) and on the individual policies of each police service. First of all, criminal records that are held in the local police record management system will be disclosed. These reports usually include information about outstanding charges, warrants, convictions, discharges, and non-guilty dispositions. Sometimes, depending on the police service and the position applied for, these reports may include information beyond criminal charges and convictions (e.g., allegations, pending charges, provincial offences).

Further, LPRCs generally also include a *CPIC Check*. This reveals criminal records held in the RCMP's Investigative and Identification data banks. The applicant may also be asked to obtain an *RCMP Report*, which is an official copy of the criminal record held by the RCMP and is only obtainable after submitting fingerprints.

Finally, if the individual is planning on volunteering with an organization that deals with vulnerable people—children, the elderly, the disabled—then the LPRC will reveal whether the individual has received a Pardon or an RS for an offence of a sexual nature.

## 17. Is an LPRC required to volunteer at a school?

Yes. LPRCs are required in order to screen out anyone who might pose a threat to school safety, and is required even where the person will be coaching his or her own child.

These searches are often preliminary searches, conducted with only the name and date of birth of the proposed volunteer. If the police find a criminal record associated with the name and date of birth submitted, that information would be disclosed (usually the reports are given to the applicant). Often, parents wishing to volunteer at their child's school are in shock when old charges appear, believing that their convictions are so old that they are gone, or that they never had a criminal record because the charges were thrown out of court. Unfortunately for them, this is not true. To add insult to injury, these people must then think of a way to tell their child and the school why they can't volunteer.

## FAMILY MATTERS

# 18. Can a record be used against a parent in family court?

Yes. It is permissible to introduce the details of a parent's criminal record during family court proceedings. Having a record will reflect negatively on the parent's character.

The parent with the criminal record should be prepared to show how he or she has been rehabilitated and has not had any further dealings with the police. It is also advisable to begin the process of having the record removed, as this will help to show the court that the person is serious about leading a crime-free life.

# 19. Can a parent lose child custody because of a criminal record?

Yes. At the very least, a criminal record will negatively affect the parent's application for custody or visitation.

Depending on the offence, a criminal record may discredit the individual's custodial ability. This means that the judge may determine that the parent is not fit to make decisions on behalf of the child, or, in fact, fit to be alone with or care for the child.

Of course, the judge will consider many factors before limiting or removing a parent's rights. Although the parents' rights are important, in family matters, the court's focus is the welfare of the child, and an old criminal record that resulted in a discharge, was an isolated event, and did not involve violence would affect custody and visitation rights far less than a criminal record that is recent and of a serious and violent nature.

# 20. Can someone with a criminal record adopt a child?

Maybe. Before adopting a child, whether in Canada or abroad, the individual will be required to provide an LPRC and an RCMP Report as part of the adoption application.

The adoption process is generally a lengthy, expensive, and complicated legal process requiring many factors to be proved and verified before the child is released into the custody of the applicants. Given the stringent regulations involved in the adoption process, in most cases, the discovery of a criminal record will result in the application being delayed, and, ultimately, being denied.

# 21. Can a person with a criminal record become a foster parent?

Maybe. Before someone can become a foster parent, there is a screening process that must be completed. As part of the screening process, every adult member of the proposed foster household over the age of eighteen must provide an LPRC. If any criminal record is discovered, the application will likely be denied.

## HOUSING

# 22. Can a criminal record prevent someone from renting a home?

Yes. In almost all cases, prospective tenants are required to complete a rental application before the landlord and tenant enter into a lease. Most rental applications include a question regarding whether the applicant has a criminal record. The application (or, in some cases, the lease itself), can sometimes give the landlord the right to make further enquiries about the applicant's criminal record.

The landlord also may require the applicant to provide an LPRC. In other cases, the landlord, having received the applicant's permission on the rental agreement, may submit the person's name and date of birth to the local police for a records check. It is in the tenant's best interest, therefore, to remove the criminal record before signing such applications. At the very least, it is prudent that these agreements are read carefully so that tenants are well aware of whether they have given consent for the landlord to conduct an LPRC.

People who need to rent before their record is removed should be ready for such a search. To prepare, tenants can make sure their deposit is refundable if the landlord decides not to rent to them, can prepare a letter explaining the incident that led to the criminal record and show remorse, and can show that they have begun the process of having the record removed.

## 23. Can a record prevent someone from obtaining a mortgage?

Yes. Many mortgage applications enquire about the applicant's criminal past and require consent for an LPRC to be conducted. In many cases, upon discovery of a criminal record, the mortgage application will be denied. Even in cases where the *spouse* of the mortgagor is discovered to have a criminal record, the mortgage will likely be denied, notwithstanding that the spouse is not named on either the title of the home or the mortgage application.

Banks don't want to take unnecessary risks. If a criminal record exists, the lenders may be concerned about the repayment of the mortgage, or the preservation of the property: for example, if the home is being paid for by proceeds of crime; if the home might be used for illegal purposes (e.g., marijuana grow house that damages the structure of the house because of the excessive moisture); or that the person might commit another crime and be arrested (e.g., sent to jail) and unable to make the mortgage payments.

DISCRIMINATION AND PEACE OF MIND

## 24. Can having a criminal record lead to future discrimination?

Yes. As discussed throughout this book, the social stigma of having a criminal record lasts longer than any court-imposed sentence. A criminal record can prevent a person from participating fully in everyday life in a number of ways—getting and keeping a job, volunteering, being admitted to school programs, immigrating to Canada, adopting a child, and travelling to the U.S.A. (for work or pleasure).

Having a criminal record can negatively influence the way that the partners of the criminal justice system perceive the individual. If the person is ever in trouble with the law again, having a record can lead to additional and/or more serious charges, more stringent bail conditions, and harsher sentences if found guilty. Further, in cases where the individual's character forms part of the decision being made by a third party, the criminal record will negatively affect the decision. For example, if the individual is driving inappropriately and a police officer is deciding whether to simply reprimand the driver or to charge him or her with a less serious provincial offence, (e.g., speeding), or to charge him or her with a criminal offence, (e.g., dangerous driving), the existing criminal record most likely will negatively impact the police officer's decision.

## 25. How does having a record affect a person's peace of mind?

Negatively. Although *peace of mind* is an intangible concept or feeling, having peace of mind is vital to having a peaceful and successful life.

Many people who have criminal records limit themselves even before obstacles arise. They refrain from applying for jobs or education programs because they fear their record will be discovered. Although not always at the forefront of their minds, they say that deep down they feel the weight of their criminal record and feel disassociated from others in the community. In my experience, removing the shame associated with having a criminal record and regaining peace of mind were the most important reasons people cited for having their criminal record removed.

## Quiz

**1. The following school programs generally require an LPRC:**
   a. Nursing
   b. Medicine
   c. Teaching
   d. Pharmacy
   e. All of the above.

**2. The following careers require an LPRC:**
   a. Airport workers
   b. Day care workers
   c. Police officers
   d. Security guards
   e. All of the above

**3. Employers:**
   a. Can never find out about an employee's criminal record
   b. Can discover if an employee has received a Pardon or RS without the individual's knowledge or consent
   c. Can discover non-convictions (e.g., dismissed and withdrawn charges, discharges, etc.)
   d. All of the Above
   e. None of the Above

**4. Having a criminal record can:**
   a. Prevent someone from being hired
   b. Prevent someone from being promoted
   c. Prevent someone from obtaining a licence
   d. Cause employees to lose their jobs
   e. All of the above

**5. Volunteers:**
   a. Are required to provide or consent to an LPRC
   b. May be denied a position because of their criminal record
   c. May be given an opportunity to explain their criminal record
   d. All of the above
   e. None of the above.

### 6. True or False:

a. An employer cannot discriminate against someone based on a pardoned or suspended criminal record (excluding sex offences)

b. People can be denied entry into certain school programs because of their criminal record

c. A person may not be able to rent an apartment or obtain a mortgage because of a criminal record

d. Having a criminal record may prevent someone from adopting a child or becoming a foster parent

e. Having a criminal record can lead to future discrimination on the part of prospective employers, police, courts, etc.

Answer Key: 1 (e), 2 (e), 3 (c), 4 (e), 5 (d), 6 true, true, true, true, true

## End Notes

1. Section 11

2. The article "Screening job applicants" is available in the May 2006 online edition of *Perspectives on Labour and Income*, Vol. 7, no. 5 (75-001-XIE).

3. U.S.A. Federal Register cite: 73 FR 18384, Document No. FR 27-08, April 3, 2008.

4. GOES Processing: www.cbp.gov

5. *Criminal Records Act* s. 5(b)

Chapter Five

# Criminal Records and Canadian Immigration

Canada has generally been a nation open to immigrants. Immigrants are foreign citizens who are, or have ever been, granted the right to live in Canada permanently. Canada accepts over 200,000 new immigrants each year, and about 20 percent of Canada's population was not born here. All immigrants must meet certain requirements to enter and stay in Canada.

Canada's security screening process determines whether a person is admissible to Canada. Considerations such as being in good health, having a valid passport or travel document, and not having a criminal record are a few of the criteria evaluated by Citizenship and Immigration Canada (CIC) and the Canada Border Services Agency (CBSA). Having a criminal record can prevent someone from entering Canada or remaining in Canada.

## VISIT | WORK | STUDY IN CANADA

Each year, more than five million people visit Canada. They are called foreign nationals—people who are not Canadian citizens or permanent residents. They come to Canada temporarily to work, study, or visit. They may also want to stay in Canada on a more permanent basis and eventually become Canadian citizens.

## 1. Can foreign nationals with a Canadian criminal record visit, work, or study in Canada?

It depends. In most cases, people with criminal records are *inadmissible* to Canada, regardless of whether the crime was committed within or outside of Canada, and regardless of whether they require a visa. To enter Canada as a visitor, people from some foreign countries are required to have a visa, while those from other countries are not.

- **No Visa Required.** Visitors who do not require a visa (e.g., American citizens) do not need prior approval before entering Canada, and are considered to have made an application to enter when they arrive at the Canadian border or at any Canadian Immigration point-of-entry (such as at a Canadian airport). At the border, the CIC officer

Through CPIC, the border officers have computer access to many data banks, including: Canadian Immigration, Interpol, RCMP, as well as those of the FBI and American Immigration.

will perform a security screening by examining the person's travel documents, by conducting computer searches, and by asking the individual several questions. If the person is flagged, either because of information the officer received electronically (such as an outstanding warrant, or a past criminal record), or because of something the person said or did during the interview, the person will be held for further questioning and inquiry.

- **Visa Required.** Visitors who require a visa, for example, those who wish to work or study in Canada, must complete a visa application and submit it to CIC at a Canadian embassy, consulate, or high commission before attempting to enter Canada. The visa application includes questions about the applicant's criminal history. If the applicant has a Canadian criminal record, he or she will need to provide further documentation, such as court and police records. An immigration officer will review the application and supporting documents and decide whether to issue a visa. If the immigration officer determines that the applicant is inadmissible because of the criminal record, the visa application will be denied.

How do people know if their Canadian criminal record makes them inadmissible? Well, the *Immigration and Refugee Protection Act (IRPA)* says that a foreign national cannot enter Canada if he or she was *convicted in* Canada for:

- a federal offence punishable by a maximum jail term of at least ten years [1]
- a federal offence punishable by way of indictment
- a federal offence where a jail term of at least six months was imposed, or
- two federal offences not arising out of a single occurrence. Although the two offences must be federal offences, it is important to note that they can be summary conviction offences (the least serious type of offences). [2]

Although the *IRPA* sets out specific parameters when the individual will be considered inadmissible, it is important to understand that people are routinely refused entry into Canada based on a criminal record that is far less serious than set out above. The CIC officers consider the entire application and make an assessment of the applicant. If the officer considers the person a threat to the Canadian public, then the visa application will be denied. Even a minor crime can prevent someone from being admitted. At the very least, a criminal record will slow down and complicate the immigration process.

## 2. Can foreign nationals with a foreign criminal record visit, work, or study in Canada?

In cases where the applicant has a criminal record from crimes committed *outside* Canada, he or she may be denied a visa or entry into Canada. The application may even be denied in cases where the criminal record is made up of non-convictions (e.g., discharges, stay of proceedings, etc.) or contains a pardon from abroad. In cases of *foreign* criminal records, individuals must provide complete details of charges, convictions, court dispositions, pardons, copies of the applicable sections of foreign law(s), and court proceedings to allow the Canadian immigration officer to determine if the applicant is admissible.

The *IRPA* states that a foreign national is inadmissible if, when the person was outside of Canada, he or she:

- Committed an offence or was convicted of an offence that, if committed in Canada, would be a federal offence punishable by a maximum jail term of at least ten years
- Committed an offence or was convicted of an offence that, if committed in Canada, would be an indictable offence
- Was convicted of two offences that, if committed in Canada, would be two federal offences not arising out of a single occurrence. Although the two offences must be federal offences, it is important to note that they can be summary conviction offences (the least serious type of offences)
- Committed a federal offence upon entering Canada (e.g., drug

trafficking), or

- Was simply believed to be part of organized crime or involved in transnational crime (e.g., human trafficking or money laundering).

## 3. Can a foreign national be removed from Canada because of a criminal record?

Yes. If a CBSA officer believes that a person is inadmissible to Canada because of a criminal record, then the officer can submit a report to the Immigration Minister. This could happen, for example, if the person was convicted of a criminal offence while in Canada, or if a foreign criminal record is discovered after the person is admitted to Canada.

If the immigration officer's report is well founded, then the person will have to attend an *Admissibility Hearing* with the Immigration Division of the *Immigration and Refugee Board (IRB)*. Here, the individual can make legal arguments and present evidence—such as submitting documents or giving oral testimony—as to why he or she should not be removed from Canada. The Immigration Division will review the evidence and make a decision. It must include reasons for the decision.

The Immigration Division may issue a removal order against the foreign national, or may allow the applicant to remain in Canada, with or without conditions. If the person is ordered to be removed, then that order becomes immediately enforceable. This means that, if there is no right of appeal, the time to appeal has expired, or if the appeal has been dismissed, then the removal order will be enforced as soon as legally possible.

## 4. What can a person do if ordered to be removed from Canada?

If removal proceedings are brought against a person because of a criminal record, the individual will have an opportunity to give evidence to show why he or she should be allowed to remain in Canada.

The individual should do whatever possible to show CIC that he or she is no longer involved in criminal activity and is now of good behaviour. One good approach is to start the process of having the record removed. Often, showing that he or she is eligible to have the record removed, that the application has been made, and providing an approximate date as to when the record will be sealed or destroyed is sufficient to persuade immigration officials to allow the individual to remain in Canada.

If, however, a removal order is made, the person must leave Canada. In such a case, if the applicant wishes to apply to re-enter Canada, the application will be more likely to succeed if the person can show that the criminal record was removed, and that he or she is committed to living a crime-free life.

## 5.  Can someone re-enter Canada after having been removed?

It depends on the type of removal order made.

- **Departure Order.** A person against whom a departure order is made has 30 days to leave Canada and is required to obtain a certificate of departure upon leaving. If he or she does not comply with either of these two conditions, the departure order *automatically* becomes a *deportation* without notice. If a person complies with the conditions, they will not be barred from applying for a visa or from seeking admission at a Canadian port-of-entry. There is no guarantee, however, that the individual will be admitted or granted a visa.

    Every foreign national who applies to enter Canada will be subject to the usual immigration screening process. This means that, at the time of re-entry, the person might be *inadmissible* for a *different* reason. For example, if the person was convicted of a crime after the departure order was issued, it is very likely that that would make the individual inadmissible. In such a case, it would be advisable to remove the criminal record before trying to re-enter Canada.
- **Exclusion Order**. This type of order prevents a person form re-entering Canada for a period of one-year from the time that their departure from Canada is confirmed. If however, the person

If a person, against whom a departure or deportation order is made, tries to re-enter Canada without written authorization, they are subject to criminal prosecution. In many cases, this leads to the arrest of the traveller by CBSA. Bail is often denied and the person may have to await trial in custody even though they wish to return to their country of nationality. Sentences often include a term of imprisonment and immediate deportation from Canada while still in custody. Of course, a conviction for unauthorized return to Canada will create a criminal record and will constitute further grounds of inadmissibility.

had made a misrepresentation during the immigration process, the time period is extended to two years. During the one- or two-year period of the order, the individual cannot re-enter Canada unless *written* authorization from CIC prior to re-entry is obtained. After the one- or two-year period expires, the individual will no longer require the Minister's consent to re-enter Canada, and will be able to apply to re-enter in the usual way.

• **Deportation Order.** This type of order prevents a person from ever coming back to Canada unless they first obtain written authorization from CIC prior to re-entry—unless they have subsequently become a permanent resident or citizen. Unlike an exclusion order, the requirement to obtain the Minister's consent is ongoing; once a deportation order is made, the person can never return to Canada unless first obtaining the Minister's consent. Once again, there is no guarantee that the Minister will grant such authorization.

## LEGALLY ENTERING CANADA WITH A CRIMINAL RECORD

### 6. How can a foreign national with a criminal record legally enter Canada?

Individuals may still be able to legally enter Canada with a criminal record, under one of the following five circumstances:

- **Temporary Resident Permit (TRP).** An individual can enter temporarily by obtaining a TRP from CIC. This document can be obtained at a visa post *outside* of Canada or in some cases from the CBSA at a *port-of-entry*. It allows the applicant to enter Canada for a *compelling, specific,* and *temporary* purpose. A TRP can be issued for a single entry or for multiple entries during a specific period of time, such as six months. It may be cancelled at any time—for example, in cases where it was obtained through misrepresentation or through the withholding of material facts.

- **Canadian Pardon or Record Suspension (RS)**. An individual with a Canadian criminal record will not be inadmissible if a Canadian Pardon, now called a Record Suspension (RS) was obtained.[3]

  The *IRPA* states: "inadmissibility ... may not be based on a conviction in respect of which a pardon has been granted. ..." An RS is obtained from the Parole Board of Canada under the rules of the *Criminal Records Act*. In cases of non-convictions (e.g., discharges, stay of proceedings, peace bond, etc.), a purge or file destruction will be required instead of a Pardon or RS.

- **Youth and Contraventions Act records.** Permanent Residents and Foreign Nationals are *not considered* inadmissible due to their charges if they have been charged with an offence under the *Contraventions Act*, or under the *Young Offenders Act*, or the *Youth Criminal Justice Act*.

- **Rehabilitation Certificate (RC)**. An individual considered inadmissible because of a criminal record can have the inadmissibility removed by obtaining an RC from CIC. Unlike a TRP, an RC *never has to be renewed*. It lasts for the lifetime of the individual, so long as he or she does not commit, or is not convicted of, any subsequent crimes that would make him or her inadmissible.

- **Deemed Rehabilitation**. An individual will cease to be inadmissible when *deemed rehabilitated* by CIC. In such cases, an application is not necessary. To be deemed rehabilitated, *five years* or *ten years* must have passed since the individual completed the sentence imposed by the court. Whether the person must wait five or ten years depends on how serious the crime was. If the charge was a *strictly summary* offence (the least serious type of offence), then the individual must wait five years. If the charge was a hybrid or indictable offence, then the individual must wait ten years. In addition to the five-year or ten-year waiting period, other criteria, such as whether the individual was charged with one or more offences, the nature of the offences, and whether there are any outstanding current charges, will be considered.

The following chart shows eligibility requirements for Deemed Rehabilitation and Rehabilitation Certificates:

| Where Charges Occurred | Reason for Inadmissibility | Eligible for Rehabilitation Certificate | Deemed Rehabilitated |
|---|---|---|---|
| INSIDE Canada | (1) convicted of an offence punishable by a maximum jail term of at least 10 years [Section 36 (1)(a)] | (1) Not applicable, Pardon or RS required | (1) Not applicable, Pardon or RS required |
| | (2) convicted of an offence where a jail term of more than 6 months was imposed [Section 36 (1)(a)] | (2) Not applicable, Pardon or RS required | (2) Not applicable, Pardon or RS required |
| | (3) convicted of an offence punishable by indictment [Section 36 (2)(a)] | (3) Not applicable, Pardon or RS required | (3) Not applicable, Pardon or RS required |
| | (4) convicted of 2 or more summary offences not arising out of a single occurrence | (4) Not applicable, Pardon or RS required | (4) 5 years after the completion of the sentence imposed |
| | (5) discharges, peace bonds, withdrawn charges, stay of proceedings | (5) Not applicable, not strictly covered under legislation; usually need to prove court outcome (proof of file destruction helpful) | (5) Not applicable, not strictly covered under legislation; usually need to prove court outcome (proof of file destruction helpful) |
| OUTSIDE Canada | (1) convicted of an offence that, if in Canada, would be an offence punishable by a maximum jail term of at least 10 years [Section 36 (1)(b)] | (1) 5 years after the completion of the sentence imposed | (1) Not applicable, must apply for certificate |
| | (2) committing an act that is an offence in the place where committed, and, if in Canada, would constitute an offence with a maximum jail term of at least 10 years [Section 36 (1)(c)] | (2) 5 years after committing the offence [Section 36 (1)(c)] | (2) Not applicable, must apply for certificate |
| | (3) convicted of an offence, that, if in Canada, would be an indictable offence [Section 36 (2)(b)] | (3) 5 years after the completion of the sentence imposed | (3) 10 years after completion of sentence imposed, and must satisfy other criteria |
| | (4) committing an act that is an offence in the place where committed, and, if in Canada, would constitute an indictable offence [Section 36 (2)(c)] | (4) 5 years after committing the offence | (4) 10 years after committing the offence, and must satisfy other criteria |
| | (5) convicted of 2 or more offences not arising out of a single occurrence, that, if in Canada, would be offences under an Act of Parliament [Section 36 (2)(b)] | (5) 5 years after the completion of the sentence imposed | (5) 5 or 10 years after completion of sentence, depending on if offence strictly summary, or could be prosecuted summarily or by indictment, and must satisfy other criteria |
| | (6) committing, on entering Canada, an offence under an Act of Parliament prescribed by regulations [Section 36 (2)(d)] | (6) 5 years after committing the offence | (6) Not applicable, must apply for certificate |

## 7.  How to determine if a person is Deemed Rehabilitated

Individuals who are unsure of whether they qualify to be deemed rehabilitated may make an official inquiry. To do this, the individual will simply complete the Application for Criminal Rehabilitation, and check the box labelled For Information Only. The Immigration Department will make an assessment based on the details of the events and provide the individual with an official response. If CIC determines that the person is deemed rehabilitated, it is in the individual's best interests to carry this official CIC letter whenever coming to Canada for presentation to CIC border officers.

The same official inquiry process can be used by those people who are unsure of whether their criminal activities, in another country, would make them inadmissible to Canada.

TEMPORARY RESIDENT PERMIT (TRP)

## 8.  What is a TRP?

If a foreign national is, upon first consideration, determined to be inadmissible, he or she *may still be admitted* as a temporary resident permit holder. As its name suggests, a TRP gives the individual temporary immigration status to enter Canada. A TRP will stipulate the time period for which it is valid, and any other conditions, such as whether the person can enter Canada only once or multiple times. A TRP can be granted to a visitor or to those who wish to work or study in Canada. Each year, over 90,000 foreign workers and over 130,000 students enter Canada temporarily.

To apply for a TRP, the individual must submit an application with all the necessary documents to a Canadian consulate outside of Canada. The application must include: copies of all court documents describing all of the charges, convictions, and sentences; a copy of the law that the individual was convicted under; police clearance certificates; letters of reference (including an employment letter, if applicable); and a personal statement from the applicant. If the applicant lived in the U.S.A. during the past ten years, he or she must also submit a police certificate from the FBI. The application must be submitted with a *non-refundable* government processing fee.

Although it may take several months for the TRP application to be processed—depending on the consulate to which the application was submitted—it will be expedited in appropriate circumstances requiring urgency. Once the individual receives a TRP, he or she may apply to enter Canada temporarily. Worth mentioning is that a single-entry TRP expires once a foreigner seeks admission to Canada, whereas a multiple-entry TRP allows the holder to enter multiple times before its expiry date.

## 9. What factors are considered in deciding whether a TRP will be granted?

When an application for a TRP is made, a CIC officer—at a visa post or a CBSA officer at a port-of-entry—will examine it carefully to decide whether to grant the permit. In most cases involving minor instances of criminality, the officer can make this decision using his or her discretion. In other, more serious cases, the officer will need guidance and/or approval from a higher authority. Generally, the officer must show that the decision is *justified* in the circumstances. Basically, it comes down to a balancing of the risk the applicant poses to Canada against the benefit to Canadians by his or her admission. Applicants will be considered an *acceptable risk* and allowed to enter if further criminal activity on their part is not expected. Officers are guided by CIC Ministry policy that sets out the following risk factors to be considered when deciding whether to grant a TRP:

- seriousness of the offence
- chance of successful settlement without committing further offences
- behavioural factors involved (e.g., drug abuse, alcoholism)
- evidence that the person has reformed or rehabilitated
- pattern of criminal behaviour (e.g., the offence was an isolated event)
- completion of all sentences, fines paid, or restitution made
- whether there are any outstanding criminal charges
- restriction of travel following probation or parole
- eligibility for rehabilitation or an RS

- time elapsed since the offence occurred, and
- controversy or risk caused by presence of the person in Canada.

Immigration officers must weigh the possible pros and cons of each case. They may also obtain and rely upon information or confirmation from third parties (such as local police services or rehabilitation counsellors).

## 10. Can a TRP be cancelled because of subsequent criminal activity?

Yes. TRPs are issued based on specific grounds of inadmissibility. If the individual's circumstances change, the TRP can be cancelled. A TRP may be cancelled at any time if an immigration officer or the CIC Immigration Division determines that the individual has failed to comply with the IRPA. For example, new grounds of inadmissibility—such as new criminal charges or convictions—could make a person an unacceptable risk.

A TRP also can be cancelled if the person engages in unauthorized employment or studies in Canada.

In such cases, the individual will be notified of CIC's intention to cancel the TRP. The individual will be given an opportunity to be heard and to provide additional information within a reasonable period of time. If, after hearing the individual's evidence, the immigration officer isn't convinced that the person should be permitted to retain the TRP, then the individual will be notified that the TRP will be cancelled. Cancellation of the TRP, in almost all cases, will require that the person leave Canada as of the date specified by CIC.

### REHABILITATION CERTIFICATE (RC)

## 11. What is an RC?

An RC is the best way for people to enter Canada legally on an ongoing basis if they do not qualify to be *Deemed Rehabilitated*. An RC *waives* the individual's *inadmissibility* to enter Canada because of a foreign criminal record. It is more difficult to obtain than the TRP but, unlike the TRP, an RC *does not expire*. An RC lasts for the *lifetime* of the individual, so long as he or she is not convicted of, or does not commit, any subsequent crimes that would make him or her inadmissible. Also, an individual with current outstanding criminal charges will not be eligible for an RC.

When the individual may be eligible to apply for an RC will depend on many factors, such as the nature and seriousness of the crime and if the individual complied with the sentence imposed. The individual must wait at least five years after completing the sentence imposed by the court before making an application. For RC purposes, the *IRPA* deems all *hybrid* offences—those that may be prosecuted either summarily or by way of indictment—to be *indictable* offences, even where they have been prosecuted summarily. (Refer to the previous chart for specific eligibility requirements)

## 12. RC application process

### Submission of Application

An *Application for Criminal Rehabilitation* must be submitted, together with all supporting documents. If the applicant is *outside* Canada, the application will be submitted to the Canadian visa post designated by CIC for this purpose and which is determined by the person's country of nationality. If the applicant lives *in* Canada, the application will be submitted to the Central Processing Centre in Vegreville, Alberta, or to the local CIC.

Calculation of the eligibility time-period to apply for an RC does not start until every part of the sentence has been satisfied. For example, if a person was ordered to pay a fine but forgot to pay the fine until years later, the time doesn't start to run until the actual date the fine was paid.

If the application satisfies CIC that the person is rehabilitated, an RC will be granted and the applicant will no longer be considered inadmissible simply because of the criminal record. Rehabilitation means that the person now leads a stable lifestyle and is unlikely to be involved in any subsequent criminal activity. Furthermore, it must be shown that the sentence imposed by the court was completed—all jail time was served, parole and probation completed, all fines, restitution, and compensation paid—as the case may be.

When making an RC application, the individual will need to provide the following:

- personal information and documents, such as name, aliases and former names, date of birth, citizenship, and copy of passport
- details of the offences committed, such as name of offence, place where it occurred, date of conviction, place of conviction, and outcome
- a copy of each court judgment made against the applicant and any other documents that relate to the sentence, parole, probation, Pardon, or RS
- a copy of the foreign law under which the applicant was charged
- detailed explanation of events that led to the offences being committed, including a description of the applicant's actions, whether weapons, drugs, or alcohol were involved, effects of the acts upon victims and others
- police clearance certificates, an FBI police certificate if the applicant lived in the United States during the past ten years, or, if living abroad but not in the U.S.A., a police certificate from the police service having jurisdiction where the applicant lives
- purpose of the applicant's proposed visit to Canada
- an explanation as to why the applicant considers himself or herself rehabilitated—such as completion of drug-rehabilitation program, employment history, community services, and so on
- a non-refundable application fee.

### Review of Application

Once the application and supporting documents are received by CIC, an immigration officer will review them to determine if the person is eligible to apply. If the immigration officer decides that the person is eligible to apply for an RC, the officer will review the application, make a positive or negative recommendation, and then forward the application to the authority that ultimately makes the final decision. For less serious offences, the authority is usually the manager of the local CIC office. For more serious offences, the CIC Minister's office will make the decision.

Some of the factors that CIC takes into consideration when deciding an RC application include:

- the number of offences and the circumstances and seriousness of each offence
- the applicant's behaviour since committing the offence(s)
- the applicant's explanation of the offences and why the individual is not likely to reoffend
- any support the applicant receives from his or her community
- why the applicant thinks he or she is rehabilitated
- the applicant's present circumstances, such as having a stable home, and being employed.

These applications can take over one year to process. Once the applicant receives an RC, the individual may then apply to enter Canada in the usual way as either a visitor or a permanent resident. See pp. 122-125 for a sample of the four-page *Application for Criminal Rehabilitation*.

## CONVENTION REFUGEES

# 13. Who is considered a Convention Refugee?

Convention Refugees are people who are living outside their national country and, because of fear of persecution, cannot be protected within their country or return to it. That fear of persecution must be well-founded and based on their race, religion, nationality, political viewpoint, or their membership in a particular social or political group. The Refugee Protection Division of CIC will make a determination as to whether the applicant will receive *Convention Refugee* or *Protected Person* status under the *IRPA*. A person who has been granted refugee protection may then apply to CIC to become a permanent resident.

# 14. Can a criminal record make someone ineligible to claim refugee status?

Yes. Generally, an individual may claim refugee protection inside or outside of Canada by notifying a CIC or CBSA officer. Once an individual is considered

[*] [+] Citizenship and        Citoyenneté et
        Immigration Canada     Immigration Canada

Language of correspondence
☐ English    OR    ☐ French

# APPLICATION FOR CRIMINAL REHABILITATION

**SECTION A    TO BE COMPLETED BY APPLICANT**

| 1 | ☐ | APPLICATION FOR APPROVAL OF REHABILITATION | 2 | ☐ | FOR INFORMATION ONLY |
|---|---|---|---|---|---|

**SECTION B    TO BE COMPLETED BY APPLICANT**

| 1 Family name | Given name(s) - Do not use initials | 2 Date of birth | YEAR | MONTH | DAY | 3 Sex ☐ Male ☐ Female |
|---|---|---|---|---|---|---|

| 4 Country of birth | 5 Citizenship | 6 Marital status | ☐ Single  ☐ Married  ☐ Widowed  ☐ Separated  ☐ Common-law  ☐ Divorced |
|---|---|---|---|

7 All other names that I use or have used (Include maiden name, previous married name(s), aliases and nicknames, legal change of name)

1) Family name              Given name(s)              2) Family name              Given name(s)

| 8 My home address is | 9 Mailing address | All correspondence should be mailed to box 8 ☐ or to: |
|---|---|---|
| No. & street                    Apt./Unit | No. & street                    Apt./Unit | |
| City/Town    Province / State / Country    Postal / ZIP code | City/Town    Province / State / Country    Postal / ZIP code | |

| 10 Home telephone no. | 11 Business telephone no. | 12 Fax no. | 13 Indicate most convenient time to reach you by telephone | Time ☐ AM ☐ PM |
|---|---|---|---|---|
| Area code  No. | Area code  No. | Area code  No. | | |

14 E-mail address (Indicating an e-mail address will authorize all correspondence, including file and personal information, to be sent to the e-mail address you specify.)

15 I may be inadmissible to Canada because of the following offence(s): (use a separate sheet if necessary, entitled #15: Offences / Convictions)

| OFFENCE(S)/CONVICTION | DATE(S) OF OFFENCE(S)/ CONVICTION | | | PLACE OF OFFENCE(S)/ CONVICTION | SENTENCE(S) | STATUTE NUMBER(S) |
|---|---|---|---|---|---|---|
| | YEAR | MONTH | DAY | | | |
| | | | | | | |
| | | | | | | |
| | | | | | | |
| | | | | | | |
| | | | | | | |

16 On a separate sheet of paper, explain in detail the events/circumstances leading to the offence(s)/conviction(s). Indicate #16: Events / Circumstances on the sheet of paper.

**WARNING**

DETAILS OF ALL OFFENCES AND CONVICTIONS MUST BE ACCURATELY RECORDED ON THIS DOCUMENT. PROVIDING FALSE OR MISLEADING INFORMATION WILL LIKELY RESULT IN A REFUSAL OF YOUR APPLICATION AND MAY PERMANENTLY BAR YOUR ADMISSION TO CANADA.

This form is made available by Citizenship and Immigration Canada and is not to be sold to applicants.
(DISPONIBLE EN FRANÇAIS - IMM 1444 F)

IMM 1444 (08-2012) E

Canadä [*]

**17** Explain the purpose of your visit or stay in Canada

**18** On a separate sheet of paper, provide reasons why you consider yourself to be rehabilitated and why you do not represent a risk to public safety. Indicate #18: Rehabilitation Factor on the sheet of paper.

**19** Addresses since the age of 18. (Use a separate sheet if necessary)

Forms will be returned if there is any period of time for which you have not shown an address. Do not use post office (P.O.) box adresses.

| DATES | | | | NUMBER AND STREET (Do not use P.O. boxes) | APT. No. | CITY OR TOWN | PROVINCE / STATE COUNTRY |
|---|---|---|---|---|---|---|---|
| FROM | | TO | | | | | |
| YEAR | MONTH | YEAR | MONTH | | | | |
| | | | | | | | |
| | | | | | | | |
| | | | | | | | |
| | | | | | | | |
| | | | | | | | |
| | | | | | | | |

**20** Provide the details of your employment history since the age of 18. Start with the most recent information. Under "OCCUPATION", write your occupation or job title if you were working. If you were not working, provide information on what you were doing (for example: unemployed, studying, travelling, in detention, etc.).

**Note: Please ensure that you do not leave any gaps in time.**

Failure to account for all time periods will result in a delay in the processing of your application.

| DATES | | | | NAME AND ADDRESS OF COMPANY (Write name in full, do not use abbreviations) | OCCUPATION |
|---|---|---|---|---|---|
| FROM | | TO | | | |
| YEAR | MONTH | YEAR | MONTH | | |
| | | | | | |
| | | | | | |
| | | | | | |
| | | | | | |
| | | | | | |

THE INFORMATION YOU PROVIDE IN THIS DOCUMENT IS COLLECTED UNDER THE AUTHORITY OF THE CANADA *IMMIGRATION AND REFUGEE PROTECTION ACT* AND IS STORED IN PERSONAL INFORMATION BANK NUMBER CIC PPU 042, 054 OR 300. THE INFORMATION IS PROTECTED UNDER THE PROVISIONS OF THE *PRIVACY ACT* AND IS ACCESSIBLE TO YOU UPON REQUEST.

**21** I certify that the information provided by me is true and complete to the best of my knowledge.
I also certify that I am not currently charged with any criminal offence.

| | YEAR | MONTH | DAY |
|---|---|---|---|
| SIGNATURE OF APPLICANT ▶        DATE ▶ | | | |

IMM 1444 (08-2012) E

**SECTION C    TO BE COMPLETED BY THE OFFICER.**

| 1 Name of originating office | 2 File no. | 3 NHQ file no. (if known) |
|---|---|---|
| 4 Cost recovery code     Fee    GST    Receipt no. | | 5 FOSS / NCMS ID no. |

| 6     Equivalent offence(s) under Canadian law | 7     Maximum penalty under Canadian law |
|---|---|
| | |
| | |
| | |
| | |
| | |

**8** Inadmissibility provision(s) ▶

- ☐ A36(1)a)    ☐ A36(1)b)    ☐ A36(1)c)
- ☐ A36(2)a)    ☐ A36(2)b)    ☐ A36(2)c)

**9** Eligible to apply for rehabilitation? ▶ ☐ Yes ☐ No

**10** Date when subject was / will be eligible ▶    YEAR    MONTH    DAY

**11** If subject is not eligible, state reason(s)

**12** Officer's recommendation

☐ I recommend approval of rehabilitation      ☐ I recommend an application for a Temporary Resident's Permit

☐ I do not recommend approval of rehabilitation      ☐ I do not recommend an application for a Temporary Resident's Permit

**13** Reasons for recommendation

| 14 Name of officer | 15 Signature of officer | Date   YEAR   MONTH   DAY |
|---|---|---|
| | | |

IMM 1444 (08-2012) E

| 16 | | 17 | |
|---|---|---|---|
| Reviewing officer's recommendation ▶ | ☐ I concur / approve | | ☐ I do not concur / approve |

**18** Comments

:

| **19** Name of reviewing officer | **20** Signature of reviewing officer | Date |
|---|---|---|
| | | YEAR    MONTH    DAY |

**21** List of documents or photocopies attached - check those attached

☐ Passport

☐ Driver's License and USA Birth Certificate (USA-born citizens only)

☐ Court judgement(s)

☐ Text of non-Canadian statutes

☐ Police certificate

☐ Documentation re: sentence, parole, probation, fine or pardon

☐ Documentation re: juvenile offender

☐ Other documentation (specify)

**I certify that a copy of these documents has been provided to the applicant and that the applicant has been given an opportunity to provide comments.**

| **22** Name of officer | **23** Signature of officer | Date |
|---|---|---|
| | | YEAR    MONTH    DAY |

**SECTION D    FOR OFFICE USE ONLY**

| | | Initials | Date |
|---|---|---|---|
| Notification by (fax/e-mail) received that authority from the Minister for relief under A36(1)(b) or A36(1)(c) was: ▶ ☐ Granted ☐ Refused | | | YEAR    MONTH    DAY |
| Authority from the Minister's delegate for relief under A36(2)(b) or A36(2)(c) granted ▶ ☐ Yes ☐ No | | | Date  YEAR    MONTH    DAY |

| Name (please print) | Title |
|---|---|
| | |

| SIGNATURE ▶ | Date  YEAR    MONTH    DAY |
|---|---|

eligible to make a refugee claim, a hearing is held by the *Immigration and Refugee Board (IRB)* to determine if the person is in need of protection.

However, the person may be ineligible to claim refugee protection because of a criminal record that includes serious non-political offences. For example, if the individual committed, or was convicted of crimes that would make him or her ineligible to make a refugee claim, the immigration hearing can be suspended and even terminated. At this point, the individual will be removed from Canada unless an appeal is granted and successfully argued.

With respect to criminal records, the *IRPA* stipulates four main categories of crimes that may make a person ineligible to claim refugee status. If the person:

- was convicted *inside* Canada for a federal offence punishable by a maximum jail term of at least ten years and the individual received a jail term of at least two years
- was convicted *outside* Canada, for an offence, which, if committed in Canada, would be a federal offence punishable by a maximum jail term of at least ten years. In these circumstances, the Minister of CIC must also believe that the person is a danger to the Canadian public.
- is simply *believed* to be part of organized crime or involved in transnational crime (e.g., human trafficking or money laundering). No conviction is required.
- committed a crime against peace, a war crime, a crime against humanity, or a serious non-political crime outside of the country of refuge. Examples of these types of crimes may include drug trafficking, sexual assault against women or children, living on the avails of prostitution, smuggling firearms, and terrorism-related offences.

## 15. Can someone lose refugee status because of a criminal record?

Yes. Generally, if an individual is determined to be a Convention Refugee after an IRB hearing, he or she can stay in Canada and become a permanent resident. However, although CIC will not normally send an individual back to the country in which the individual feared persecution, a criminal record may cause them to do so. Whether CIC will deport the individual from Canada depends on the nature and seriousness of the crime, and on any other factor that CIC determines is relevant to the proceedings. For example, if the person committed a crime after being granted refugee status, or lied or withheld important facts about a past criminal record when making their application, CIC would consider these to be relevant factors in making its decision.

If an individual is given an order to be removed from Canada, he or she may make an application for a *Pre-removal Risk Assessment (PRRA)*. This is an assessment of the risk the individual would face if sent back to his or her home country. If the PRRA application is successful and it is proven that deportation would endanger the person's life, then the applicant will be allowed to stay in Canada. Otherwise, the person will be removed from Canada.

If a person can show that he or she is committed to living a crime-free life by applying for an RS, CIC will often allow the person to stay in Canada until it is received. For example, the following immigration letter on p.128, among other things, asks to see evidence that a formal Pardon application (as it was then called) had been submitted.

## PERMANENT RESIDENTS

## 16. Who is considered a permanent resident?

A permanent resident is someone who has been granted the right to live permanently in Canada. Permanent residents have more rights than visitors or refugees but not all the rights of Canadian citizens. Permanent residents can enter legally and permanently live in Canada so long as they comply with certain conditions.

## 17. Can a criminal record make someone ineligible for permanent residence status?

Yes. Applicants for permanent residence in Canada may not be eligible to acquire that status, or even to enter or stay in Canada, if they have a criminal record.

CPIC Report

Citizenship and
Immigration Canada

Citoyenneté et
Immigration Canada

File No.

Citizenship and Immigration Canada
200 Town Centre Court
Suite 380
Scarborough, Ontario
M1P 4X8

Toronto, Ontario

Dear Client:

This refers to your request, pursuant to subsection 114(2) of the Immigration Act for consideration on humanitarian and compassionate grounds.

As the information on your file is now outdated, we request your assistance in completing and returning the following:

1. ☐ Background questionnaire in detail
2. ☒ *In Canada Application For Landing* (IMM5001)
3. ☒ Copy of your passport
4. ☐ Proof of relationship to your relative
5. ☐ Proof of sponsor's status in Canada
6. ☒ Proof of savings
7. ☐ Proof of income of sponsor or yourself
8. ☒ Other:  4 passport size photographs
            Provide proof Pardon has been requested from the National Parole Board

**A determination on your case will be based on previously supplied information and information which you are asked to provide in this letter.** It is imperative that you provide full particulars of your case. You will be contacted if an interview is required. Please do not contact us unless instructed to do so as unnecessary case inquiries reduce the time we can spend in processing our clients' applications.

In closing, may I remind you that it is your responsibility to ensure that you keep us advised of any change of address by calling our general phone line 973-4444.

Thank you for your cooperation and patience.

Yours truly,

Citizenship and Immigration Counsellor

\* NOTICE

*The Scarborough Citizenship and Immigration Centre is closed to the public.*
*You will be NOTIFIED if an interview is required. Please call (416) 973-4444 for*
*all other Citizenship and Immigration Services.*

Canada

Citizenship and Immigration Canada Letter asking for proof that a Pardon had been applied for

Further, it is important to understand that if *any mem*ber of the family who is listed in the permanent residence application is *inadmissible* because of a cri*minal record,* everyone who is part of the family application will be inadmissible.

Schedule A of the Immigration Application which asks if the applicant, or any member of the family, has a Criminal Record

The form on p. 129 is page 1 of Schedule A of the application for permanent residence status. Question 6 deals with various things that could make a person inadmissible, including if the principal applicant or any of the family members listed in the application has a criminal record.

## 18. Can someone lose permanent residence status because of a criminal record?

Yes. Even if an individual has been a permanent resident for many years or since childhood, a criminal record can preclude the individual from applying for citizenship, cause the individual to lose permanent residence status, and at worst, it may cause the person to be removed from Canada. Permanent residence status also can be removed for a number of other reasons, including if the person: lived outside of Canada for more than three years in any five-year period; falsified documents when applying for permanent residence status; or lied or falsified documents when applying for refugee status.

The relevant fact is whether CIC considered this information when granting residency status or whether the information is *new* to CIC. If CIC had knowledge of the criminal record and still granted permanent residence status, then the criminal record will have no further impact. If, however, new information is brought to the attention of CIC, such as a very old criminal record they didn't know about, or a new charge altogether, it will complicate and could jeopardize the person's immigration status. If the permanent resident is charged with a crime, the police will report this fact to the CBSA. From this point forward, the CBSA will investigate the severity of the crime and determine what affect it will have on the individual's immigration status.

The *IRPA* says that a permanent resident cannot enter Canada if he or she:

- was *convicted inside* Canada for a federal offence punishable by a maximum jail term of *at least ten years*
- was *convicted inside* Canada for a federal offence which included a jail term of *more than six months*, or
- committed an offence or was convicted of an offence *outside* Canada that if committed in Canada *would be a federal offence* punishable by a maximum jail term of at least ten years.

The following CIC letter shows that the immigration application was put on hold until CIC had an opportunity to review the court records.

Citizenship and        Citoyenneté et
Immigration Canada    Immigration Canada

**INTERVIEW CALL-IN NOTICE**

*APPLICATION FOR PERMANENT RESIDENCE IN CANADA*

CANADA IMMIGRATION CENTRE
P.O. BOX 1010, STATION "B"
MISSISSAUGA, ONTARIO
L4Y 3W3

| | HWY 401 |
|---|---|
| | **WATLINE AVE** |
| *NORTH* ↑ | MATHESON BLVD |
| H W Y 10 | HWY 403 |
| | Q.E.W. |

Client Identification Number ▮▮▮▮▮▮

▮▮▮▮▮▮▮▮▮▮▮▮

This office has scheduled an interview for you. The date and time of your appointment is indicated below. To cancel or change the time of the interview, please call (905) 507-2012. You are required to present yourself to this office at least 20 minutes prior to your interview time. If an interpreter is required, you must provide your own. **Failure to appear for your interview may result in your application being refused.**

**INTERVIEW DATE** _____ **TIME** _____ **ROOM NO** _____

**YOUR** _____ **MUST ACCOMPANY YOU TO THE INTERVIEW.**

**PLEASE BRING THE INFORMATION REQUESTED BELOW**

COMPLETED FORMS:

OTHER DOCUMENTS:

[ X ] OTHER: WE REQUIRE A COPY OF THE COURT RESULTS/CONVICTION CERTIFICATES, FOR VANCOUVER AND TORONTO, BEFORE WE CAN PROCEED FURTHER WITH YOUR CASE.

C. TOUT

IMMIGRATION OFFICER

**YOU MUST BRING THIS FORM WITH YOU TO THE INTERVIEW**
YOU MUST ATTEND THIS OFFICE AT LEAST 20 MINUTES
PRIOR TO YOUR SCHEDULED INTERVIEW TIME

Citizenship and Immigration Canada Letter asking for copy of the applicant's Criminal Record

CANADIAN CITIZENSHIP

A Canadian citizen is a person who either was born in Canada, was born to a Canadian parent abroad (except those who were born outside of Canada to Canadian citizen parent[s] who were also born outside of Canada), or who, after applying, was granted Canadian citizenship by CIC. A Canadian citizen enjoys full legal status—such as legal rights, privileges, and duties—in Canada. The legislation that governs how a person can become a Canadian citizen is the *Citizenship Act*.

## 19. Can a criminal record make someone ineligible to become a Canadian citizen?

Yes. In addition to the "language and knowledge of Canada" requirements, in order to be eligible to apply for Canadian citizenship, a person must be at least eighteen years of age and have resided in Canada as a permanent resident for at least three of the past four years. In calculating that three-year period, time spent in pre-trial custody, doing community service, on probation or parole, or in jail cannot be counted.[4]

In the citizenship application, the individual will be asked to provide detailed information about any criminal offences, whether committed inside or outside of Canada.

Applicants will likely not be granted Canadian citizenship if they:

- are currently on probation, parole, or in jail
- are currently charged with an indictable criminal offence or an offence under the *Citizenship Act*
- in the three years prior to applying, or during the application process, have been convicted of an indictable criminal offence, or an offence under the *Citizenship Act*
- are, or have ever been, under a removal order
- have been charged with:
  ◊ an offence related to certificates of citizenship (e.g., using a certificate to impersonate another person, knowingly permitting

another person to use his or her certificate to impersonate the applicant, trafficking in certificates, etc.)

◊   an indictable offence for which no final outcome has been obtained
- have charges pending because the charges were stayed[5]
- are under investigation (by Canadian federal law enforcement) or have been convicted of certain crimes against humanity or war crimes (including murder, extermination, enslavement, deportation, imprisonment, torture, sexual violence, etc.)
- have had Canadian citizenship taken away (revoked) in the past five years, or
- have committed an offence outside of Canada that is considered an offence in Canada that would make applicants ineligible for citizenship.

At the very least, a criminal record will slow down and complicate the citizenship application process.

## 20. Can someone lose Canadian citizenship status because of a criminal record?

Yes. While rare, an individual who has been granted a certificate of citizenship can actually have his or her Canadian citizenship *revoked*. This can happen if the person committed offences during the process of obtaining his or her Canadian citizenship or permanent residence status. Such offences include making false representations, knowingly concealing material circumstances, or offences relating to fraud.

In the above circumstances, the individual does not need to be convicted of these offences to lose citizenship status. The CIC Minister simply needs to be *satisfied* that a prohibited offence took place and, at that point, an application can be made to the Federal Court for a judicial review of the decision. A sample *Application for Canadian Citizenship* (pages 1 and 4) follows.

Citizenship and   Citoyenneté et
Immigration Canada   Immigration Canada

## APPLICATION FOR CANADIAN CITIZENSHIP - ADULTS
### (18 years of age and older)
### UNDER SUBSECTION 5(1)

| FOR OFFICIAL USE ONLY |
|---|
| UCI no. |
| Certificate no. |

**NOTE:** The information you provide should not be limited by the space allowed to answer a question. If you need more space, attach another sheet of paper. Indicate the number of the question you are answering.

Refer to the guide for specific instructions.
Please PRINT in ink or TYPE.

**1. A** Language you prefer for:

Service: ☐ English   ☐ French

**B** I have special needs that require accommodation

☐ No   ☐ Yes ▶ If yes, please explain: _____

**2.** I have applied for Canadian citizenship before

☐ No   ☐ Yes ▶ When? _____ Year

**3. A** Name (<u>exactly</u> as it is shown on my immigration document)

Last name (surname/family name) _____

Given name(s) _____

**B** Request for a different name to appear on certificate and please indicate/select reason below: (subject to approval by Citizenship and Immigration Canada)

☐ Truncated (shortened) name on immigration document   ☐ Legal name change

☐ Minor change in spelling   ☐ Significant change in spelling

Last name (surname/family name) _____

Given name(s) _____

**C** List any other names used including <u>name at birth</u>, maiden name, previous married name(s), aliases and nicknames. These names will not appear on your citizenship certificate.

Provide details: _____

Last name (surname/family name) _____

Given name(s) _____

| FOR OFFICIAL USE ONLY |
|---|
| Space reserved for applicant's label |

**4. A** Birth details as shown on my immigration document

Date ▶ Year | Month | Day     Place ▶ Town/City _____

Country _____

**B** Personal information

Sex ▶ ☐ Male ☐ Female   Height ▶ _____ cm OR _____ ft _____ in   Colour of eyes ▶ _____

Marital status ▶ ☐ Never married ☐ Married ☐ Common-law ☐ Widowed ☐ Divorced ☐ Legally separated

**5. A** Home address

| No. and street | | Apt. no. |
|---|---|---|
| City/Village | Province | |
| Country | | Postal code |

**B** Mailing address (if different from home address)

| No. and street | | Apt. no. |
|---|---|---|
| City/Village | Province | |
| Country | | Postal code |

This form is made available by Citizenship and Immigration Canada and is not to be sold to applicants.
(DISPONIBLE EN FRANÇAIS - CIT 0002 F)

CIT 0002 (01-2013) E

 Canada

**7. Language evidence**

**A** If you are between 18 and 54 of age you **must** submit acceptable proof that demonstrates that you have adequate knowledge of English or French. Please check the appropriate box to indicate which one of the following forms of proof you are submitting with your application:

☐ Results of a CIC-approved third-party language test; **or**

☐ Diploma, certificate or transcript of a secondary or post-secondary education in English or French, in Canada or abroad; **or**

☐ Evidence of achieving CLB/NCLC 4 in a government-funded language training program

☐ If you successfully completed LINC (Language Instruction for Newcomers to Canada), classes during the period from January 2008 to October 2012 but did not receive a certificate*

\* CIC has previously collected information about the results of your LINC language training for a statistical purpose but CIC would like to obtain and use this information for purposes of verifying your language results. By signing the consent form section 9E of this application, you authorize CIC to use the information that has been already collected to verify whether you have adequate knowledge of English or French.

**B** I have a disorder, disability or condition that is cognitive, psychiatric or psychological in nature which prevents me from submitting proof of language with my application. Note: You must submit supporting evidence.

☐ No   ☐ Yes   ▶ If yes, please explain.

---

**8. PROHIBITIONS UNDER THE *CITIZENSHIP ACT***

**A** Are you now or have you ever been in the last 4 years: • an inmate of a penitentiary, jail, reformatory, or prison?  ▶ ☐ No ☐ Yes

• on probation?  ▶ ☐ No ☐ Yes

• on parole?  ▶ ☐ No ☐ Yes

**B** In the past 3 years, have you been convicted of an indictable offence (crime) or an offence under the *Citizenship Act*?  ▶ ☐ No ☐ Yes

**C** Are you now charged with an indictable offence (crime) or an offence under the *Citizenship Act*?  ▶ ☐ No ☐ Yes

**D** Are you now, or have you ever been, under a removal order (have you been asked by Canadian officials to leave Canada)?  ▶ ☐ No ☐ Yes

**E** Are you now under investigation for or charged with a war crime or a crime against humanity or have you ever been convicted of a war crime or a crime against humanity?  ▶ ☐ No ☐ Yes

**F** In the past 5 years, have you had Canadian citizenship which has been taken away (revoked)?  ▶ ☐ No ☐ Yes

I have read and understand the prohibitions under the *Citizenship Act*.

If you have checked "YES" to any of the prohibitions listed above, provide details below. If applicable attach court documents.

## Quiz

**1. A foreigner with the following cannot generally enter Canada:**

    a. A conviction within Canada for a federal offence punishable by a maximum jail term of at least 10 years

    b. A conviction within Canada for a federal offence where a jail term of at least 6 months was imposed

    c. A conviction outside Canada that, if committed in Canada, would be an indictable offence

    d. If the person committed a federal offence upon entering Canada (such as an offence under the *Criminal Code*, or *Customs Act*)

    e. All of the above

**2. Foreigners who cannot enter Canada because of their criminal record can:**

    a. Never enter Canada

    b. Try to satisfy the Minister of CIC that they have been rehabilitated after waiting at least 5 years after completing their sentence

    c. Obtain a Record Suspension for Canadian convictions before trying to enter

    d. Apply to enter Canada as a temporary resident permit holder

    e. (b), (c), and (d)

**3. After being removed from Canada, foreigners can re-enter if:**

    a. They were removed pursuant to a Departure Order and are not inadmissible when they return to Canada

    b. They were removed pursuant to an Exclusion Order and have obtained written authorization from the Minister of CIC prior to returning to Canada

    c. They were removed pursuant to a Deportation Order, so long as they wait 5 years prior to returning

    d. All of the Above

    e. (a) and (b)

**4. Permanent residents cannot enter Canada if:**

    a. They were convicted in Canada for a federal offence punishable by a maximum jail term of at least 5 years

    b. They were convicted in Canada for a federal offence that included a jail term of more than 3 months

    c. They committed an offence abroad that, if committed in Canada, would be considered an offence punishable by a maximum jail term of at least 5 years

   d. (a) and (c)
   e. None of the above

**5. A person will be ineligible for Canadian citizenship if:**
   a. Charged with an indictable offence for which no final outcome has been obtained
   b. Convicted of an indictable offence, in the 3 years prior to applying, and for which a Pardon or Record Suspension has not been received,
   c. Convicted of a summary conviction offence, and is currently on probation
   d. (a) and (b)
   e. (a), (b), and (c)

**6. True or False:**
   a. Temporary residents cannot lose their status because of their criminal record
   b. Permanent residents cannot lose their status because of their criminal record
   c. A foreigner can be removed from Canada because of a criminal record, even after having entered legally
   d. If someone claims refugee protection and has a criminal record, he or she may be deemed ineligible and removed from Canada
   e. While rare, people who have been granted a certificate of citizenship can lose citizenship status because of a criminal record

Answer Key: 1 (e), 2 (e), 3 (e), 4 (e), 5 (e), 6 false, true, true, true

# End Notes

1. Federal offences include offences under the *Criminal Code, Controlled Drugs and Substances Act, Firearms Act, Customs Act,* and so on.

2. *IRPA* s. 36.

3. *IRPA* s. 36 (3). Under the new Canadian Pardon law, the term "Record Suspension" replaced the word "Pardon."

4. Also, if the applicant was detained on charges and ultimately found not-guilty by reason of insanity, the detention time cannot be counted.

5. A *stay of proceedings* means there was no finding of guilt, but the case was not closed. The file will stay open for one year to give the Crown time to produce new evidence that could secure a conviction.

Chapter Six

# Travelling to the U.S.A. with a Criminal Record
### – I-194 Entry Waivers –

## I-194 U.S.A. ENTRY WAIVERS

## INADMISSIBILITY AND BEING DENIED ENTRY AT THE BORDER

In the past, Canadians with criminal records may have passed through the American border after only answering a few standard questions about their citizenship and the purpose of their trip. They were lucky. Since the tragic events of September 11, 2001, their luck has been running out. The intensified security at the American borders and improved technology have given U.S.A. Customs and Border Patrol officers (CBP) quicker and deeper insight into the RCMP data banks. During routine security checks, CBP officers can now easily access Canadian criminal records contained in both the RCMP Investigative and Identification data banks. All the CBP officer needs is the person's name and date of birth to obtain detailed criminal record information. That information is then instantly downloaded into their FBI computer system where it will remain forever—even if the person eventually gets a Record Suspension (formerly called a Pardon).

One way to avoid this mess and enter the United States legally, without the shame and turmoil of being refused on the spot, is to obtain a U.S.A. Entry Waiver. Applicants must be prepared to disclose their entire criminal past and submit official documents and explanations about their crimes. Those who have never been stopped at the border and are not keen to make a Waiver application might consider removing their Canadian criminal record before going to the U.S.A. If photographs and fingerprints are completely destroyed, or where a Pardon or Record Suspension has been granted and the U.S.A. did not have prior knowledge of the criminal record, they won't find it.[1]

## 1. Can American Immigration officers access Canadian criminal records?

Yes, in most cases. When Canadian law-enforcement officers charge someone with a crime, they almost always take photographs and fingerprints. A copy of this local police file is then entered into CPIC Investigative data bank and, also, the RCMP creates its own file in the Identification data bank, where a fingerprint section number (FPS) is assigned to the person's name and date of birth.

The RCMP's Investigative and Identification data banks are accessible to

American Customs officers through CPIC searches. The American *National Crime Information Centre (NCIC)* is their counterpart to our CPIC. When a person attempts to enter the U.S.A., American *Customs and Border Patrol (CBP)* officers have the authority to conduct a CPIC check via NCIC using the person's name and date of birth.

If a criminal record exists in one of these data banks, the CBP officer will discover it. Even in cases that did not result in a finding of guilt (e.g., cases that were thrown out of court or where the person was found to be innocent) and which are supposed to be *restricted*, the fact that a criminal record exists will be revealed because the criminal record and the person's name and date of birth are associated with an RCMP fingerprint section (FPS) number. Where the details of the crime and the outcome are not instantly available, the simple fact that an FPS number exists is sufficient to have the file downloaded and for the person to be turned away at the border.

Many would argue that those charges that resulted in a *not-guilty* outcome for which disclosure is *restricted* are never disclosed. Although *not-guilty* charges do not appear on *hard copy certified RCMP reports*—issued for American travel purposes—those charges together with their FPS number *are* routinely disclosed at the border during a computer search. The CBP officers can easily identify the FPS number and will usually tell the person some details of the information that they see—such as what the offence was—and then ask for further details. Sometimes, the CBP officer will print out parts of the criminal record information and give it to the person.

The letter that follows shows that as far back as 1997, American CBP officers were able to access detailed information from the RCMP Identification data bank. Today, this type of information can be accessed and downloaded faster and more easily. Once the American CBP officer downloads the person's criminal record information into their system, it will be retained forever. The U.S.A. will identify the individual as being an *Illegal Alien* and assign a lifetime Alien Number (A#) to them. From then on, every time the person tries to cross the border, he or she will be stopped because of their criminal record.

## 2. Can someone who has a criminal record legally enter the U.S.A.?

According to American immigration laws, a person can be denied entry into the United States for several reasons, including:

- being convicted of a *crime involving moral turpitude (CIMT)*
- being convicted of a drug-related offence[2]
- being convicted of two or more offences for which the total jail sentence was at least five years
- if a CBP officer knows or has reason to believe that the individual has ever been engaged in (among other things) drug-trafficking, human-trafficking, money-laundering, espionage, terrorism, torture, smuggling other people into the U.S.A., and so on.

The Jay Treaty (1794) and subsequent legislation have recognized certain rights of Native people. Under article III, those qualifying for Native status (50% Aboriginal Blood) can cross the border freely.

Under any of these circumstances, it is illegal to enter the U.S.A. with a criminal record, unless a person is an American citizen, has Native American status, or has received advanced permission from American Immigration such as a U.S.A. Entry Waiver.

The key thing to remember is that a CBP officer has the authority to refuse someone entry for any reason that the officer feels might be a threat to the U.S.A. It is not *necessary* that the person have a conviction to be turned away at the border. In fact, no criminal record needs to exist to be denied entry. For example, if during an interview with a CBP officer, a person simply admits to having committed an act that the CBP officer believes would constitute a criminal offence, then the person will almost certainly be refused. So, people must be aware of self-incrimination when being interviewed at the border.

Determinations as to who will be admitted are made at the discretion of the CBP officers on a case-by-case basis in light of all the relevant and available facts. The border officers do not have the means or the authority to review all the details of a crime. Their job is to keep the U.S.A. safe and to screen out all the *undesirable people.* That's why what actually happens is that the officers make a quick, on-the-spot assessment, and, in most cases, will not let in anyone with a criminal record. Instead, they will tell the person to make a formal application for a Waiver. This way, they are sure the application for entry will be thoroughly reviewed by their *Admissibility Review Office (ARO),* and they don't have to take any chances of letting in someone who is inadmissible. The following letter was given to a Canadian citizen by American Immigration officers at Pearson Airport. The person was questioned and fingerprinted by CBP officers before being handed this letter, which advises that a Waiver is required.

### UNITED STATES DEPARTMENT OF JUSTICE
### IMMIGRATION AND NATURALIZATION SERVICE
#### LESTER B. PEARSON INTERNATIONAL AIRPORT
#### TORONTO, CANADA

AT THIS POINT IN TIME, YOU DO NOT APPEAR CLEARLY ADMISSABLE TO THE UNITED STATES AS A TEMPORARY VISITOR FOR PLEASURE. IN AN EFFORT TO SATISFY IMMIGRATION OFFICIALS OF YOUR STATUS AND INTENTIONS, YOU MAY PROVIDE THIS OFFICE WITH THE ITEMS CHECKED BELOW.

THIS LIST IS INTENDED TO BE USED AS A GUIDELINE TO ASSIST YOU IN RETURNING WITH THE NECESSARY MATERIALS TO SUFFICIENTLY MEET THE BURDEN OF PROOF INCUMBENT UPON YOU AS AN APPLICANT FOR ADMISSION TO THE UNITED STATES. THIS LIST SHOULD NOT BE CONSIDERED ALL INCLUSIVE. **THE FINAL DECISION OF ADMISSION IS ALWAYS MADE BY AN IMMIGRATION INSPECTOR AFTER ALL ITEMS/FACTS ARE CONSIDERED.**

[ ] **EVIDENCE OF EMPLOYMENT**
   ie: recent pay stubs, employment ID, letter of employment, etc.

[ ] **EVIDENCE OF FOREIGN RESIDENCE**
   ie: various utility bills-recent phone, gas, electric, water, recent rent receipts, copy of mortgage, deed, etc.

[ ] **EVIDENCE OF FINANCIAL ABILITY**
   ie: bank statements, savings and checking acount transaction books, income tax forms, etc.

[ ] **EVIDENCE OF FINANCIAL ASSISTANCE**
   ie: unemployment insurance, mothers assistance, welfare, disability, in the form of current stubs, receipts, government correspondence.

[ ] **EVIDENCE OF EDUCATIONAL TIES**
   ie: valid school ID, letter from school official, current course registration, etc.

[ ] **CONFIRMED RETURN TICKETS**
   ie: plane, train, bus, etc. (date specific; non-refundable)

[ ] **SUFFICIENT FUNDS FOR INTENDED LENGTH OF STAY**
   ie: cash, travellers checks, personal checks, credit cards, etc.

[ ] **CONTACT PERSON**
   ie: family member, friend, or individual whom you are travelling to see in the US.

[ ] **ADDRESS/TELEPHONE NUMBER WHERE YOU CAN BE REACHED IN THE U.S.**

[X] **OTHER:** *YOU NEED TO OBTAIN AN I-194 WAIVER FROM USINS FOR YOUR CONVICTION IN HAMILTON, ONTARIO ON 5/3/91 FOR THEFT UNDER $1000 AND GIVEN FINE OF $250*

DATE: 07/04/1997

TIME: 9 6 6

TERMINAL:

*HAND DELIVERED TO:*

USA Immigration Letter showing they have access to the RCMP data bank

CRIMES INVOLVING MORAL TURPITUDE

## 3.   What is a Crime Involving Moral Turpitude (CIMT)?

There is no statutory definition or definitive list of what constitutes a *Crime Involving Moral Turpitude (CIMT)* in the U.S.A.

In fact, the American courts have made inconsistent determinations for some crimes. For example, over time, impaired driving offences have been found to be both crimes involving and not involving moral turpitude. Such inconsistency causes much confusion to those of us trying to nail down what crimes would render someone inadmissible. But surely the courts have said something more about the matter?

Well, in a U.S.A. Board of Immigration Appeals decision (which is generally the highest administrative body for interpreting and applying immigration laws), it was stated quite unhelpfully that:

Although impaired driving charges are not currently considered crimes involving moral turpitude, as of 2012, in some cases, individuals with only one impaired charge are now being asked to undergo a psychological examination before being admitted to the U.S.A.

Moral turpitude refers generally to conduct that shocks the public conscience as being inherently base, vile, or depraved, contrary to the rules of morality and the duties owed between man and man, either one's fellow man or society in general. Moral turpitude has been defined as an act which is per se morally reprehensible and intrinsically wrong ... so it is the nature of the act itself and not the statutory prohibition of it which renders a crime one of moral turpitude.[3]

This type of statement does not clear up the problem. Over time, people have tried to review the large volume of decisions from American administrative bodies and the courts, and from these decisions draw conclusions about which crimes would render someone inadmissible to the U.S.A. Unfortunately, for practical purposes, this doesn't really work either, and this is why:

Neither the seriousness of the offence nor the severity of the sentence imposed will determine whether a crime is a CIMT. Rather, it is also a question of the offender's intent. American law says that if a crime was comprised of an element of specific and malicious intent (or such negligence and reckless conduct that it would be regarded by law as equivalent to such intent) on the part of the offender, then it will be a CIMT. If this wasn't confusing enough, being convicted of conspiring or attempting to commit a CIMT also counts, as do convictions for aiding and abetting or being an accessory in the commission of a CIMT. In reality, no one can be sure what crimes will be considered a CIMT at any given time. The following U.S.A. Immigration letter clearly shows that it reserves the right to change its policies when, in rendering a decision about the offences of assault and mischief, it stated, "… they are not, *at this time*, considered *by this service*, to be crimes involving moral turpitude."

When someone who has a Canadian criminal record arrives at an American border, a CBP officer does not have the time to analyze the criminal offences with respect to their *inherent* properties, understand the individual's intent with respect to whether that falls within the CIMT category, and finally determine whether the crimes involve moral turpitude. When making timely decisions at the border and given the complexity in determining if a crime is a CIMT, it is impossible to expect a CBP officer to know with certainty what crimes involve moral turpitude. That is why CBP officers err on the side of safety.

What really happens is CBP officers turn away almost everyone with an FPS number, even though a large number of these people have not committed a crime that would make them inadmissible (e.g., charges with *not-guilty* outcomes). Even in cases where people have brought all the appropriate court documents with them, proving that the charges were thrown out of court, the CBP officer will often refuse them entry. At the very least, these people will experience delays and uncertainties at customs. This can be very humiliating and humbling, and if travelling by air, it is not uncommon for the individual to miss his or her flight.

So, figuring out if a crime is a CIMT is, to a large extent, merely an academic exercise. For practical purposes, people with criminal records who want to enter the U.S.A. legally and with as few problems as possible should submit a formal Waiver application.

**U.S. Department of Justice**

Immigration and Naturalization Service

130 Delaware Avenue
Buffalo, New York 14202

A   77   8

21 St. Clair Ave. E. Suite PH
Toronto, ON Canada
M4T 1L9

NOV X 3 1997

Dear M

Reference is made to your application for advance permission to enter the United States as a nonimmigrant, submitted to this office on May 9, 1997.

Records at this office indicate the following:

| Date and Place | Charge | Disposition |
|---|---|---|
| 02- 3-1995<br>Oshawa, ON | (1) Assault A Peace Officer Sec 270<br>(1) (A) CC<br>2 Chgs<br>(2) Mischief Over $1000 Sec 430<br>(3) CC | (1) 45 Days Intermittent On Each Chg Conc & Probation 6 Mos On Each Chg<br>(2) Susp Sent & Probation 1 Yr |

On February 3, 1995 you were convicted of two (2) charges of Assault a Peace Officer and one (1) charge Mischief Under $1000. For the first convictions you served 45 days intermittent and 6 months probation on each charge and for the second conviction you received a suspended sentence and 1 year probation. While Assault of A Peace Officer and Mischief Under $1000 are deemed to be serious, they are not, at this time, considered by this service to be crimes involving moral turpitude.

You may wish to retain this letter for presentation to United States Immigration authorities if you should apply for entry in the future.

Very truly yours,

John J Ingham
District Director

USA Immigration Letter showing what constitutes a Crime Involving Moral Turpitude can change

# 4. How can people prove their crime is not a CIMT?

The only way to definitively prove to a CBP officer that a particular crime is not a CIMT is to have an official letter from U.S.A. Immigration stating this fact. And, as ridiculous as it seems, the only way to receive such a letter is to make a formal application for a Waiver.

When applying for a Waiver to legally enter the U.S.A., there are two possible successful outcomes.

- If the ARO determines that the crime was *not* a CIMT, the individual will receive an official *letter* stating this fact.
- If the crimes are determined to involve moral turpitude, and if the application is successful, the individual will receive a *Waiver*.

Either way, whenever the individual wants to enter the U.S.A., he or she will need to carry the *Waiver,* or the *letter* stating that the crime was not a CIMT. Only presenting one of these official documents will prove to the CBP officer that the person is no longer inadmissible due to a criminal record.

That this type of letter should be presented at the border is evidenced in the samples on pp. 148-149. The first is a letter from the American ARO, stating, "To help facilitate future travel, it is recommended that you carry this letter for presentation to the inspecting officer." A similar statement appears at the bottom of the second (much older) letter issued by the American Immigration office (INS). Since these letters *never expire*, both are still valid today. Essentially, letters such as these act as *Permanent Waivers* and those people who were issued one should treat it like gold. In fact, it is prudent to make photocopies and have them notarized in case the original is lost or damaged.

# 5. Are there any crimes that would not prevent someone from entering the U.S.A.?

Legally, yes. From a practical perspective, however, a person often will be refused entry into the U.S.A. if the CBP officer sees that a criminal record file exists in the RCMP data banks, even if the offence is one that would not render the person inadmissible.

**U.S. Customs and Border Protection**
Admissibility Review Office
2825 Worldgate Drive
Herndon, VA 20598

A2

February 2, 2011

Dear Mr.

This correspondence is in reference to your Form I-192, Application for Advance Permission to Enter as Nonimmigrant. Your application was submitted on or about September 1, 2010 because you may be inadmissible to the United States under Section 212(a)(2)(A)(i)(I) of the Immigration and Nationality Act (INA), as amended. The noted section of the INA states, in part, that an alien who has been convicted of a crime involving moral turpitude is inadmissible to the United States.

A review of the record establishes that on September 6, 2006, you were convicted Toronto, Ontario, Canada, of Assault in violation of Section 266 of the Canadian Criminal Code. As a result of this conviction, your sentence was suspended and given 3 years probation.

Upon examination of the statute under which you were convicted, Section 266 of the Canadian Criminal Code, this office concludes that this conviction does not, in whole or part, constitute a crime involving moral turpitude. As such, this conviction does not have an effect on admissibility to the United States under Section 212(a)(2)(A)(i)(I) of the INA

It is the determination of this office that you are eligible for travel to the United States. Your inspection, upon applying for admission to the United States, will be conducted in the normal process accorded an applicant seeking admission into this country. To help facilitate future travel, it is recommended that you carry this letter for presentation to the inspecting officer.

Sincerely,

Michael D. Olszak
Director
Admissibility Review Office

USA CBP "N/A" Letter stating that the applicant is not 'inadmissible'

**U.S. Department of Justice**

Immigration and Naturalization Service
130 Delaware Avenue
Buffalo, New York 14202

A   -25

DEC 3 0 1998

Dear M———

Reference is made to your application for advanced permission to enter the United States as a nonimmigrant, originally submitted to this office November 1 , 1998.

Records at this office indicate the following:

| Date and Place | Charge | Disposition |
|---|---|---|
| 1995-01-1<br>Oshawa, Ontario | Driving While Ability Impaired | $750 & Prohibited<br>Driving 18 Months |
| 1997-01-03<br>Toronto, Ontario | Escape Lawful Custody | Conditional Discharge<br>Probation 7 Months |

On January  1, 1995 you were convicted of Driving While Ability Impaired in Oshawa, Ontario, for which you received a sentence of $750 fine and prohibited driving for 18 months.  On January 3, 1997 you were convicted of Escape Lawful Custody in Toronto, Ontario, for which you received a conditional discharge and probation for 7 months. While you did commit and were convicted of two serious criminal charges, the crimes committed therein are not considered crimes involving moral turpitude.  As a result, you are not inadmissible to the United States based on the above convictions.

Your inspection upon applying for admission to the United States will be conducted in the normal inspectional process accorded an applicant seeking entry to this country.

You may wish to retain this letter for presentation to the United States Immigration authorities if you should apply for entry in the future.

Very truly yours,

John J. Ingham
District Director

USA Immigration "N/A" Letter from 1998, which is still valid

Offences that are *not supposed to* render a person inadmissible are:

- purely political offences
- a conviction for a single youth crime[4] where more than five years have passed. If, however, the person was between fifteen and eighteen years old, they may still be inadmissible if they were tried and convicted at that time as an adult for serious offences involving violence, or if there is a pattern of criminal misconduct as a youth.
- crimes for which the maximum punishment is one year or less and the actual punishment imposed, if convicted, was six months or less. For example, this would apply to strictly summary offences in Canada where the maximum punishment is six months.

If a pattern of crime as a youth exists, physicians can be called to examine the person to determine inadmissibility on the grounds of having a physical or mental disorder that poses a threat to themselves and others.

These exemptions do not apply to convictions for drug offences. The U.S.A. considers drug offences as a separate category that *almost always* renders a person inadmissible.

Keep in mind that when it comes to entering the U.S.A., it is the individual's burden to prove that he or she is admissible—for example, by showing police and court records, and the relevant *Criminal Code* section. In reality, the person's chances of getting in are slim. Furthermore, those who carried such documents and were admitted in the past would still have to go through the same process every time they wanted to enter the U.S.A. Showing documents about a criminal record at the border and having to explain the situation takes time, can be embarrassing, and, quite frankly, is not a realistic or reliable approach.

EFFECT OF A CANADIAN PARDON OR RECORD SUSPENSION

## 6. Can someone with a conditional or absolute discharge enter the U.S.A.?

In Canada, a discharge means that a person was *found guilty* but was *not convicted*. A discharge can be either *absolute* (where no punishment or conditions are imposed) or *conditional*, which carries a punishment (usually a small fine or probation).

Technically speaking, while the U.S.A. *does not* consider absolute discharges as *convictions* for the purpose of immigration law, they *do consider* conditional discharges to be convictions. This means that having a conditional discharge may make someone inadmissible if it is in relation to a CIMT or drug offence. Either way, it is unlikely that a CBP officer will endeavour to make this distinction and render a decision on the spot. There is a high probability that the CBP officer will turn the person away no matter what the outcome of the charges were.

As previously mentioned, the best solution is to submit a Waiver application and the ARO will determine if the person is inadmissible. If a Waiver is *not needed*—because the crime was not a CIMT—the individual will be given an official ARO letter stating that fact, which will need to be produced every time they cross the border. The Waiver application fee is not refunded. Showing up at the border without this letter (or the Waiver if the crime was a CIMT) is risky, and will most likely result in the person's being turned away.

## 7. Can someone on probation or parole enter the U.S.A.?

The American government does not have special rules for people whose jail sentences were suspended or for those who were given probation or given early release and are on parole. Their laws focus on the fact that the person was convicted. The fact that the person was relieved in whole or in part of the penalty imposed does not matter. If the offence for which the person received a suspended sentence or was granted probation or parole was a CIMT or related to drugs, then he or she will be considered inadmissible.

Also, where the crime is considered a CIMT, individuals who have not completed their court-ordered sentence (e.g., still on probation or parole) will not be eligible for a Waiver. They must wait until the sentence is completed and then apply for a Waiver to legally enter the U.S.A.

## 8.  Can someone with a Canadian Pardon or Record Suspension enter the U.S.A.?

U.S.A. immigration law does not recognize a Canadian Pardon or Record Suspension (RS).[5] CBP officers are required, under the American Immigration and Nationality Act, to look at a person's convictions to determine if they are allowed to enter the United States. The Board of Immigration Appeals has repeatedly stated that no effect is to be given to a rehabilitative statute that purports to expunge, dismiss, cancel, vacate, discharge, or otherwise remove a record of conviction. And that is precisely what the Canadian *Criminal Records Act* does—it allows people to obtain an RS that effectively removes their criminal record.

So what does this mean in practice? Well, if a person tried entering the U.S.A. *before* receiving a Pardon or RS, and the CBP officer discovered the criminal record information during a routine screening, then the information would be downloaded into the American computer system. The criminal record information will stay in their system even after the individual obtains a Canadian Pardon or RS or otherwise removes the criminal record in Canada. From then on, the American officials can easily access the information and will use it to deny the individual entry into the United States, unless a Waiver is obtained.

If, however, a person's criminal record was *never discovered* by CBP officers before the individual received a Pardon or RS (or had the record destroyed as in the case of not-guilty outcomes), then the CBP officers will *not* be able to access it because it is no longer in either of the RCMP data banks accessible to the U.S.A.

Once someone's RCMP record has been pardoned, suspended, or otherwise removed, a CPIC check will not show any Canadian criminal record. In the case of Canadian Pardons and Record Suspensions, the criminal record is sealed in a separate data bank.[6] In the case of non-convictions, when the record is removed properly, it is either purged (transferred to a separate data bank and then destroyed) or completely removed and transferred to the arresting police force for destruction. In either situation, the U.S.A. will no longer have access to these records.

Many people whose records were never discovered by the U.S.A. are confused as to whether they have to admit a past criminal history after they have removed their criminal record. This is a very interesting situation. From the perspective of Canadian law, the crime has been removed from public record and the person is supposed to answer no if asked, "Do you have a criminal record?" In fact, Canadian human rights laws make it illegal to discriminate against a person who has received a Pardon or an RS for their criminal record.[7] Further, section 11 of the Canadian *Charter of Rights and Freedoms* establishes that if a person is found guilty and punished for a crime, he or she is not to be tried or punished for it again.

The U.S.A., however, only recognizes Canadian criminal laws that gave rise to the criminal record. It does not recognize Canadian laws that pertain to criminal record removal and the right not to be discriminated against once the record has been removed. This means that, when it comes to criminal records and admitting Canadians into the U.S.A., our record removal laws—purges, destructions, Pardons, Record Suspensions—our human rights laws, and Canada's *Charter* are *not* recognized by the U.S.A.

If the U.S.A. has no *prior* knowledge of the record that was removed and therefore will not be able to access it, the question is: Should a person admit to a past criminal record that no longer exists under Canadian law? I will leave that decision up to the individual.

## 9. Does a criminal record affect NEXUS and FAST Card applications?

Yes. NEXUS and FAST (Free and Secure Trade Program) card applications will likely be denied if the applicant is discovered to have a criminal record.

As part of their Western Hemisphere Travel Initiative (WHTI),[8] the American government has been promoting Trusted Traveler Programs. For Canadians, the NEXUS and FAST card applications are the most popular of these programs. The purpose of these programs is to allow frequent travellers to cross the border faster. The FAST card is for truckers while the NEXUS card is for others who travel frequently across the border. For example, truckers with a FAST card are permitted to use a specially designated lane when driving their load across the border, and those with a NEXUS card use special expedited lines at major airports. In order to gain such privileges, these programs require the individual to complete an application and undergo a security screening. The applicants must become members by completing an online application,[9] after which they will be interviewed and their relevant documents will be reviewed. The applications all have questions about criminal records. Those with criminal records will need to produce further documentation and their application will usually be denied.

## 10. How does having a criminal record affect Snowbirds?

*Snowbirds* is a term used to describe Canadians who travel to the warmer climate of the southern American states during the winter months. Most of these people are retired seniors. Most Snowbirds are aware of American laws that deal with how long Canadians are legally permitted to stay in the U.S.A. Many, however, are not aware that their past criminal record may catch up with them and prevent them from enjoying their vacation—especially in cases where they have crossed the border many times without a problem. They are under the mistaken belief that their record is so old that it no longer exists. But this is not so. In the course of removing criminal records for many years, I have seen convictions from as far back as the 1930s.

Even young offender records created under prior legislation may still be on record at the RCMP. So, to be safe, Snowbirds can see what is still on file by submitting their fingerprints to the RCMP for certification. There are no special exemptions for Snowbirds with regard to having a criminal record. If their criminal record is discovered during a routine screening by a CBP officer, they will be refused entry to the U.S.A.

## 11. What if someone attempts to enter the U.S.A. after having been refused?

If someone with a criminal record, and no Waiver, is caught trying to enter the U.S.A. after already having been refused entry, American CBP officers are permitted to take severe measures. If the person is travelling by automobile, the CBP officer can confiscate the vehicle—even if the individual with the criminal record is not the driver or the owner! In some cases, the vehicles are returned to the owner after an application is made; in other cases, the vehicles are not returned, rather, they are sold at a U.S.A. government auction.[10]

If the person is travelling by bus, he or she will be removed and sent back to Canada. If travelling by airplane, the individual will be refused entry, the ticket will be stamped *VOID*; and cancellation insurance cannot be collected. If the person is a trucker, the cargo could be seized. It is also common, if someone is stopped a second or third time, for the individual to be detained, fingerprinted, and handcuffed. In some cases, people have also been banned from entering the U.S.A. for up to twenty years. As you can imagine, these experiences can be quite devastating.

Worth mentioning is that it is much easier to get caught a second time, because after a person has been stopped and refused entry the first time, the U.S.A. will have created their own files. This means the individual's criminal record is automatically accessed during a routine border screening as soon as the CBP officer enters the person's name and date of birth into their computer system. Furthermore, repeated unsuccessful attempts to enter the U.S.A. greatly reduce an individual's chance of being granted a Waiver.

## U.S.A. ENTRY WAIVERS

# 12. What is a Waiver? (I-192, I-194)

A Waiver[11] is an official American document that allows otherwise inadmissible people, such as those with criminal records, to enter the United States legally. The application is sometimes referred to as an I-192 because that is the number of one of the forms used in the application. Once the Waiver is granted, it is actually called an I-194. The I-194 together with the cover letter must be presented to the CBP officer every time the person wishes to enter the U.S.A.

Following is an example of a Waiver, which is valid for three years:

**U.S. Customs and Border Protection**
Admissibility Review Office
12825 Worldgate Drive
Herndon, VA 20598-1340

A0
October 4, 2011

Dear

Your Form I-192, Application for Advance Permission to Enter as a Nonimmigrant, has
been approved. Enclosed is a copy of your Form I-194, Notice of Approval of Advance
Permission to Enter as a Nonimmigrant. The terms and conditions of the approval are:

> You are granted multiple entries into the United States at various ports of entry as a
> visitor for business and pleasure for a period of stay to be determined by the admitting
> officer, provided that you are not inadmissible to the United States under any other
> section of the law other than Sections 212(a)(2)(A)(i)(I) and 212(a)(6)(C)(i) of the
> Immigration and Nationality Act, as amended.

<u>VALID THREE YEARS FROM THE DATE OF APPROVAL</u>

This letter and the Form I-194 must be presented to the Customs and Border Protection
Officer when you make an application for admission into the United States.

Sincerely,

Michael D. Olszak
Director
Admissibility Review Office

USA Entry Waiver Cover Letter

**U.S. Customs and Border Protection**
Admissibility Review Office
12825 Worldgate Drive
Herndon, VA 20598-1340

**FILE:** A0                                    **DATE:** October  4, 2011
**IN RE:**

**APPLICATION**: Temporary admission to the United States pursuant to Section 212(d)(3)(A)(ii) of the Immigration and Nationality Act.

**The applicant has been found to be ineligible to receive a nonimmigrant visa under Sections 212(a)(2)(A)(i)(I) and 212(a)(6)(C)(i) of the Act.**

| Nationality: | Date and Country of Birth: | | Country of Residence: |
|---|---|---|---|
| CANADA | 2/ 7/1969, | | CANADA |
| Occupation: | | Employer: | |
| Coach | | | |
| Purpose in seeking entry into the United States and destination: | | | |
| Business and Pleasure | | | |
| Plans regarding travel to the United States and period of temporary stay: | | | |
| Will enter at various ports-of-entry to various destinations in the U.S. | | | |
| Basis of favorable action: | | | |
| Humanitarian | | | |

**ORDER:** It is ordered that the application be granted for the above indicated purpose, subject to revocation at any time, valid as set forth below.

**ENTRY: Multiple entries as a visitor for business and pleasure for a period of time not to exceed that authorized at entry.**

**PERIOD OF TEMPORARY STAY: To be determined by the admitting officer.**

**VALID THREE YEARS FROM THE DATE OF APPROVAL**

Michael D. Olszak
Director
Admissibility Review Office

Form I-194
(Rev. 1-2-82) Y

USA I-194 Entry Waiver

## 13. Who grants Waivers?

The *Department of Homeland Security (DHS)*—through the ARO—will review all Waiver applications. The ARO will first decide whether the crime was a CIMT. They will then decide if a Waiver should be granted and, if so, how long it will be valid.

### ELIGIBILITY
## 14. When is someone eligible to apply for a Waiver?

Technically speaking, a person can apply for a Waiver at any time. Practically speaking, however, the chance of an application being successful will depend on several factors, one of which is how much time has passed since the crime was committed. In other words, the longer it has been since the crime was committed, the better the chance of being granted a Waiver.

That being said, it is recommended that individuals submit their application well in advance of the date they intend to visit the United States because the application review time at the ARO varies and can take as long as one year or more. Also, there are several documents that must be submitted in addition to the application forms, and these documents, such as an RCMP Certified Criminal Record Report, can take several months to collect, adding more time to the process.

### APPLICATION
## 15. What are the Waiver application requirements?

The current non-refundable Waiver Application fee is USD $585. Since that fee must be drawn on an American financial institution, it is easiest to pay by credit card or exact U.S.A. cash.

Applicants will be required to complete forms, have their fingerprints taken, submit supporting documents, and pay a U.S.A. government processing fee.

The Waiver application package must include the following:

- Original Form I-192, with original signature (sample two-page form follows on pp.160-161), and if an attorney was retained to complete the application on behalf of the applicant, a G-28 must also be filed

- Evidence of citizenship
- U.S.A. Fingerprint chart FD-258 (to be completed by a U.S.A. CBP officer at a designated location)
- A completed and signed Form G-325A, which is used to provide biographical information about the applicant (sample form on p.162)
- A certified RCMP criminal record report, including the applicant's fingerprints
- A statement from the applicant regarding the purpose of the intended visit to the U.S.A. (e.g., business, vacation, medical treatment, study, etc.)
- A copy of the official court record, from the actual court of conviction, indicating plea, indictment, disposition, and sentence for each and every crime committed
- A statement in the applicant's own words and signed by the applicant, explaining the circumstances of each arrest, conviction, and sentence imposed
- Evidence or explanation of the applicant's reform, such as counselling or rehabilitation programs completed, current employment, marital status, community service, and so on.

OMB No. 1615-0017; Expires 03/31/2013

**I-192, Application for Advance**
**Permission to Enter as Nonimmigrant**
[Pursuant to Section 212(d)(3)(A)(ii) of the INA]

**Department of Homeland Security**
U.S. Citizenship and Immigration Services

(Read instructions to the form.)
Type or Print in Black Ink

**Fee Stamp**

**File No.** A-

I hereby apply to the Secretary of Homeland Security for permission to enter the United States temporarily under the provisions of section 212(d)(3)(A)(ii) of the Immigration and Nationality Act (INA).

| 1. Full Name | 2. Date of Birth *(mm/dd/yyyy)* |
|---|---|

| 3. Place of Birth *(City-Town, State/Province, Country)* | 4. Present Citizenship/Nationality |
|---|---|

5. Present Address, Telephone Number, and E-Mail address

6. All addresses at which I have resided during the past 5 years *(Use a separate sheet of paper, if necessary.)*

| 7. Desired Port of Entry into the United States | 8. Means of Transportation |
|---|---|

| 9. Proposed Date of Entry | 10. Approximate Length of Stay in the United States |
|---|---|

11. My purpose for entering the United States is: *(Explain fully)*

12. I believe that I may be inadmissible to the United States for the following reason(s) and no others:

13. ☐ have ☐ have not previously filed an application for advance permission to enter as a nonimmigrant

on _____ , _____ , at _____.

**If you are an applicant for T and U nonimmigrant status, you do not need to answer questions 14 through 17.**

14. Have you ever been in the United States for a period of 6 months or more? If yes, when, for how long, and in what immigration status?

Form I-192 (Rev. 03/09/12) Y

Entry Waiver Application Form I-192

15. Have you ever filed an application or petition for immigration benefits with the U.S. Government, or has one ever been filed on your behalf? If yes, list the applications and/or petitions, the filing locations, and describe the outcome of each application/petition (for example: denied, approved, pending).

16. Have you ever been denied or refused an immigration benefit by the U.S. Government, or had a benefit revoked or terminated (including but not limited to visas)? Describe in detail.

17. Have you ever, in or outside the United States, been arrested, cited, charged, indicted, fined, or imprisoned for breaking or violating any law or ordinance, excluding minor traffic violations? Describe in detail. Include all offenses where impaired driving may have been an issue.

**18. Applicant's Signature and Certification**

I understand that the information herein contained may be used in any proceedings (including civil, criminal, immigration, or any other judicial proceeding) hereafter instituted against me.

I certify that the statements above and all attachments hereto are true and correct to the best of my knowledge and belief.

_____   _____
(Signature of Applicant)                                         (Date)

**Signature of the Applicant/Signature of Guardian or Family Member (if Applicant is unable to sign)**

**19. Preparer's Signature and Certification**

I declare that this document was prepared by me at the request of the applicant or qualified relative/legal guardian of the applicant, and it is based on all information of which I have knowledge and/or was provided to me by the above named person in response to the exact questions contained on this form. I have not knowingly withheld any information.

_____   _____
(Signature)                                       (Address)                     (Date)

| RECEIVED | TRANS. IN | RET'D TRANS. OUT | COMPLETED |
|----------|-----------|------------------|-----------|
|          |           |                  |           |

Entry Waiver Application Form I-192

Department of Homeland Security
U.S. Citizenship and Immigration Services

OMB No. 1615-0008; Expires 08/31/2012

## G-325A, Biographic Information

| (Family Name) | (First Name) | (Middle Name) | ☐ Male  ☐ Female | Date of Birth (mm/dd/yyyy) | Citizenship/Nationality | File Number  A |
|---|---|---|---|---|---|---|

| All Other Names Used (include names by previous marriages) | City and Country of Birth | U.S. Social Security # *(if any)* |
|---|---|---|

| | Family Name | First Name | Date of Birth (mm/dd/yyyy) | City, and Country of Birth (if known) | City and Country of Residence |
|---|---|---|---|---|---|
| Father | | | | | |
| Mother (Maiden Name) | | | | | |

| Current Husband or Wife (If none, so state) Family Name (For wife, give maiden name) | First Name | Date of Birth (mm/dd/yyyy) | City and Country of Birth | Date of Marriage | Place of Marriage |
|---|---|---|---|---|---|

| Former Husbands or Wives (If none, so state) Family Name (For wife, give maiden name) | First Name | Date of Birth (mm/dd/yyyy) | Date and Place of Marriage | Date and Place of Termination of Marriage |
|---|---|---|---|---|
| | | | | |

**Applicant's residence last five years.  List present address first.**

| Street and Number | City | Province or State | Country | From Month | Year | To Month | Year |
|---|---|---|---|---|---|---|---|
| | | | | | | Present Time | |
| | | | | | | | |
| | | | | | | | |
| | | | | | | | |
| | | | | | | | |

**Applicant's last address outside the United States of more than 1 year.**

| Street and Number | City | Province or State | Country | From Month | Year | To Month | Year |
|---|---|---|---|---|---|---|---|
| | | | | | | | |

**Applicant's employment last five years.  (If none, so state.) List present employment first.**

| Full Name and Address of Employer | Occupation (Specify) | From Month | Year | To Month | Year |
|---|---|---|---|---|---|
| | | | | Present Time | |
| | | | | | |
| | | | | | |
| | | | | | |
| | | | | | |

**Last occupation abroad if not shown above. (Include all information requested above.)**

| This form is submitted in connection with an application for: ☐ Naturalization  ☐ Other (Specify):  ☐ Status as Permanent Resident | Signature of Applicant | Date |
|---|---|---|

If your native alphabet is in other than Roman letters, write your name in your native alphabet below:

**Penalties:** Severe penalties are provided by law for knowingly and willfully falsifying or concealing a material fact.

**Applicant:** Print your name and Alien Registration Number in the box outlined by heavy border below.

| Complete This Box  (Family Name) | (Given Name) | (Middle Name) | (Alien Registration Number)  A |
|---|---|---|---|

Form G-325A (Rev. 08/08/11) Y

USA G-325 Biiographic Form, part of Waiver Application

PROCESS
# 16. What criteria are used to decide whether a Waiver will be approved?

To determine the applicant's eligibility for a Waiver, a number of factors are weighed, and each decision is made on a case-by-case basis. The criteria used include the following:

- The type of offences committed, that is, did the crimes involve moral turpitude, and, if so, what category of crimes they were
- The seriousness of the offences committed (i.e., did the prosecutor proceed summarily or by indictment)
- The number of offences committed
- How recently the offences were committed (as opposed to when the case went to trial, which can often be years later)
- Whether the applicant completed the sentence imposed by the court (e.g., paid fines, completed probation, etc.)
- The applicant's personal history (e.g., long criminal history or single lapse in an otherwise clean record)
- Whether the applicant has demonstrated rehabilitation since the offence was committed (e.g., obtaining a Canadian Pardon or RS, or completing a counselling or drug-rehabilitation program, if applicable)
- Whether the applicant has steady employment and enough money to support himself or herself while in the U.S.A.
- Whether the applicant has a stable home life and ties to the community
- The reason or purpose for the applicant's wanting to enter the U.S.A., and
- Recommendations or supporting letters from prominent members of the community attesting to the individual's good moral character, reputation, and behaviour.

# 17. When will a Waiver application be denied?

A Waiver application can be denied for many reasons, such as: the application was not completed properly; the processing fee was not paid; all necessary supporting documents were not provided; the applicant did not show sufficient rehabilitation, and so on.

In most cases, if the ARO is proposing to deny the Waiver application, they will send an I-72 Form (p. 168) to the applicant, listing their reasons and giving the person a deadline within which to respond (usually eighty-seven days). The applicant will then have the chance to do whatever is requested within the designated time-period given. Usually the ARO will need further documentation. Sometimes, however, the ARO may request that the applicant undergo a psychological or physical examination. Although psychological and physical examination requests have not always been common, as of 2011 they are being requested more often.

## 18. How long does it take to get a Waiver approved?

Collecting and preparing the application forms and all of the supporting documents can take anywhere from three to ten months. In addition, it will take approximately five to twelve months for the ARO to review the application. Therefore, it is best to start the application well in advance of the date that the applicant wishes to enter the U.S.A.

EXPLORATION AND RENEWAL
## 19. How long are Waivers valid? Can they be renewed?

Waivers are issued for periods ranging anywhere from six months to five years. The most common terms are for one year, three years, and five years. However, most Waivers allow the person to enter the U.S.A. on multiple occasions until the Waiver expires.

In cases where a person has submitted a Waiver application for an offence that is determined *not* to be a CIMT, the ARO will issue a letter stating that a Waiver is not needed. Although this type of letter is not actually a Waiver, it is used like a *Permanent* Waiver because it does *not* expire, and because it will be needed to show to the CBP officers each time the person goes to the U.S.A.

In cases where the crime is determined to be a CIMT, a Waiver may be issued.

The length of time for which a Waiver will be valid depends on many factors, and includes the nature and number of offences, how long ago the offences were committed, the length of the criminal record, the individual's personal situation, and whether the individual has been issued a Waiver in the past.

In the past, people could obtain *Border Cards* (laminated two-sided cards), which were commonly referred to as permanent Waivers (see sample that follows). In fact, the Border Card was valid *indefinitely*, until revoked by the U.S.A.— which did happen a number of years ago when those in existence were revoked and Border Card applications discontinued.

If someone wants to continue travelling to the U.S.A., it is a good idea to apply for a Waiver renewal well *before* the current Waiver expires. If approved, the new Waiver will take effect *after* the expiration of the current Waiver. This means that the applicant gets the full benefit of the time-period of each Waiver. This is good news because, as mentioned, the Waiver application is costly, and it takes about one year to collect all documents and for the ARO to process it.

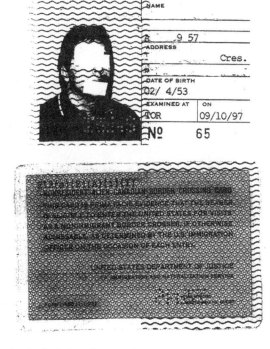

USA Border Card which no longer exists

EFFECT OF WAIVER

## 20. Can someone with a Waiver go to the U.S.A. whenever they want?

Almost always. In most cases, a Waiver is valid for multiple entries until it expires. Therefore, someone in possession of a valid Waiver may travel freely to the U.S.A. so long as he or she brings all other necessary documents that are normally required to cross the border (e.g., passport). As noted, however, Waivers expire and must be renewed for the individual to have legal permission to continue travelling to the U.S.A.

## 21. Can someone with a Waiver still be denied entry into the U.S.A.?

Yes. Having a Waiver means that *inadmissibility* based on a person's *criminal record* is *waived*. In other words, the Waiver allows the applicant to legally enter the U.S.A. with a Canadian criminal record. However, anyone can still be refused entry into the U.S.A. for various other reasons (e.g., not having enough funds for the length of stay in the U.S.A., not having proper immigration status in Canada, etc.).

## 22. Do people need to apply for a Waiver if they have never been refused entry?

If a person wants to travel to the U.S.A. with a Canadian criminal record, a Waiver is required to enter the U.S.A. legally.

Essentially, the individual will be admitting to, and giving details about, his or her criminal record to the American federal government. Once a Waiver application is submitted, the U.S.A. will download the details into their files and they will never be removed, regardless of whether a Canadian RS was subsequently granted or the criminal record file is later destroyed in Canada. Once a Waiver application is submitted, the individual will then require a Waiver for the rest of his or her life (or need to carry the letter stating that the crime did not render them inadmissible—also issued by the U.S.A.).

## 23. Can someone with a criminal record enter the U.S.A. if there is a family emergency?

In some circumstances, a permit, referred to as Advance Parole, can be obtained to allow a person to enter the U.S.A. while the Waiver application is being processed.[12]

Such permits, however, are difficult to obtain and are only granted for urgent humanitarian reasons, such as emergency medical treatments or to attend the funeral of a close family member. The decision whether to grant such a document is made on a case-by-case basis, and, if permission is given, it will be for a single and temporary entry.

## 24. Does someone need a Waiver if only "stopping over" in the U.S.A.?

Yes. Any time people enter the U.S.A.—even where a person does not leave the airplane on a "stop over" en route to another country—they are required to clear American Customs. Therefore, even on a stopover flight, to legally enter the U.S.A. with a criminal record, a Waiver is required. Since there is a good chance the criminal record will be revealed, without a Waiver the individual can be denied entry, the airplane ticket can be voided, and the individual can be sent back. Consequently, it is a good idea for people with criminal records either to fly directly to their final destination and bypass the U.S.A. entirely, or to obtain a Waiver.

## 25. Can a Canadian Permanent Resident apply for a Waiver?

Yes. If someone is a Permanent Resident of Canada and he or she has a criminal record, in addition to obtaining a visa,[13] a Waiver will also be required. These applications are currently required to be completed online.[14] Once the person begins a new application, an identification number will be assigned to the file.

**U.S. Customs and Border Protection**
Admissibility Review Office
12825 Worldgate Drive
Herndon, VA 20598-1340

<u>NAME AND ADDRESS OF APPLICANT/PETITIONER</u>

| | |
|---|---|
| | NAME OF BENEFICIARY |
| | K , B |
| | DATE   September   , 2011 |
| PLEASE COMPLY WITH THE BELOW CHECKED ☒ INSTRUCTIONS. | FILE NO.   A |
| | FORM NO.   I-192 |

☒    1. A review of our law enforcement database revealed that you have a pending case with Brampton Court. Provide a certified copy of court records showing the final disposition of this pending case.

The evidence submitted in response to this request should be submitted at one time within 87 days of this request. Your application will be deemed abandoned and action thereon will be terminated if you fail to respond to this request.

Form I-72
(REV 4-1-83) COMPUTER GENERATED

**PLEASE RETURN THIS LETTER AND ALL ATTACHMENTS WITH YOUR RESPONSE**

USA Proposal to Deny Waiver Application - Deficiency Letter I-72

The visa application is quite extensive and includes:

- Personal information, such as name, date and place of birth, current address
- Passport information
- Date of trip to the U.S.A. and the place where the applicant will be staying
- Purpose of travelling to the U.S.A.
- Travel companion(s) (if any)
- Employment information, and so on.

The application also includes questions about whether the applicant has a criminal record and details about the crimes committed. Once the visa application is completed and submitted online (including a photo that must be uploaded), the applicant must then contact the American consulate to set up an appointment for an interview with a consular officer. At the interview, the applicant will have to submit the Waiver application and supporting documents (e.g., court records, RCMP report, etc.).[15] The wait time for an interview and for the visa application to be processed varies, depending on the individual consulate office.

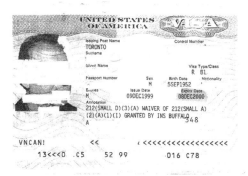

Canadian Passport stamped with a USA Visa which includes a Waiver of the criminal record

## 26. Can people apply for a Waiver on their own?

Yes—although it is not recommended. Most people choose not to prepare their own application because it is an extremely subjective, difficult, and lengthy process, and government rules and policies change frequently without notice. Without specialized knowledge that only practical experience can give you, the Waiver process can be quite daunting. Applications prepared without professional help frequently undergo delays in processing and will often be denied because they are incomplete or incorrect.

That's where the services of a lawyer or an agent can be critical.

## Quiz

**1. Does a criminal record prevent someone from entering the U.S.A.?**
   a. Almost always
   b. No, never
   c. No, so long as the person fully and honestly explains the details of the criminal record to a CBP officer
   d. It depends on whether the offence is considered to be a crime involving moral turpitude or related to drugs
   e. It depends on whether the offence is considered serious according to Canadian law

**2. A crime involving moral turpitude:**
   a. Makes someone inadmissible to enter the United States (unless the person has a Waiver)
   b. Includes acts and omissions that shock the public conscience as being inherently base, vile, or depraved
   c. Includes murder, fraud, sexual assault, kidnapping, and money laundering
   d. Does not generally include common assault, disorderly conduct, firearms violations, and traffic violations
   e. All of the above

**3. What is a Waiver?**
   a. A document that prevents a CBP officer from seeing a Canadian criminal record
   b. A document allowing inadmissibility—because of a criminal record—to be waived
   c. A document that guarantees that a person will be admitted into the U.S.A.
   d. A document that gives U.S.A. immigration officials the right to search someone's person, vehicle, and property at the border
   e. None of the above

**4. A Waiver:**
   a. Is issued by the U.S.A. Department of Homeland Security
   b. Can be requested at any time
   c. Can take up to 12 months to be issued
   d. Has an expiration date
   e. All of the above

**5. If someone tries to enter the U.S.A. after being refused because of a criminal record:**
   a. The vehicle the person is in could be confiscated
   b. The person risks being detained, handcuffed, fingerprinted, and sent back to Canada
   c. If someone is a trucker, their cargo could be confiscated
   d. The person could be banned from entering the U.S.A. for a number of years
   e. All of the above

**6. True or False:**
   a. The U.S.A. recognizes Canadian Pardons and Record Suspensions
   b. The U.S.A. may grant special permits for urgent humanitarian reasons for people to enter the U.S.A. while their Waiver application is being processed
   c. CBP officers cannot access Canadian criminal records
   d. Criminal records do not affect NEXUS and FAST card applications
   e. Crimes involving moral turpitude are defined in the U.S.A. *Immigration and Nationality Act*

Answer Key: 1 (a), 2 (e), 3 (b), 4 (e), 5 (e), 6 false, true, false, false, false

## End Notes

1. The only exceptions are, if:
- the criminal record is so serious that it is located in the Interpol system,
- the criminal record was so serious that it was transferred by the RCMP to the FBI,
- the person has disclosed the record on an immigration application (e.g., study or work permit, green card, FAST card, etc.)
- the person is involved in an unresolved criminal matter (e.g., commits a subsequent crime or there is a warrant out for their arrest, etc.). In these circumstances a CBP officer will be able to find and download the information.

2. USA *Immigration and Nationality Act*, section 212 (a) 2 Criminal and Related Grounds

3. *Matter of Luaiva Tui FUALAAU (1996), Matter of Danesh,* 19 I&N Dec. 669 (BIA 1988); *Matter of Flores,* 17 I&N Dec. 225, 227 (BIA 1980), and *Matter of P-6* I&N Dec. 795 (BIA 1955)

4. A crime that was committed when the person was under eighteen years of age.

5. As of March 2012, new Canadian pardon laws replaced the word "Pardon" with the term "Record Suspension."

6. No one has access to pardoned criminal records without the permission of the Minister of Public Safety Canada, and that permission will only be given in rare cases, such as if the individual is subsequently charged

with a crime.
Section 6 (2), *Criminal Records Act*, (R.S.C., 1985, c. C-47)

7. Section 3 (1), *Canadian Human Rights Act*, (R.S.C. 1985)

8. U.S.A. Federal Register cite: 73 FR 18384, Document No. FR 27-08, April 3, 2008.

9. GOES Processing: www.cbp.gov

10. Code of Federal Regulations: 8 CFR Part 274 , "Seizure and forfeiture of Conveyances"

11. "Advanced Permission to Enter as a Non-Immigrant"

12. Application for Travel Document Form I-131

13. Nonimmigrant Visa Application DS-160, current fee USD $140

14. https://ceac.state.gov/genniv/

15. Application for Waiver of Grounds of Inadmissibility I-601, current fee USD $585

Chapter Seven

# Removing Criminal Records

Parole Board of Canada (PBC)
Pardons And Record Suspensions For Convictions

New Pardon Law, Bill C-10

Eligibility

Application

People who have never been involved with the police tend to oppose the removal of criminal records. In over twenty years of helping people to remove their records, I have learned that much of the public still perceives those with criminal records to be "dangerous" offenders. This is a misconception. According to Statistics Canada (2010), over 70 percent of crimes were non-violent—such as property crimes, failing to appear in court, and mischief. Furthermore, about 25 percent of the people in the RCMP Identification data bank had minor offences on their record and had never even been convicted. Their cases resulted in *discharges* or *not-guilty* outcomes.

Fortunately, those who are no longer involved in criminal activity have the opportunity to make a fresh start and a positive change in their lives by removing their criminal records. Removing the stigma associated with a criminal past is a vital part of developing an improved self-image. When the weight of a criminal record is lifted, people feel a new sense of freedom and peace, allowing them to become more productive. Those who have cleared their records can pursue opportunities that were previously out of reach. The most significant being the ability to get employment and thereby acquire the necessities of life: namely, food and housing. This benefits not only themselves and their families, but all of society as well. For example, statistics show that people who received their Pardons did, in fact, learn from their mistakes and have become rehabilitated, as 96 percent of them remain crime-free. That's why the government has a vested interest in seeing people remove the barriers created by a criminal record.

Unfortunately, the fact that the Pardon System worked did not prevent the government from changing the law. On March 13, 2012, Bill C-10, the *Safe Streets and Communities Act*, was given Royal Assent (became law). It was a grouping of nine existing bills (proposed laws) and affected several *Acts* of Canada, including the *Criminal Code* and the *Criminal Records Act (CRA)*. The *CRA* is the law that governs Pardons and Record Suspensions (for convictions) and purges (for offences that were discharged). It is important to understand that the new Pardon law does not affect those whose records consist solely of non-convictions. It replaced the word *Pardon* with *Record Suspension* (an unrecognized term) and made it more difficult (and in some cases impossible) for people to seal their records.

This chapter will discuss the various methods of removing criminal records.

It is not a step-by-step how-to guide as there are too many variables that could exist in any one situation. Given the number of unique circumstances surrounding people's lives and the various types of criminal records, providing the reader with an answer for every scenario is not possible, and attempting to do so would be irresponsible. Consequently, if you have a cluster of issues surrounding your particular situation, such as an immigration application pending or a job opportunity, you might want to refer to other chapters while reading this one.

## 1. Do criminal records disappear automatically?

Not in most cases. Individuals must take active steps to remove, seal, or destroy a criminal record. The only two situations where a criminal record is supposed to be removed automatically are:

- **Youth Criminal Records.** Generally, when the non-disclosure date has been reached, youth criminal records cannot be disclosed and are purged from the RCMP's Identification data bank.[1] In many cases, youth records also are automatically sealed by the local police service that laid the charges. It is still prudent, however, to get confirmation in writing that the youth files are sealed, not only by the RCMP, the local police, and the court, but also by any community organizations or other individuals who may have created a criminal record file while providing services to the young person in connection with his or her rehabilitation and reintegration.

- **Absolute and Conditional Discharges Registered *after* July 24, 1992.** After one year (for absolute discharges) or three years (for conditional discharges) have passed from the final court date, these records are automatically purged from the RCMP's Identification data bank. This law does not apply to discharges registered *before* July 24, 1992—although the RCMP often purges these records if they come across them. Furthermore, this is a federal law and does not have authority over what the courts and the local police services do with such files. In many cases, the police will retain this information until the individual takes steps to remove it.

## 2. How long are criminal records kept?

Apart from the two exceptions previously mentioned, a criminal record is generally retained for a very long time or indefinitely, unless the individual takes active steps to remove it. For example:

- **RCMP.** The RCMP retains criminal record information in its Identification data bank until a person turns eighty, provided that there has been no criminal activity reported in the ten years prior.[2]

  The information contained in the RCMP's *Investigative* data bank is retained until the provider of the information (i.e., the local police service that uploaded the information) has removed it.

- **Local Police Service.** Criminal record information is retained in the data banks of each Canadian local police service according to the retention period set out in the individual policies of each service. Generally, criminal records containing convictions are retained by the local police services indefinitely, until the individual's death, or until the individual reaches the age of eighty (provided at least forty years have passed with no criminal activity). Other types of criminal records—such as *not-guilty* outcomes, and incident reports—can remain on police files indefinitely or until the retention period outlined in the police bylaws has been reached.

  For example, occurrence reports, (i.e., no charges have been laid), remain on file until the time period set out in the retention schedule of each local police service. Such retention periods usually range from about five to ten years, depending on the individual police service. The interesting thing to note here is that the information will be associated not only with the suspect, but also with the complainant, alleged victim(s), and witness(es). This means that a police records search under any of their names could pull up this police report. Often, people inexperienced with police reports misread or confuse the findings. The offence is generally listed in a larger font, while the notation or key to reading the report is listed in a smaller font at the bottom of the report.

For example, the letters s, o, v, w mean suspect, other, victim, and witness. The person reading the report may wrongly assume that the applicant was the suspect, when, in fact, he or she might have been the witness.

- **Court.** Local courts retain criminal record information according to the policies of the individual court and the outcome of the charge (e.g., conviction, acquittal, etc.). Timeframes vary from one year to indefinitely. Once the time has passed, the file may be destroyed, sealed, or transferred to archives. If a Pardon or a Record Suspension (RS) has been awarded, the court records are sealed and/or transferred to the Parole Board of Canada (PBC) to be sealed with the Pardon or the RS.

> In my experience, anything on a police file is viewed negatively and with suspicion by much of society. Even in cases where the person is not the suspect or the accused, but is actually the witness or victim, the decision-maker reading the record may not approve the application. Some employers feel that to be a witness (especially in more than one incident) must mean that the person was involved in the crime, or simply that he or she has a propensity to be around crime and would, therefore, not be suitable as an employee. Any kind of police record can be damaging. The fear of having one's name listed in a police report, therefore, is one reason why crimes are sometimes not reported.

- **U.S.A. Immigration / FBI.** Although many of the American states do have Pardon Programs for criminal records created in the U.S.A., they do *not* remove Canadian criminal record information once they have accessed it through the RCMP data banks and downloaded it into their system—even if the government of Canada has awarded a Pardon or an RS.

- **Other Agency, Organization, or Individual.** What other agencies do with criminal record information is more difficult to know. Privacy laws prohibit both individuals and organizations from retaining someone's personal information once the purpose for obtaining it no longer exists.

Although not all organizations are vigilant in destroying criminal record files, the good news is that a search of police and RCMP records will not reveal information held by other types of organizations (except other federal authorities like Citizenship and Immigration Canada).

## 3. What are the different methods of removing a criminal record?

How a criminal record will be removed depends on a variety of factors, such as: the outcome of the charges, the number of charges, and the policies of the charging police service. Generally speaking, however:

- if the outcome resulted in a *not-guilty verdict*, a *destruction* of the person's fingerprint and photographs and the *destruction* or *sealing* of the outcome record is required
- an offence that was *discharged* requires a *purge* and a *destruction*, and
- a *conviction* requires a *Record Suspension*.

### POLICE DESTRUCTION AND PURGES

## 4. What is a not-guilty outcome?

For record removal purposes, not-guilty outcomes include: acquittals, withdrawn and dismissed charges, charges that were stayed, and peace bonds. These types of criminal records can be destroyed or sealed only by the charging police service.[3]

Charges may be withdrawn under regular circumstances or under the various provincial alternative measures programs, such as Ontario's diversion program, whereby the person's charges are withdrawn provided they make a donation to a charity, such as the Salvation Army, or attend a program for counselling.

For record removal purposes, peace bonds are treated like not-guilty outcomes, even though the person must sign a form admitting to guilt and must follow the conditions set out in the peace bond.

## 5. What is a destruction?

The criminal record file of a not-guilty outcome is under the legal jurisdiction of the charging police. If that police service agrees, it will usually destroy the person's fingerprints and photographs and destroy or seal the charge outcome records. Most times, the charging police service will also request the RCMP to return its copy of the criminal record file for destruction. In the case where photographs, fingerprints, and other records held by police are permanently destroyed, they can never resurface or be accessed again.

See pp. 183-185 for letters from:

- Durham Regional Police, confirming (i) that the RCMP returned its copy of the record to them, and (ii) that the destruction of fingerprint and photograph records had been completed

  _Some police services allow the individuals to be present at the police station when their fingerprints and photographs are destroyed._

- Toronto Airport Detachment of the RCMP, confirming that it had destroyed its records (individual RCMP detachments will only destroy not-guilty records in their possession if they were also the charging police), and
- Ontario Provincial Police, confirming that the RCMP file was cancelled, that the OPP charge files were sealed, and that the individual's fingerprints were destroyed.

## 6.  When is someone eligible for a destruction?

The following chart sets out the eligibility time frames adopted by *most* police services.

### Eligibility Time Periods for Destructions

| Outcome | Date Eligible | Date when application can be submitted |
|---|---|---|
| • Withdrawn<br>• Acquitted<br>• Dismissed | Date withdrawn | Must wait five months after date withdrawn before applying |
| Withdrawn (Through Alternative Measures Program, e.g., Diversion Program) | Date withdrawn | Date withdrawn (unless file transferred to the RCMP, then must wait five months before applying) |
| Stayed Charges | One year from date Stayed | One year from date Stayed |
| Peace Bond | Upon Expiration of Peace Bond (usually one year) | Upon expiration of Peace Bond |

In addition to these basic guidelines, the individual police services may have further policies regarding what they will and will not destroy. The criteria used by police services for making their decision can include such things as the nature of the offence and whether there are any other charges on the individual's record. It should be noted that the policies of some police services are to *not* destroy fingerprints, photographs, and criminal record files relating to not-guilty

March 16, 2012

Pardons Canada
901-45 St. Clair Ave W
Toronto, Ontario
M4V 1K9

Re:

Dear Pardons Canada:

This letter is to advise you that all relevant documents have been received from the RCMP.

Be advised that fingerprints and photographs of your client that were taken by this Service have been destroyed.

Please notify your client that destruction has taken place.

Kathy Massey
Supervisor, Records Unit

KM:ll

Durham Regional Police Service | Oshawa 905-579-1520
Police Headquarters, 605 Rossland Road East | Toll Free 888-579-1520
Box 911 Whitby, Ontario L1N 0B8 | Fax 905-666-8733

www.drps.ca

Durham Police Letter confirming RCMP files were returned for Destruction

| Royal | Gendarmerie |
|---|---|
| Canadian | royale |
| Mounted | du |
| Police | Canada |

Royal Canadian Mounted Police
Toronto Airport Detachment
255 Attwell Drive,
Etobicoke, Ontario.
M9W 7G2

Pardons Canada
45 St. Clair Ave. W.Ste 901
Toronto, Ontario.
M4V 1K9

Security Classification/Designation
Classification/désignation sécuritaire

**Confidentiel**

Your File   Votre référence

Our File   Notre référence

2007-02-21

Dear Madame or Sir

**Destruction of fingerprints of** ███████████████ (B.███████)

1. Please be advised that the fingerprints of ████████████████ have been destroyed as per your request and OM 19.8.4.3.1 RCMP.

*C O'Keefe*
Cst. C. O'Keefe #41099

*S.A. Daley*
S.A. Daley Sgt. NCO I/c
Toronto Airport Detachment
Immigration and Passport Section

# Canada

RCMP Local Detachment Letter confirming the Destruction of fingerprints

Ontario Provincial Police | Police provinciale de l'Ontario |  | **Kenora Detachment**
Box 1010, 350 Hwy 17A
Kenora, Ontario
P9N 3X7

Telephone: (807) 548-5534
Facsimile: (807) 548-8381

File Reference:

Pardons Canada
45 St. Clair Ave West
Suite 901
Toronto, ON
M4V 1K9

Attn: ████████ Records Department

**RE: ██████████ - Destruction Request**

Please be advised that we were notified by the RCMP 05 December 2011 that the FPS file for ██████████, had been cancelled. The charges of Criminal Harassment and FTC w/undertaking have been sealed. Fingerprints were destroyed.

If you have any further questions, please contact Jane Dolinski at (807) 467-2111.

Yours truly,

D. Lucas, Inspector
Detachment Commander

DL/jd

"POLICING" A PARTNERSHIP WITH THE COMMUNITY

Ontario Provincial Police Letter confirming RCMP Fingerprint Section (FPS) Number was cancelled

For acquittals, withdrawn and dismissed charges, although a person is eligible for a file destruction immediately at most police services, they must wait five months from the court date to send a request. The time delay ensures that the file has been forwarded to the RCMP and that it may then be requested back by the police.

outcomes under certain circumstances. In such cases, the not-guilty record is disclosed, just as is a record of conviction (that has not been pardoned or suspended). Some of the devastating results of the police refusing to destroy offence information that resulted in not-guilty outcomes include:

- disclosure of the information on a police records check for employment purposes
- delay or denial of Canadian Immigration applications
- discovery of the record at the U.S.A. border. If the charging police do not recall the information from the RCMP, that information is disclosed during routine *computer* searches at the Canada/U.S.A. border.

The police justification for keeping information related to not-guilty outcomes is that it may be required for investigative purposes. The individual maintains that this type of policy violates his or her *Charter* rights and his or her rights under privacy laws. Simply stated, the issue is a much-debated one, wherein the rights of law-enforcement agencies to be able to do their job effectively and the rights of the individual to be free of persecution must be balanced. Some individuals have gone so far as to take legal action to force the charging police service to destroy information related to their not-guilty outcomes. Many of these cases have succeeded.

Ironically, the police services that do not destroy or even seal certain charges that resulted in *not-guilty* outcomes, will remove or seal charges that *did* result in a finding of guilt—*discharges* and *convictions.* This is not just. The end result is that people who were found not-guilty often can be treated more harshly, in that they will have a criminal record forever, while those who were found guilty and even convicted have their records sealed both at the federal and local police levels.

Since local police policies across the country are constantly changing, it is difficult for the average person to know what to do. In some cases, having charges at more than one police service can further complicate the destruction or sealing of records, and, if done incorrectly, can result in revealing the information to other police services instead of having it destroyed.

Although the destruction of files relating to not-guilty outcomes should be the least complicated and most successful of applications, it is not.

## 7.   How long does a destruction take?

A destruction of fingerprints, photographs, and the outcome record usually takes six to sixteen months to complete. This includes time taken acquiring a copy of the record and ensuring that both local police records and the RCMP copy are destroyed.[4]

## 8.   What are the benefits of a destruction?

Technology makes a criminal record far more likely to be discovered than ever before. As mentioned, being able to produce a clear police report is essential to many important aspects of a person's life—such as securing an apartment, a job, or a volunteer position, being bonded, career licensing, educational opportunities, and travelling to the U.S.A. The benefits of having a not-guilty file destroyed include:

- An LPRC will no longer show the charge.
- Police information that is destroyed can never resurface.
- The American officials will not be able to access the information from the RCMP—providing that the U.S.A. did not have a copy of this information prior to the destruction, and provided that the charging police requested and destroyed the RCMP file as well as their own.

Of course, one of the most important reasons for removing a criminal record is to attain a sense of freedom and peace of mind. The person can make a fresh start and once again feel like an equal member of society. This makes for a better citizen, parent, and community member.

## 9.  What information is not destroyed?

Most police services will not destroy incident reports relating to the not-guilty charge until the expiration-time specified in their bylaws. Each police service has its own bylaws, so the time periods vary. Further, as previously mentioned, some police services have policies that outline specific categories of offences they will not destroy, as well as other ancillary reasons for denial.[5] Still other police services, while refusing to destroy their records, do agree to seal them for LPRC purposes.

The bottom line is that each police service has the legal jurisdiction to deal with the criminal records it has created. Of course, they must do so within the confines of the laws of Canada, (particularly the *Charter* and privacy laws). If someone has had dealings with the police, it is always a good idea to find out what information they intend to keep on file. If the person feels that the police are retaining information that they are not legally permitted to keep, they can make a formal request that it be destroyed and, failing that, legal action may be taken.

### RCMP DESTRUCTION AND PURGES

## 10. What are discharges?

A *discharge* means there is a finding of *guilt* but *no conviction*. This may seem confusing because the legal concept of a discharge is difficult to grasp at first. Essentially, instead of saying to the accused, "You are convicted," the judge would say, "You are discharged." In either case the offence can be the same, and so, too, can the punishment. But how criminal records resulting from a conviction or a discharge are removed is very different. The conviction requires an RS while the discharge requires a purge (by the RCMP) and also a destruction or purge by the local police.

There are two types of discharges: *absolute* and *conditional*. With an absolute discharge, there is no sentence or condition to be satisfied. A conditional discharge, as the name suggests, carries one or more conditions that must be met

# Toronto Police Service

40 College Street, Toronto, Ontario, Canada. M5G 2J3
(416) 808-2222  FAX (416) 808-8202
Website: www.TorontoPolice.on.ca

William Blair
Chief of Police

*Criminal Records Unit*
File Number: ...█████

March 28, 2012

Pardons Canada
45 St. Clair Avenue West, Suite 901
Toronto, Ontario
M4V 1K9

Dear Sir/Madam:

**Re:** ██████████████████████████████

This will acknowledge your letter/application received February 9, 2011.  I confirm that your client's fingerprints, photographs and record of disposition, held by this Service and the R.C.M.P. as a result of your client's charge(s), have been destroyed.

Please note that the destruction only relates to your client's fingerprints, photographs and the record of disposition.  You may contact Criminal Records at (416) 808-8268 should you have any further questions relating to the fingerprint and photograph destruction.

Note:  The relevant Toronto Police Service Record of Arrest report pertaining to this incident will be retained in accordance with the City of Toronto Municipal Code, Chapter 219, Article 1. Questions concerning this retention should be directed to Records Release at (416) 808-8244.

Sincerely,

Fahreda Caissie, Group Leader
Information Access
Records Management Services

FC:ma

*To Serve and Protect - Working with the Community*

Toronto Police Letter confirming Destruction of Photographs, Fingerprints and Record of Disposition

by the accused—typically, probation for one year or completion of community service.

## 11. What is a file purge?

The RCMP is responsible for purging those criminal records that result in an absolute or conditional discharge. When a file is purged, the RCMP transfers it to a special repository (data bank) awaiting final destruction. The law mandating that the RCMP purge discharge records is section 6.1 of the *Criminal Records Act (CRA)*. Once the file has been purged the *CRA* states, "No record of a discharge ... that is in the custody of the Commissioner or of any department or agency of the Government of Canada shall be disclosed to any person, nor shall the existence of the record or the fact of the discharge be disclosed to any person, without the prior approval of the Minister ..."[6]

See samples of the following on pp. 191-193:

- OPP letter explaining that the RCMP purged the absolute discharge and that the OPP has agreed to the destruction of the person's photographs and negatives
- Calgary Police Service letter confirming that the RCMP's file has been closed (purged), and that fingerprints and photographs held by the Calgary Police Service were destroyed, and
- RCMP letter explaining that the applicant's RCMP record "... has been removed and transferred to a 'special repository' in accordance with ... the *Criminal Records Act*..." This means that the record was a discharge (or a youth record), not an adult conviction.

## 12. When is someone eligible for a file purge?

A person is eligible to have a discharge purged once the waiting period has been met: one year for absolute discharges, and three years for conditional discharges, regardless of any punishment imposed (e.g., probation or fine payment). The waiting period begins to run from the final court date. The RCMP automatically

| Ontario<br>Provincial<br>Police | Police<br>provinciale<br>de l'Ontario |  | **Peterborough County Detachment**<br>**Détachement du comté de Peterborough** |
|---|---|---|---|

P.O. Box 477      C.P. 477
453 Lansdowne Street East    453, rue Lansdowne Est
Peterborough ON K9J 6Z6    Peterborough ON K9J 6Z6

Tel: (705) 742-0401      Tél. : (705) 742-0401
Fax: (705) 742-9247     Téléc. : (705) 742-9247

File Reference: ▮▮▮

May 23, 2007

Pardons Canada
45 St. Clair Ave. W.
Ste. 901
Toronto, Ontario
M4V 1K9

▬▬▬▬▬▬▬

▬▬▬▬▬▬▬

Re:    **Destruction of Fingerprints/Photographs**

      DOB: ▬▬▬▬▬▬▬

The Peterborough County O.P.P. charge of Assault 266 CC for the above noted person was given an Absolute Discharge in Provincial Court, Peterborough, Ontario on ▬▬▬▬▬▬▬

Correspondence received from RCMP indicates that due to the disposition on this charge ▮▮ ▬▬▬▬ fingerprints have been transferred to the Special Fingerprints Repository and can only be disclosed for identification purposes. Therefore, her photographs and negatives will be destroyed June 8, 2007 at 10:00 a.m. ▬▬▬▬▬ is welcome to attend our office to witness the destruction or accept this letter as proof that it was done.

Yours truly,

*[signature]*

Graham Gleason
A/Detachment Commander #5801

:sb

Ontario Provincial Police inviting applicant to attend at the police station to witness the Destruction

CALGARY
POLICE
SERVICE

Vigilance
Courage
Pride

2012 March 13

Pardons Canada
Suite #901
45 St.Clair Ave. West
Toronto, Ontario
**M4V 1K9**

**Attention:**

**Re:** ████████████████████
**Your File:**

In response to your letter dated 2011 October 06, we have had confirmation from RCMP OTTAWA that their file for above subject has been closed.

This letter is to confirm that the fingerprints and photograph held by Calgary Police Service were withdrawn from our files and destroyed this date.

Yours truly,

Todd Zelensky, A/Inspector
i/c Investigative Support Section

TZ/wg

Calgary Police Letter confirming the destruction of both the RCMP and the Calgary police files

Royal
Canadian
Mounted
Police

Gendarmerie
royale
du
Canada

Your File  Votre référence

Our File  Notre référence
FPS # ████████

Re: **REQUEST FOR CRIMINAL RECORD**
(for the purpose of an Application     for
Pardon)
Form NPB 301-A

Please be advised that all information contained on your criminal record has been removed and transferred to a special repository in accordance with either the Criminal Records Act or the Young Offenders Act pending destruction. Information contained in this special repository is unavailable to law enforcement agencies unless further criminal activity resumes.

Since a pardon under the Criminal Records Act cannot be obtained for any of these dispositions, should you have other convictions for which a pardon is required, it is suggested that you continue the pardon process. In continuing this process, please refer to steps two and three of your Pardon Application Booklet.

Objet: **DEMANDE DE CASIER JUDICIAIRE**
(en vue d'une demande de
réhabilitation)
formulaire CNLC 301-1A

La présente tient à vous informer que le contenu de votre casier judiciaire a été rayé et transféré dans un répertoire spécial, en conformité avec la Loi sur le casier judiciaire ou la Loi sur les jeunes contrevenants, en attente de sa destruction. L'information que contient ce répertoire n'est pas disponible à l'organisme responsable de l'application de la loi sauf lorsqu'il s'agit de récidive.

Il n'y a pas lieu de présenter une demande de réhabilitation pour les accusations transférées dans le répertoire spécial, cependant si vous avez été condamné pour d'autres accusations qui nécessitent une réhabilitation, je vous suggère de continuer ce processus. Afin de continuer le processus de réhabilitation, s'il vous plaît voir les étapes deux et trois du Livret de demande de réhabilitation.

Groupe des pardons et des droits de la personne,
Sections des dossiers judiciaires,

C D rw

for   D.A. Thibodeau Cpl.,
Pardons and Human Rights Unit,
Criminal History Section.

Canadä

RCMP Report stating record was Purged

Even if the eligibility period has passed, some police services will not destroy the photographs, fingerprints, and outcome records if an unexpired prohibition order exists (e.g., if the person's driver's licence is suspended).

purges discharges registered after July 24, 1992, after the waiting period has been met. In order to ensure that the purge has been completed, and for those discharges prior to July 24, 1992, not covered by this law, it is a good idea to get written confirmation of whether a record still exists at the RCMP. Once the RCMP purge is completed, it is necessary to remove the record at the local police.

## 13. How long does it take for a file to be purged?

A file purge usually takes four to sixteen months to complete (which includes destroying or sealing the records at the local police).

## 14. What are the benefits of a file purge?

As with destructions, the benefits of having a criminal discharge record purged, and being able to provide a clear police report are many and can often affect the most important aspects of a person's life. With a purge:

- An RCMP records check will no longer show the information.
- The American officials will not be able to access the information from the RCMP—providing that the U.S.A. did not have a copy of this information *prior* to the purge.

If the discharge is also destroyed (or sealed) at the local police service, some further benefits are:

- An LPRC will no longer show the charge.
- Police information that is destroyed can never resurface.

PAROLE BOARD OF CANADA (PBC)
PARDONS AND RECORD SUSPENSIONS FOR *CONVICTIONS*

## 15. What is a conviction?

A *conviction* means that someone was charged with an offence under a federal law (usually the *Criminal Code*), went to court, and was found guilty and convicted.

## 16. What is the *Criminal Records Act (CRA)*?

The *CRA* is federal legislation that governs Pardons, Record Suspensions (RS), and RCMP purges in Canada.[7] Among other things, it deals with matters such as who can apply for an RS, when and how an application can be made, who can order an RS, what the effect of having an RS is, and how it can be revoked.

Further, notwithstanding that the word *Pardon* was replaced by the term *Record Suspension*, there are still over 400,000 Pardons in existence. The *CRA* continues to govern these Pardons, both in terms of the effect of a Pardon, as well as when they can be revoked or cease to have effect.

It is important to note that the *CRA* is a federal law and, as such, only applies to records kept within federal departments and agencies. This means that the *CRA* has no power over provincial and municipal police and court records. That said, once provincial and municipal law-enforcement agencies and the courts have been notified that an RS has been granted, they will almost always cooperate by restricting access to these records. So too will provincial courts.

## 17. What is the history of the *CRA*?

The *CRA*'s author—lawyer and Member of Parliament, Don Tolmie—came up with the idea of a Pardon Program for Canada in 1968, after hearing about an injustice in Nova Scotia. A city councillor had been forced to resign his seat when a defeated opponent revealed that the councillor had been convicted of theft a decade earlier. Tolmie felt that while people make mistakes, they shouldn't have to deal with the stigma for the rest of their lives. He said: "Obviously, it is illogical and completely unjust to add to his punishment, which a competent court decided upon, by saddling him with a record in perpetuity and hounding and harassing him to his dying day." As chair of the Justice Committee in 1969, Tolmie drafted the legislation, presented it as a private member's bill, and was ultimately successful in making it into a law in 1970. To this day, thanks to Tolmie's efforts, over 400,000 people have been pardoned under the *CRA*.

The Pardon Program is the single most successful program ever administered by the federal government. Over the past forty years, the program has had a consistent success rate of 96 percent.

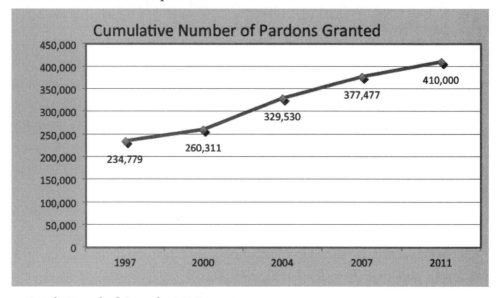

Parole Board of Canada, 2012

Unfortunately, in March 2012, the government went against the steadfast rule: *if it ain't broke, don't fix it*, and proceeded to change the Pardon law. It is my contention that the new law, with its longer waiting periods, has created an environment in which the crime rate will likely increase. This will have far-reaching negative consequences, not only for those individuals directly involved and their families, but also for the rest of us, and our families, as we likely will experience higher unemployment and crime rates.

NEW PARDON LAW, BILL C-10

## 18. What are Pardons and Record Suspensions (RS)?

The new Pardon law came into effect as of March 13, 2012. Apart from the difference in terminology and some eligibility (and non-eligibility) rule changes, the effect of a Pardon and of an RS is the same.[8]

Once a Pardon or an RS[9] has been awarded, the CRA requires the RCMP (and any other federal government department or agency having a copy of the record in their custody), to keep the record separate and apart from other criminal records and not to disclose it. In addition, the Minister requests all other persons (who are not under federal jurisdiction) having custody or control of any judicial record of conviction about the person to seal those records and not disclose them on police records searches.[10] The criminal record is not destroyed through either of these processes. Rather, it is hidden and cannot be disclosed through a criminal records check unless (i) the Pardon or RS is revoked or ceases to have effect, (ii) it falls within the rules for sex-related offences, or (iii) the permission to disclose it has been obtained from the federal Minister of Public Safety.

Pardons that have previously been granted or issued (and have not been revoked or ceased to have effect) remain valid and in force notwithstanding the new term *Record Suspension*.

## 19. What are the benefits of having a Pardon or an RS?

Individuals with a criminal record are often at a serious disadvantage with many aspects of regular day-to-day life. Some of the benefits of being awarded a Pardon or an RS, as with destructions and purges, include such things as:

- An RCMP records check will no longer show the information.
- The American officials will not be able to access the information from the RCMP—providing that the U.S.A. did not have a copy of this information *prior* to the Pardon or RS.
- Local police services also seal their records (although not obligated to do so), and an LPRC will no longer show the charge.

- Canadian human rights laws forbid discrimination against the individual based on a pardoned or suspended record.

Further, here's what the Supreme Court and the National Parole Board said about the effect of a Pardon:

> A pardon does not have an absolute effect and does not erase the past. Neither a discharge nor a pardon allows a person to deny that he or she was found guilty of an offence. The facts surrounding the offence did occur, but the pardon helps obliterate the stigma attached to the finding of guilt. Consequently, when the time period provided for in the *Criminal Records Act* elapses or a pardon is granted, the opprobrium that results from prejudice and is attached solely to the finding of guilt must be resisted, and the finding of guilt should no longer reflect adversely on the pardoned person's character. It must be presumed that the person has completely recovered his or her moral integrity.

Also, the Chairperson of the National Parole Board (NPB) (now the PBC) stated, "... the pardons system has a dual benefit: to assist the individual with a criminal record in moving forward in his or her rehabilitation, and to enhance the safety of communities by motivating the individual to remain crime-free and to maintain good conduct."[11]

In cover letters sent to applicants who had been awarded Pardons, the Director of the NPB stated, "This [pardon] signifies the intent of Parliament that a person to whom a pardon has been awarded, under the CRA, should no longer be made to suffer any legal disabilities or penalties imposed as a result of a conviction."[12]

Here's what those who have been given a second chance have to say...

> Jeff H., "*It has been a long time since I've been able to say that I am truly free. Some of the obstacles I have had to endure were job searching, school functions with my kids, and just the scared feeling whenever I see a police car or hear a siren.*"

Thompson H., "*Even if the criminal record is old, it lingers as a sour reminder of past mistakes. Having received my pardon has released me from my past. It has given me a new beginning.*"

Marcia B., "*I couldn't believe that I would get a chance at a new life again. Even now, I still cannot believe it. I have a pardon. I can apply to any job I want. I no longer feel depressed and feel the need to hide.*"

Robert B., "*Having my pardon has given me hope that I can overcome what I have done in my past and do great things in our society. It has given me a sense of purpose, and the drive to be the man I truly want to be and hold my head high.*"

Edmondo S., "*I would like to extend my appreciation on helping me start a new clean life. Sometimes you have so many plans on what you would like to do with your life, however, sometimes it doesn't always work. Having a criminal record prevented me from doing a lot with my life—no matter how small the charges were—a record is a record.*"

## 20. What are the limitations of a Pardon or an RS?

- **Local Police and Courts.** Both Pardons and Record Suspensions are awarded under the *CRA*, which is a Canadian federal law. This means that provincial and municipal police and courts are not under a legal obligation to maintain pardoned or suspended records separately, or to prevent their disclosure. Having said this, however, police services and courts across Canada do comply with the federal law. This may be because police and courts in our country give value to the federal law and to the success of the Pardon Program, as well as the fact that these records can be accessed if the person does reoffend. The practical result of their compliance therefore, is that if a person has a Pardon or an RS (except in the case of sex offences), his or her record, or the fact that it has been pardoned or suspended, will not be disclosed in a standard LPRC.

- **Sex Offences**. Those with Pardons or Record Suspensions for a sex offence cannot be employed by or volunteer to work with vulnerable people without having their record divulged. As set out in the *CRA*, a notation of the sex offences listed in the schedule, for which a Pardon or an RS was awarded, will be made in the RCMP data bank so that the record can be *flagged*.

- **Foreign Governments.** Most foreign governments will require an RCMP records check to be submitted with a work or study visa application. After a Pardon or an RS has been awarded, an RCMP records search will produce a "no criminal record" result. However, if the foreign government had knowledge of the record *before* the Pardon or RS was awarded, they may have downloaded a copy into their own data banks. Under those circumstances, applicants will likely have to provide further explanations or complete an additional process specific to that country's laws (e.g., U.S.A. Entry Waivers).

- **Prohibitions.** Prohibition orders, such as a driver's licence suspension or firearms ban, that are still in effect, will not prevent someone from obtaining a Pardon or an RS;  However, they are *not* terminated because a Pardon or an RS was ordered.

## 21. Is a Canadian Pardon or RS recognized outside of Canada?

- **Pardon.** Many countries have some sort of system in place for pardoning crimes. If the country was aware of or had a copy of the Canadian criminal record *prior* to the Pardon or RS having been awarded, showing them that the record was removed, will improve the chances of having an immigration application accepted. Having said that, however, having a Pardon or an RS does not guarantee that the record will not continue to be a barrier.

- **Record Suspension.** Since this new term is not internationally recognized (nor defined in any dictionary), individuals wanting to show that their record has been forgiven by way of a *"Record Suspension having been ordered,"* will likely have to explain that, in Canada, it is now the same as having a criminal record pardoned. They may have to include parts of the *CRA* to support this statement.

## 22. Is a separate RS required for each conviction?

No. As long as the individual completed the punishment imposed by the court, and no subsequent criminal behaviour is recorded, all convictions can be simultaneously removed and sealed once the eligibility requirements have been met. An RS is an all-or-nothing proposition, meaning that it will not be ordered for *any* of the convictions, unless *each* of the convictions has reached its eligibility date.

## 23. When an RS is ordered, what happens to the non-convictions?

If someone has both *convictions* and *non-convictions* on the criminal record, the non-convictions will be sealed together with the convictions once an RS is ordered. No separate application is necessary.

The non-convictions, however, can impact whether the individual's application will be successful. The PBC will look at the nature of the non-convictions and the date when they occurred. If the non-convictions occurred *subsequent* to the *last* conviction, the PBC might decide that the individual is *not* of *good behaviour* and may go on to deny the application.

## 24. Who can apply for an RS?

Any adult, if convicted of an offence under a Canadian federal law,[13] may apply for an RS. This is true even if the person is not a Canadian citizen, does not have any other type of Canadian immigration status, or lives outside of Canada. Offences committed by youth generally do not require an RS to be removed. However, there are instances where young offender records are considered to be part of the person's adult criminal record. In those instances, an RS would be needed.

Where someone is convicted of a crime *outside* of Canada, they can apply for a Canadian RS if they were transferred to Canada under the *Transfer of Offenders Act,* or the *International Transfer of Offenders Act.*

Following are fingerprints taken by the Slovakian police for a Slovakian citizen who had committed an offence while in Canada. These fingerprints were sent to the RCMP for certification and then submitted with the Pardon application.

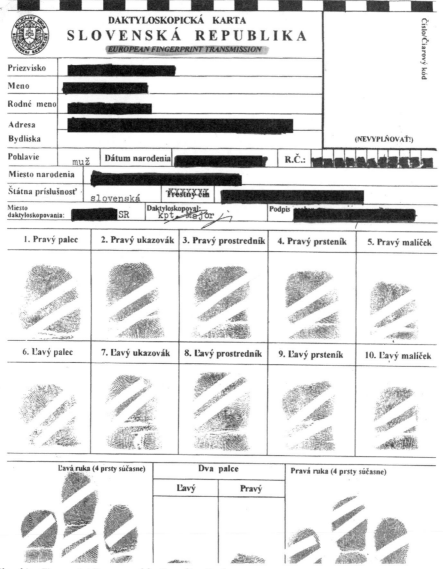

Slovakian Fingerprint Forms used for Canadian Pardon

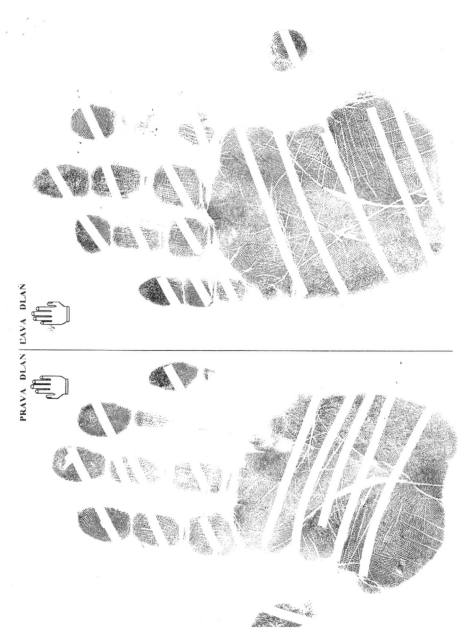

Slovakian Fingerprint Forms used for Canadian Pardon

## 25. Who can award an RS?

The Parole Board of Canada (PBC) is a federal agency, within the portfolio of Public Safety Canada, which has authority to deal with day parole and full parole under the *Corrections and Conditional Release Act*, and the authority to award, deny, and revoke Pardons and Record Suspensions under the *CRA*. The PBC's national office in Ottawa is where the RS applications are submitted and reviewed.[14] The processing and governing of Pardons and Record Suspensions comprises a relatively small part of the PBC's operations.

Interestingly, the Pardon Program, which has had a consistent 96 percent success rate over the last 40 years, recently came under attack, resulting in the current legal changes, whereas the parole programs as well as the statutory release laws that are also overseen by the PBC have not been changed. The success rates of those programs are as follows:

Successful Completion Rates for Federal Conditional Release
**Day parole**: 87.4 percent (13.6 percent breached their parole conditions or committed another offence while out on parole.)
**Full Parole**: 76.5 percent (23.5 percent breached their parole conditions or committed another offence while out on parole.)
**Statutory Release**: 62.4 percent (37.6 percent breached their parole conditions or committed another offence while out on parole.)  Note: statutory release is a release granted by law and usually is not a PBC decision.[15]

Not only are these programs not nearly as successful as the Pardon Program, the cost of preparing a parole review by the PBC is about $2,000 per inmate (with a total annual cost of about $35 million). The inmate does not have to cover any of these costs, whereas the RS applicant must pay the federal government's cost to process the application (currently $631).

## 26. Can someone obtain an RS for any type of crime?

An RS can be obtained for almost all types of crimes. The exceptions are:

- if the person was convicted of a Schedule 1 offence under the CRA.

Schedule 1 offences are mostly related to sexual offences involving children, but also include sexual offences related to young people under the age of eighteen,[16] or

- if the person was convicted of "more than three offences each of which either was prosecuted by indictment or is a service offence that is subject to a maximum punishment of imprisonment for life, and for each of which the person was sentenced to imprisonment for two years or more."[17]

ELIGIBILITY
## 27. When is someone eligible to apply for an RS?

Generally, people are eligible to apply for an RS once they have completed the sentence imposed by the court and have waited the necessary time period. Waiting periods depend on the seriousness of the case—whether the court proceeded summarily (less serious offences) or by indictment (more serious offences). The following chart sets out the time frames listed in the *CRA*. New legislation has increased the waiting period for summary offences from *three* to *five* years, and indictable offences from *five* to *ten* years.

These time-frames do not include the time it takes to complete the sentence, collect the application documents, and the amount of time that the application will remain at the PBC (waiting to be assigned and then processed). Adding these together, it means that for summary conviction offences, it will take about seven years, and for indictable conviction offences it will take about thirteen years from the final court date before the individual can have their crimes pardoned through the RS process.[18]

Unfortunately, the new law has made the prospect of obtaining an RS impossible for some, and so far in the future for others that they might become discouraged from living a crime-free life while waiting to be eligible. We have removed their hope of a fresh start. Instead of making our *streets safer*, this change will likely have the opposite effect.

Given how pervasive police records checks have become, a person's job prospects are extremely limited when they have a criminal record. As a result of this new law, people will be living in our communities who, for a very long time, will find it almost impossible to get a decent job and acceptable housing. As most people with criminal records are also parents, this new law will have a large negative impact on our communities. When people are out of work for long periods of time, there are serious consequences to their home life, to our economy, and to society. Only time will show what the repercussions of this legislation will be.

| Record Suspension Eligibility: Waiting Periods | | |
|---|---|---|
| **Legislation** | **Conviction Details** | **Waiting Period** |
| ***Criminal Code* and other federal statutes** | Summary | 5 years |
| | Indictable | 10 years |
| ***Transfer of Offenders Act*** | All | 10 years |
| ***National Defence Act*** | Fine of more than $2,000 Detention for more than 6 months Person was dismissed from the service Imprisonment for more than 6 months Punishment more than imprisonment for less than 2 years  s. 139(1) | 10 years |
| | Service offence (other than above) | 5 years |
| **Those Not Eligible** | (1)  If convicted of a Schedule 1 offence and exception does not apply. (2)  Those convicted of more than 3 indictable offences where more than 2 years jail was ordered for each of the offences. | No Record Suspension Allowed |

## 28. What is included in a "sentence" for the purpose of determining eligibility?

A sentence is considered completed when the individual has:

- **paid all fines, surcharges, costs, restitution, and compensation orders in full**. The waiting period starts at the time the final payment is made. That means that if the payment is made three years after the court ordered the fine, that is the date when the waiting period begins.
- **served all jail time ordered by the court.** Even if the individual is released from jail early, either due to statutory release or parole, the entire jail time ordered by the judge must pass before the waiting period begins. It is also important to note that any time spent in jail

*prior* to sentencing (often referred to as *dead-time*) is *not* included in calculating eligibility for an RS.

- **satisfied all conditions of a probation order.** Often, if a probation officer considers someone under a probation order to be of good conduct, the individual may be allowed to stop reporting before the probation time is completed. This has *no bearing* when calculating eligibility. Unless a judge subsequently reduces the probation time, the entire probation time originally ordered must be completed.

*Prohibitions* (such as driver's-licence suspensions or not being allowed to possess firearms) are *not* included in calculating eligibility.

## 29. How can the "good conduct" assessment affect eligibility for an RS?

An important factor that the PBC considers when evaluating RS applications—outside of completing the sentence ordered by the judge and waiting the requisite period of time—is *being of good conduct.* The concept of good conduct is given a broad and comprehensive interpretation. The PBC officer in charge of processing the file will pursue investigations to confirm whether the individual has led a crime-free life after the conviction, as well as having generally been of good behaviour.

In determining if the applicant was of good conduct, the PBC does not only consider subsequent *convictions*, but may deny an RS on the basis of *any* subsequent infractions of the law. For example, criminal charges, even where they resulted in a *not-guilty* outcome, might be sufficient to deny the application. In fact, in some cases, provincial offences, such as unpaid parking tickets or speeding violations, are the basis for a denial. The severity of the charge, how recent the event was, and the applicant's explanation of the events, are all factors that the PBC officer will consider.

Statistics show that only 2 percent of the applications (that are accepted for processing) are denied, suggesting that most applicants have remained crime-free and have been of good conduct.

It is important to understand that the CRA gives the PBC "absolute discretionary powers" to make the final decision as to whether an RS application will be successful. Only one PBC officer, who then makes his or her recommendations to the Board, usually reviews each application. The PBC officer's recommendation is almost always followed by the Board.[19]

In the letter on p. 209, the PBC officer was proposing to deny the application because—among other things—they had received information that the applicant had been "verbally abusive" at a Human Resources Centre.

## 30. When should someone start preparing an RS application?

Given the importance of obtaining an RS, individuals should start collecting the necessary documents well in advance of their eligibility date—except, of course, for documents that expire, which should only be obtained close to the submission date. Collecting documents in advance will not change the eligibility date, but the benefit is that the file will be prepared and ready for submission, as soon as the waiting period is met.

Further, analyzing all the necessary documents in advance may lead to the discovery of problems —such as an unpaid fine—which can then be remedied before the application is made. Indeed, analyzing the criminal record in advance, may lead to the discovery that the person was not even convicted, and therefore needs a destruction or purge, both of which can be requested much sooner than an RS.

At the very least, preparing an RS application in advance gives people hope and helps keep them crime-free. In turn, this will allow them to make plans, such as enrolling in education or work programs, and applying for jobs, with the knowledge that the criminal record will not be a noose around their necks for life.

## 31. Obtaining an RS before eligibility: Royal Prerogative of Mercy

A *conditional pardon*, which would allow the record to be sealed before eligibil-

**I✦I** Government    Gouvernement
of Canada    du Canada

National    Commission nationale des
Parole Board    libérations conditionnelles

Ottawa, Ontario    Ottawa, (Ontario)
K1A 0R1    K1A 0R1

Our File:  ██████████    Date: 2000/11/03
Your File:

Pardons Canada    BULK

████████████████
████████
██████████████████

Dear Sir/Madam:

RE:  ██████████

_____

This is further to a request for pardon under the *Criminal Records Act*.

Having reviewed the results of the inquiries, the National Parole Board proposes to deny the pardon, based on the following:

Your client rececently came to the attention of the police in March 1999 as he was reported to have been verbally abusive to staff at the Human Resource Centre. He refused to leave despite several requests to do so. He also has two traffic violations for speeding in 1997 and 1999. Police also report that he was not truthful on his pardon application about his previous addresses for the past five years. He indicated that he had lived at ██████████████████ for the past five years. A drivers licence check indicates, however, that he has lived at other addresses and cities. Given all these factors, the Board is not convinced at this time that Mr. ██████ meets the good conduct criteria and proposes to deny your client's pardon.

If you so wish, you may make written representations you feel may assist your client's case and cause the Board to render a positive decision.

The written representations, which may be made with or without an assistant, should include comments with regards to the Board's proposal to deny and any other information that reflects good conduct. You may also provide details of any exceptional circumstances that you feel may assist your client's case.

Please return this letter along with the written representations within sixty days.

## Canada    PROTECTED

National Parole Board Letter identifying reasons why applicant is not of good conduct

ity is reached, is almost never granted.

The Royal Prerogative of Mercy (RPM) is a *discretionary* power based on an ancient right of the monarchy to grant mercy. In Canada, the Governor General or the Governor in Council has the power to exercise this right. The Governor in Council will grant clemency upon recommendation from the Minister of Public Safety, who, in turn, receives recommendations from the PBC.

Although few people make these applications, and they are almost never granted, under the *Criminal Code*, the Governor in Council can grant any of the following types of mercy:[20]

- **Free Pardon**: If the person is innocent, the Free Pardon recognizes that the conviction was in error and erases both the consequences and the record of conviction.
- **Conditional Pardon**: This refers to either of these two situations:
  1. The criminal record is kept separate and apart from other criminal records *prior to eligibility* (five or ten years, whichever is applicable).
  2. Parole in advance of the eligibility date under the *Corrections and Conditional Release Act* in cases of life and indeterminate sentences.
- **Remission of fine, forfeiture, and pecuniary penalty**: If ordered, this can erase all or part of the monetary penalty that was imposed by the court.

Under the RPM, the role of the PBC is to review clemency applications and make their recommendations to the Minister.[21] The guidelines that the PBC uses to review the RPM applications are strict and include such statements as "intended only for rare cases," and "undue hardship … out of proportion to the nature and seriousness of the offence."

As you will see from the graphs on p. 211-212, clemency is only granted in extreme situations (only 3 percent of applications). Further, the statistics do not separate the applications by type, which means that approval for conditional pardons is an even smaller percentage of the total RPM applications *granted* (the rest being Free Pardons and remission of fines applications).

One successful case that I was involved with concerned a woman with a unique government position hanging in the balance. This brave woman had survived serious physical and mental abuse from early childhood. As a result, she had turned to drugs and alcohol to kill the painful memories. She eventually began committing crimes in order to sustain her drug habit. After many hard years, this woman became clean and sober. She went back to school and successfully completed her university degree. Unfortunately, federal policy prohibited her from being hired unless she had been granted a Pardon. The job she was offered was very senior and one for which her life experiences made her ideal. Given her circumstances, I felt that this woman's case was indeed rare. We argued that denying her this chance after all she had been through would most definitely cause a hardship out of proportion to the nature and seriousness of her offences (which were mostly small thefts). Giving details of her childhood and struggles with rehabilitation, and her perseverance in educating herself, we succeeded in having the request granted.

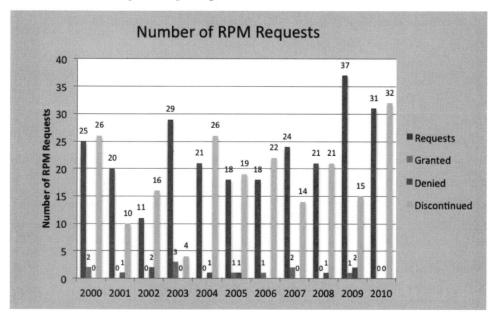

Parole Board of Canada, 2012

All other RPM applications I have seen have failed. In one such case, the Pardon applicant was terminally ill and had requested a conditional pardon so that she could die knowing she had been forgiven. Her application for an RPM was refused. Consequently, in her will, she requested that if her Pardon was granted prior to her death, it be put in her coffin. Although the RPM application was denied, her Pardon was granted just prior to her death and her wish to have it buried with her was fulfilled.

## Percentage of RPM Requests Granted

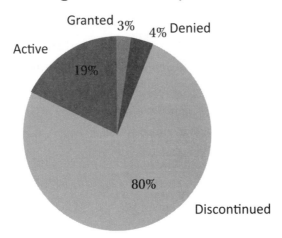

Parole Board of Canada, 2012[22]

Now that the waiting periods for RS eligibility have been increased, people must suffer the effects of a criminal record much longer. Consequently, we may see an increase in the number of RPM applications as people try to speed up the process.

APPLICATION
## 32. What is included in an RS application?

For most people, there are nine steps in the RS application process. For those who are or were in the Canadian Military, there are ten steps, as one additional document is required.

**1. Certified RCMP report**. A certified copy of the individual's criminal record or a certification that *no criminal record* exists must be obtained from the RCMP. This step involves submitting a current set of fingerprints and a small processing fee to the RCMP. RCMP staff match the individual's fingerprints to his or her Fingerprint Section (FPS) number and the criminal record associated with that number. Using fingerprint information ensures that the correct criminal record is being released.

Many local police services, especially in cities, do not provide this service. Individuals, if they are completing this application on their own, must find a private company that provides this service and is accredited by the RCMP. Furthermore, many fingerprinting companies no longer use ink or paper forms; rather, fingerprints are taken digitally and sent electronically to the RCMP. For those living in rural areas, however, local police detachments may still offer old-style ink-and-paper fingerprinting services.[23] Notwithstanding this fact, it is often better for those living in rural areas to drive to the nearest city to have their fingerprints taken digitally. Digital prints are processed faster, thereby saving the applicant two to five months processing time.[24]

**2. Analyze the Criminal Record**. Before proceeding further, it is imperative to determine if an RS is required. Using the certified RCMP report, other available police or court records, and the information that the individual knows about his or her record, it can be determined if the person needs an RS or if a file destruction or purge is required. If the analysis of the criminal record is not done properly, the record might not be removed correctly, and will almost certainly resurface in the future (usually at the most inopportune time).

**3. Proof of Convictions.** Sometimes, the charging police do not report all convictions to the RCMP. Therefore, convictions may exist that do not appear in the certified RCMP record report. In order to obtain an RS for all convictions, the details of missing convictions must be proven by obtaining a court record from the court where the case was heard, or by a police report from the charging police. Proof of conviction must include the offence, the final court date, the

The court or police service also may report charges that resulted in non-convictions, and which did not appear on the RCMP report. Although these charges do not require an RS, they are, in fact, sealed with the convictions once an RS is ordered. In deciding whether an individual is of good conduct, the PBC can deny an RS application based on non-convictions.

court location, the sentence received, and the name of the charging police service. The police and the court charge a range of fees for providing these documents.

Following is a sample of a Toronto Police records search revealing seven charges resulting in non-convictions that were *in addition* to those charges and convictions appearing on the person's RCMP report.

### TORONTO POLICE SERVICE

#### Details of Police Records Check - Pardon

Name: ████████████                    Date of Birth: **1958**████

The following is a detailed account of police information for the above named as identified in the attached Summary of Local Police Records Check.

| DATE OF DISPOSITION | CHARGE/OFFENCE TYPE | DISPOSITION | COURT |
|---|---|---|---|
| 1997. | Possession under $5000 (2 charges) | Withdrawn | 126 Court – Old City Hall |
| 1998. | Fraud over $5000 (2 charges) | Withdrawn | Superior Court – 361 University Ave. |
| 1999 | Fraud over $5000 (2 charges) | 10 months on each charge concurrent | Superior Court – 361 University Ave. |
|  | Fraud over $5000 | Withdrawn |  |

TORONTO POLICE SERVICE
POLICE REFERENCE / LOCAL RECORDS CHECK
(40 College Street, Toronto, Ontario M5G 2J3)

VERIFIED: _____*Manoul*_____  DATE: *Oct 14/09*

Toronto Police Records Check showing withdrawn charges that were Not on RCMP report

### 4. Certified PBC Court Information Form, Affidavits, and Third-party Letters. A Certified Court Information Form is required for each conviction that was prosecuted summarily and where less than ten years have passed since the sentence was completed, and if the person was ordered to pay a fine, cost, surcharge, restitution, or a compensation order. Even if ten years have passed since the sentence was completed, and there was no monetary payment ordered, it is still a good idea to obtain a court record if the case was prosecuted

summarily, as these files are processed faster at the PBC.

### Court Errors

The courts can make clerical errors completing these forms and it is up to the applicant to scrutinize them carefully to ensure every detail has been properly completed. If the court record was not completed properly, and the individual did not find the error, the PBC will return the application. By the time the PBC reviews the application, sends it back, another court record is obtained and the application is resubmitted, the LPRC and the RS application likely will have expired. The file will then be rejected for the second time.

### Payments to Victims or Third Parties

In cases where payments were ordered to be made directly to the victim (i.e., a restitution or compensation order), proper documentation from the individual or company, such as a letter or an affidavit, is necessary to prove that restitution was, in fact, paid.

### Court Records for Other Types of Applications

For people making other types of applications that may require court records—such as U.S.A. Entry Waiver applications, visas to study or work in other foreign countries, or Canadian Immigration applications—a second copy of the PBC Court Information form may not be adequate. Foreign countries require documents to be completed according to their own policies, procedures, and forms, and these records should be obtained before an RS is ordered as court records are sealed and will no longer be available afterwards.

A sample of the the two-page PBC *Court Information Form*, as well as a letter confirming *restitution* was paid can be seen on pp. 217-219. The victim in this case was the Government of Canada.

**5. Military Conduct Sheet.** If the applicant is, or ever has been, a member of the Canadian Forces, then a *Military Conduct Sheet,* or written confirmation of its non-existence, must be obtained. A military conduct sheet for current members is only valid for six months from the date it is issued.

**6. PBC Local Police Records Check (LPRC).** The applicant must obtain an LPRC from the police service where he or she currently lives and for each city or town where he or she has lived (for a period of three months or more) in the past five years. Using the PBC's form, the local police are required to disclose the existence and details of convictions, if any, which are in addition to those appearing in the RCMP data banks, as well as all information related to incidents involving police and all charges (including provincial convictions and charges), as well as their outcomes. LPRCs are only valid for *six months* from the date they are issued.

Logically, it would seem that this form should be completed at the last minute to ensure that it does not expire. However, the LPRC processing time at each police service varies. It depends not only on the policies of each police service, but also on the demands on the resources of the particular police service at any given time. This is tricky. While you don't want the form to expire, you also don't want to waste months waiting for the LPRC to be processed. It gets even more complicated if there is more than one check required (which is often the case).

If the individual lives outside of Canada, an LPRC must be obtained from the police in that region as well.

See pp. 221-224 for a sample of the two-page LPRC form, as well as copies of two foreign LPRCs. One is from Ecuador and the other from Germany (both show "no criminal record").

**7. Identification and Immigration Documents.** If the applicant was born *in* Canada, or was born *outside* Canada and is *not* living in Canada, then only a copy of an official document proving his or her *identity* (and not immigration status) must be submitted with the application. Examples of appropriate documents include a copy of a driver's licence or a foreign identification card.

If the applicant is currently *living in* Canada but was born *outside* of Canada, then he or she must provide copies of valid *Canadian Immigration* documents, such as Canadian citizenship or Permanent Resident Card. If the person does not have Canadian immigration status, then an official document stating this fact must be included with the application.

**8. Record Suspension Application Form.** In addition to being completed properly, this form must be signed and dated by the applicant. It is only valid for six

Parole Board
of Canada

Commission des
libérations conditionnelles
du Canada

**Protected when completed**

# Court Information Form

### For the purpose of a Record Suspension Application
### Please print clearly using blue or black ink. You must answer all questions.

## SECTION A: PERSONAL INFORMATION – You must answer all questions.

1. **What is your full legal name?** (You must fill in your name and date of birth at the top of page 2 as well.)

    Last Name: _____ Given Name(s): _____

2. **Have you ever used another name other than your legal name above?**

    NO ☐  YES ☐  → If YES, please write the other names that you have used here. If you do not give all of the names that you have used in the past, your application will be returned to you.

| Previous Last Name(s) | Previous Given Name(s) |
|---|---|
|  |  |
|  |  |
|  |  |

3. **What is your gender?** MALE ☐ FEMALE ☐     4. **What is your date of birth?** Y Y Y Y M M D D

## SECTION B: CONTACT INFORMATION – You must answer all questions.

5. **What is your mailing address?**

    _____

    Apartment/House Number and Street Address      City/Town      Province      Postal Code      Country

6. **What is your telephone number?** ( _____ ) _____ - _____

## FOR COURT USE ONLY. DO NOT WRITE IN THIS SECTION.

Name and Address of Court:          Telephone Number ( _____ ) _____ - _____

Court Name          Street Address          City/Town          Province          Postal Code

## OFFENCE INFORMATION – FOR COURT USE ONLY. DO NOT WRITE IN THIS SECTION.

**OFFENCE INFORMATION #1**

| Offence Description | Sentence | Place of Sentence | Date of Sentence |
|---|---|---|---|
|  |  |  | Y Y Y Y M M D D |

Method of Trial: ☐ Summary   ☐ Indictable   ☐ Unable to Confirm     Court Reference # _____

If Unable to Confirm Method of Trial, State Reason Why: _____

Have all Fines, Surcharges, Restitutions, Compensation Orders and Other Costs Been Paid in Full? ☐ NO ☐ YES

If They Have Been Paid in Full, What Was the Date of the **Last** Payment? Y Y Y Y M M D D

If No, How Much is Outstanding? $ _____

☐ **Our records have been destroyed;**
    however we can confirm there are **no outstanding monies** owed with regard to this case.

**Please turn this form over. →**

*Parole Board of Canada* ■ *Toll-free Info line 1-800-874-2652 – www.recordsuspension.gc.ca*

Canadä

Parole Board
of Canada

Commission des
libérations conditionnelles
du Canada

Page 2 of 2

**Protected when completed**

# Court Information Form

### For the purpose of a Record Suspension Application
### Please print clearly using blue or black ink. You must answer all questions.

## APPLICANT INFORMATION – YOU MUST FILL IN THIS INFORMATION.

Indicate the full legal name and date of birth of the applicant provided on the front of this form:

Full legal name: _____    Date of birth: [Y Y Y Y M M D D]

## OFFENCE INFORMATION – FOR COURT USE ONLY. DO NOT WRITE IN THIS SECTION.

### OFFENCE INFORMATION #2

| Offence Description | Sentence | Place of Sentence | Date of Sentence Y Y Y Y M M D D |
|---|---|---|---|

Method of Trial:   ☐ Summary    ☐ Indictable    ☐ Unable to Confirm    Court Reference # _____

If Unable to Confirm Method of Trial, State Reason Why: _____

Have all Fines, Surcharges, Restitutions, Compensation Orders and Other Costs Been Paid in Full? ☐ NO  ☐ YES

If They Have Been Paid in Full, What Was the Date of the **Last** Payment? [Y Y Y Y M M D D]

If No, How Much is Outstanding? $ _____

☐ **Our records have been destroyed;**
 however we can confirm there are **no outstanding monies** owed with regard to this case.

### OFFENCE INFORMATION #3

| Offence Description | Sentence | Place of Sentence | Date of Sentence Y Y Y Y M M D D |
|---|---|---|---|

Method of Trial:   ☐ Summary    ☐ Indictable    ☐ Unable to Confirm    Court Reference # _____

If Unable to Confirm Method of Trial, State Reason Why: _____

Have all Fines, Surcharges, Restitutions, Compensation Orders and Other Costs Been Paid in Full? ☐ NO  ☐ YES

If They Have Been Paid in Full, What Was the Date of the **Last** Payment? [Y Y Y Y M M D D]

If No, How Much is Outstanding? $ _____

☐ **Our records have been destroyed;**
 however we can confirm there are **no outstanding monies** owed with regard to this case.

### OFFENCE INFORMATION #4

| Offence Description | Sentence | Place of Sentence | Date of Sentence Y Y Y Y M M D D |
|---|---|---|---|

Method of Trial:   ☐ Summary    ☐ Indictable    ☐ Unable to Confirm    Court Reference # _____

If Unable to Confirm Method of Trial, State Reason Why: _____

Have all Fines, Surcharges, Restitutions, Compensation Orders and Other Costs Been Paid in Full? ☐ NO  ☐ YES

If They Have Been Paid in Full, What Was the Date of the **Last** Payment? [Y Y Y Y M M D D]

If No, How Much is Outstanding? $ _____

☐ **Our records have been destroyed;**
 however we can confirm there are **no outstanding monies** owed with regard to this case.

## COURT AUTHORIZATION – Please sign, date, and stamp this form.

Name of Authorized Officer of the Court: _____

Signature: _____

Date: [Y Y Y Y M M D D]

Please put
Court seal or
stamp here.

PBC/CLCC 0301E (2012)

Human Resources    Développement des
Development Canada    ressources humaines Canada

Program Integrity          Intégrité des programmes
Income Security Programs    Programme de la sécurité du revenu
16th Floor, Tower "B"       16ième étage, Tour «B»
Place Vanier               Place Vanier
355 River Road             355, chemin River
Vanier, Ontario, K1A 0L1    Vanier (Ontario) K1A 0L1

Fax. (613) 952-0865

Our File: ████

April 12, 1996

 Avenue
Toronto, Ontario

Dear ████

From July 1992 to September 1994, you obtained from the Government of Canada the sum of $9,084.63 to which you were not entitled under the Old Age Security Act. On March 25, 1996, you pleaded guilty to the charge of fraud contrary to Section 380(1)(a) of the Criminal Code of Canada. At that time, you were ordered to make restitution in the amount of $9,084.63.

Please be advised we have received a cheque in the amount of $9,084.63 and have applied this restitution amount against your debt to the Crown. Income Security Programs now consider this matter concluded.

*Pat Hill*

Pat Hill
Chief
Investigations & Recovery

c.c.:

Barrister & Sollicitor

# Canada

Human Resources Development Canada Letter confirming restitution paid for Old Age Security payments obtained by fraud

months from the date signed.

The two-page Record Suspension Application Form is reproduced on pp. 226-227.

**9. Measurable Benefit / Sustained Rehabilitation Form.** This form was introduced after the new Pardon law came into force on March 13, 2012. It is comprised of four questions aimed at identifying if applicants are *rehabilitated*, how they would *benefit* from an RS, and *details of the crimes* committed.

The two-page Measurable Benefit / Sustained Rehabilitation Form is reproduced on pp. 229-230.

**10. Submitting the Application.** The completed and signed RS application, together with all supporting documents and the processing fee must be submitted to the Clemency and Record Suspension Division of the PBC in Ottawa.[25] Since February 23, 2012, the processing fee has increased to $631. Only certified cheques, money orders, or bank drafts payable to the Receiver General for Canada will be accepted. Personal cheques will not be accepted.

The application cannot be submitted electronically because it contains original documents.

The first PBC fee for a pardon application was $50, introduced in 1994. It was increased to $150 in 2010, and yet again to $631 in February 2012. Although there was some discussion about establishing a two-tier fee system, (whereby those with indictable offences would pay more than those with only summary convictions, to reflect the increased expenses associated with processing files containing indictable offences), this proposal was not adopted.

# 33. Completed Pardons and Record Suspensions, and how they make people feel

The true meaning and effect of a Pardon and an RS can be brought to mind by reading some heartfelt and typical sentiments expressed in just a few of the thousands of letters we received at Pardons Canada:

> John C., (Teacher) *"The positive difference in my life is already evident. I am motivated and my psychological outlook has changed towards being emotionally enhanced for the better good.*

Parole Board
of Canada

Commission des
libérations conditionnelles
du Canada

**Protected when completed**

# Local Police Records Check Form

**For the purpose of a Record Suspension Application**

**Please print clearly using blue or black ink. You must answer all questions.**

## SECTION A: PERSONAL INFORMATION – You must answer all questions.

1. **What is your full legal name?** (You must fill in your name and date of birth at the top of page 2 as well.)

   Last Name: _____  Given Name(s): _____

2. **Have you ever used another name other than your legal name above?**

   NO ☐   YES ☐ → If YES, write these other names below or your application will be returned to you.

   | Previous Last Name(s) | Previous Given Name(s) |
   |---|---|
   | | |
   | | |
   | | |

3. **What is your gender?** MALE ☐  FEMALE ☐    4. **What is your date of birth?** Y Y Y Y M M D D

5. **Do you have a Driver's Licence?** NO ☐  YES ☐ → If YES, what is your Driver's Licence number?

   Number: _____  Province: _____

## SECTION B: MAILING AND RESIDENCE INFORMATION – You must answer all questions.

6. **What is your mailing address?**

   _____

   Apartment/House Number and Street Address      City/Town      Province      Postal Code      Country

7. **What is your telephone number?** ( _____ ) _____ - _____

8. **What addresses have you lived at in the last 5 years?** Include your current address. **P.O. Boxes will not be accepted.**

   | Apartment/House Number and Street Address | City/Town | Province | Country | From Y Y Y Y M M | To Y Y Y Y M M |
   |---|---|---|---|---|---|
   | Current Address | | | | | Present |
   | Previous Address | | | | | |
   | Previous Address | | | | | |
   | Previous Address | | | | | |

## SECTION C: APPLICANT AUTHORIZATION – You must sign and date here.

9. **You must write in the name of the Police Service, and then <u>you</u> must sign and date this form.**

   I hereby authorize (write in name of Police Service here) _____
   to release to the Parole Board of Canada information that the Police is allowed to divulge.

   Sign here: _____  Date: Y Y Y Y M M D D
            (Applicant's Signature)

10. **Ask the Police Service to fill in the <u>back</u> of this form.** Include this form in your application with the front side filled in **by you** and the back side filled in by the **Police Service.**

**Please turn this form over. →**

■◆■  Parole Board   Commission des
      of Canada      libérations conditionnelles
                     du Canada

Page 2 of 2

**Protected when completed**

# Local Police Records Check Form

### For the purpose of a Record Suspension Application
**Please print clearly using blue or black ink. You must answer all questions.**

---

**SECTION D: FOR POLICE USE ONLY. DO NOT WRITE IN THIS SECTION.**

Indicate the full legal name and date of birth of the applicant provided on the front of this form:

Full legal name: _____   Date of birth: `Y Y Y Y M M D D`

**Are There Convictions in Addition to Those Appearing on CPIC?**  ☐ NO  ☐ YES

**Conviction(s) in Addition to Those Appearing on CPIC**

| Offence Description | Sentence | Place of Sentence | Arresting Police Service | Date of Sentence | | | | | | |
|---|---|---|---|---|---|---|---|---|---|---|
| | | | | Y | Y | Y | Y | M | M | D | D |
| | | | | | | | | | | |
| | | | | | | | | | | |
| | | | | | | | | | | |
| | | | | | | | | | | |
| | | | | | | | | | | |
| | | | | | | | | | | |
| | | | | | | | | | | |

**List all Information Related to Incidents Involving Police and All Charges Regardless of Disposition Including Provincial Convictions/Charges.**

| Nature of Occurrence | Outcome | File Number | Date of Occurrence | | | | | | |
|---|---|---|---|---|---|---|---|---|---|
| | | | Y | Y | Y | Y | M | M | D | D |
| | | | | | | | | | |
| | | | | | | | | | |
| | | | | | | | | | |
| | | | | | | | | | |

**Police Representative Information:**

Police Service Name: _____

Police Representative Name: _____   Telephone Number: ( _____ ) _____ - _____

Signature: _____

Date: `Y Y Y Y M M D D`   | Internal Use Only |

Please put
Police Service
seal or
stamp here.

PBC/CLCC 0301E (2012)

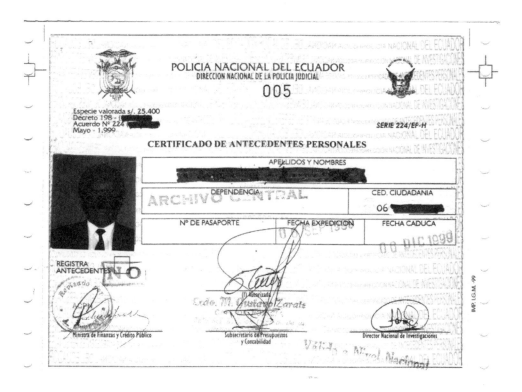

Local Police Records Check from Ecuador used for Pardon Application

# DER GENERALBUNDESANWALT
## BEIM BUNDESGERICHTSHOF

Der Generalbundesanwalt beim Bundesgerichtshof 53169 Bonn

Frau

71

Heidelberg

Bonn, den **20.01.2000**

Dienstgebäude: Heinemannstr. 6

Telefon: 01888 583 0

Aktenzeichen:
U00,
-NB-DTV/---/-

(bei Rückfragen bitte angeben)

## Führungszeugnis

über

### Angaben zur Person

| | | |
|---|---|---|
| Geburtsname | : | |
| Familienname | : | |
| Vorname | : | |
| Geburtsdatum | : | |
| Geburtsort | : | |
| Staatsangehörigkeit | : deutsch | |
| Anschrift | : | 71 |
| | Heidelberg | |

Inhalt: **Keine Eintragung**

Local Police Records Check from Germany used for Pardon Application.

*In short: Cheerful and balanced."*

Lisa P., (Single mother) *"You have given me another chance and its [sic] greatly appreciated. I can now move on with my life and career and better my future for me and my son."*

Mike A., (Law-enforcement) *"Thank you again for not only the opportunity to set my own life straight, but the chance to prevent many other people from making the same mistakes. That is the foundation for my application into law-enforcement; not solely to bring the guilty to justice, but to prevent people from making mistakes that will force them into crime."*

Li C., (Software executive) *"I know that committing a crime is unacceptable, so thank you everyone for making it forgivable."*

Christine M., (Retired senior) *"Thank you for helping me get my pardon. I am very appreciative of the fact that people are given the opportunity to be granted a pardon for a past mistake. I enjoy doing volunteer work within the community and I could not do this with a criminal record. It is a great sense of relief when you can plan to do things and not have to worry."*

Robert S., (Carpenter) *"To me a pardon means not feeling like a criminal anymore. It also means that I paid my debt to society and I can start a clean slate, with employment, apartment rental, and not being left out anymore. A pardon also reduces the stress of feeling guilty; it means that I've been forgiven."*

Garth W., *"This pardon to me is a new and more positive chapter in my life. I consider this a GIFT from Pardons Canada and the National Parole Board. I intend to make good use of it in a positive way in the community. I owe it to myself, my family, friends, and the community."*

Parole Board
of Canada

Commission des
libérations conditionnelles
du Canada

**Page 1 of 2**

**Protected when completed**

# Record Suspension Application Form

**Please print clearly using blue or black ink. You must answer all questions.**

## SECTION A: PERSONAL INFORMATION – You must answer all questions.

1. **What is your full legal name?** (You must fill in your name and date of birth at the top of page 2 as well.)
   Last Name: _____  Given Name(s): _____

2. **Have you ever used another name other than your legal name above?**
   NO ☐   YES ☐ → If YES, write these other names below or your application will be returned to you.

   | Previous Last Name(s) | Previous Given Name(s) |
   |---|---|
   | | |
   | | |
   | | |

3. **What is your gender?** MALE ☐  FEMALE ☐     4. **What is your date of birth?** Y Y Y Y M M D D

5. **Were you born in Canada?** NO ☐  YES ☐ → If NO, see STEP 5 of the Record Suspension Application Guide.

6. **Do you have a Driver's Licence?** NO ☐  YES ☐ → If YES, what is your Driver's Licence number?
   Number: _____  Province: _____

7. **Are you employed?** NO ☐  YES ☐ → If YES, who is your employer?
   Employer Name: _____

## SECTION B: CORRESPONDENCE AND RESIDENCE INFORMATION – You must answer all questions.

8. **What is your Mailing Address?**
   *(All information about a decision will be sent to your current address)*

   _____

   Apartment/House Number and Street Address     City/Town     Province     Postal Code     Country

9. **Do you want information in English or French?** English ☐  French ☐

10. **What addresses have you lived at in the last 10 years?** Include your current address. **P.O. Boxes will not be accepted.**

| Apartment/House Number and Street Address | City/Town | Province | Country | From Y Y Y Y M M | To Y Y Y Y M M |
|---|---|---|---|---|---|
| Current Address | | | | | Present |
| Previous Address | | | | | |
| Previous Address | | | | | |
| Previous Address | | | | | |
| Previous Address | | | | | |

**Please turn this form over. →**

■✦■  Parole Board   Commission des
      of Canada      libérations conditionnelles
                     du Canada

Page 2 of 2

**Protected when completed**

# Record Suspension Application Form

**Please print clearly using blue or black ink. You must answer all questions.**

## APPLICANT INFORMATION – YOU MUST FILL IN THIS INFORMATION.

Indicate the full legal name and date of birth of the applicant provided on the front of this form:

Full legal name: _____   Date of birth: Y Y Y Y M M D D ⎣⎯⎯⎯⎯⎯⎯⎯⎯⎦

## CONTACT INFORMATION – You must answer all questions. The Parole Board will need to contact you directly.

11. Telephone Number: (      )        -           → Can we leave a voicemail message? YES ☐ NO ☐

     If you do not have a telephone, provide a mailing address: _____

12. **Can we contact someone else about your application?**

     NO ☐  YES ☐ → If YES give us their name and telephone number:

     Name: _____   Telephone Number: (_____)_____-_____

13. **Have you ever been a member of the Canadian Forces?**

     ☐ NO            ☐ YES – Former             If **YES,** See Step 3 of the Record
                     ☐ YES – Current            Suspension Application Guide and
                     ☐ YES – Former or Current Reserve Member   fill in the information below.

     Military Service ID Number: _____

     Date of Enrolment: Y Y Y Y M M D D ⎣⎯⎯⎯⎯⎯⎯⎯⎯⎦   Date of Discharge: Y Y Y Y M M D D ⎣⎯⎯⎯⎯⎯⎯⎯⎯⎦

     Provide the complete mailing address of your unit (your commanding officer may be contacted).

| Unit Name | Sub-Unit Name | Street Address or P.O. Box Number | City/Town | Province | Postal Code |
|---|---|---|---|---|---|

## CONVICTION INFORMATION – You must answer all questions.

14. **Do you have any other convictions that do not appear on your Criminal Record?**

     NO ☐  YES ☐ → If YES provide details below:

| Offence | Arresting Police | Sentence | Date | Court (Street/City/Province) |
|---|---|---|---|---|
| Offence | Arresting Police | Sentence | Date | Court (Street/City/Province) |
| Offence | Arresting Police | Sentence | Date | Court (Street/City/Province) |

## APPLICANT AUTHORIZATION – You must answer all questions.

15. The information you provide in this application is collected under the authority of the *Criminal Records Act* for the purpose of processing your request for a record suspension. You have the right to the correction of, access to and protection of, your personal information under the *Privacy Act*. Personal information collected through the processing of your application will be stored in Personal Information Bank Number PBC PPU 010 and can be accessed and assessed for accuracy by sending a written request to the Access to Information and Privacy Coordinator, Parole Board of Canada, 410 Laurier Avenue West, Ottawa, ON K1A 0R1. Exempt personal information obtained from external partners in the course of processing this application cannot be provided upon request.

You must sign and date this form to confirm the following: I understand that the information may be used in a record suspension decision, to conduct inquiries, and may be used in summary form for reporting, quality control, performance measurement, evaluation, research purposes and to establish an inventory of record suspensions. I grant permission for the disclosure of relevant personal information about me with justice system participants as defined in the *Criminal Code*, as may be deemed necessary for the purpose of the investigation related to this application and for the purpose of any record suspension decision.

**I certify that the statements made by me in this application are true and complete. Failure to sign this authorization will result in your application being returned to you as incomplete.**

Sign here: _____   Date: Y Y Y Y M M D D ⎣⎯⎯⎯⎯⎯⎯⎯⎯⎦
                    (Applicant's Signature)

PBC/CLCC 0301E (2012)

Michael K., "*When I had my criminal record, I was very unhappy and I worried that someone would find out. This caused me not to sleep well and I was scared. It feels like I have a new life.*"

Erney G., "*I want to express my appreciation for getting my freedom of the criminal record which has been like a shadow in my life in Canada. I have no words to describe how grateful I am today for being able to have the same opportunities as the rest of the people in Canada have. Being able to apply for a better job, knowing that I can walk the streets freely without being discriminated by those who do not understand, or are quick to judge.*"

Following are samples of both old-style Pardon documents and the current RS documents (see pp. 234-240). As you can seen from the older cover letter, the federal government was "pleased to inform" the individual of the granting of a Pardon and the Solicitor General's office gave his "best wishes for" the person's future success, as well as highlighting the main positive benefit of having a Pardon, namely that the individual could not be discriminated against.

The current cover letter of the PBC simply states that an RS was ordered. It then says that the "criminal record held by federal departments ... will be sequestered from other criminal records."[26] This is not plain and clear language. Given that Canada is made up of a large number of new immigrants, it might be a better idea to say what happens to the record in a way that most people would understand (e.g., sealed and kept separate from).

After that, the new letter goes on to highlight what an RS does *not* do. Although the legal benefits are the same as a Pardon, the new approach does not give people what they really need, the reassurance from the government that they have merited their new opportunity to start fresh. It seems that this letter was drafted in an effort to impart a lot of information and pre-empt further enquiries to the PBC staff. The result, however, is that the values and forward thinking that gave rise to the Pardon system seem to have been diluted in the process.

Parole Board
of Canada

Commission des
libérations conditionnelles
du Canada

**Page 1 of 2**

**Protected when completed**

# Measurable Benefit/Sustained Rehabilitation Form

**For the purpose of a Record Suspension Application**
**Please print clearly using blue or black ink. You must answer all questions. Attach additional pages if required.**

**What is your full legal name?** (You must also fill in your name and date of birth at the top of page 2 and any additional pages that you attach to this form.)

Last Name: _____    Given Name(s): _____

What is your date of birth? | Y | Y | Y | Y | M | M | D | D |    Signature: _____

**1. Clearly indicate how a record suspension would provide you with a measurable benefit <u>and</u> how it would sustain your rehabilitation into society as a law abiding citizen.**

_____

_____

_____

_____

_____

_____

_____

_____

_____

**2. Describe all positive changes you have already made to improve your situation since your conviction. You may include supporting documents.**

_____

_____

_____

_____

_____

_____

_____

_____

**Please turn this form over. →**

*Parole Board of Canada* ■ *Toll-free Info line 1-800-874-2652 – www.recordsuspension.gc.ca*    Canadä

▌◆▌ Parole Board    Commission des
         of Canada       libérations conditionnelles
                         du Canada

**Protected when completed**

# Measurable Benefit/Sustained Rehabilitation Form

**For the purpose of a Record Suspension Application**
**Please print clearly using blue or black ink. You must answer all questions. Attach additional pages if required.**

Indicate the full legal name and the date of birth of the applicant provided on the front of this form

Full legal name: _____    What is your date of birth?  Y Y Y Y M M D D

**3.  Information on the offence(s). Describe the circumstances and how/why each of the offences was committed.**

**4.  For all sexual offences, include the age of the victim. Provide official documentation if available.**

# Canada

PARDON

HIS EXCELLENCY THE GOVERNOR GENERAL IN COUNCIL, on the recommendation of the Parole Board, is pleased hereby to grant to ~~████████████~~ a pardon, in respect of the offence of breach of the Narcotic Control Act, of which he was convicted on the seventh day of May, 1982;

AND this pardon is evidence of the fact that the Parole Board, after making proper inquiries, was satisfied that ~~████████████~~ was of good behaviour and that the conviction should no longer reflect adversely on his character and, unless subsequently revoked, this pardon vacates the conviction in respect of which it is granted and, without restricting the generality of the foregoing, removes any disqualification to which ~~████████████~~ is, by reason of the conviction, subject by virtue of any Act of Parliament or a regulation made thereunder.

GIVEN at Ottawa, this twenty-first day of May, 1992.

By Order,

*J. Coronelle*

DEPUTY REGISTRAR GENERAL

RECORDED 18th June, 1992
Film ██ Document ██
P.C. 1992-██ - /██████ 1992

Old-Style Pardon: Original is legal-sized with original seal

Solicitor General
of Canada

Solliciteur général
du Canada

JUN 2 6 1992

Dear

    I am pleased to inform you that the Governor-in-Council has granted you a pardon under the provisions of the <u>Criminal Records Act</u>.

    This pardon removes any disqualification to which you were subject by virtue of any Act of the Parliament of Canada. Your criminal record is now sealed and it may not be disclosed without the prior approval of the Solicitor General of Canada.

    I am enclosing an extract from the <u>Criminal Records Act</u> regarding the effect of the pardon, the custody of the record, and the circumstances under which the pardon may be revoked. Further documentation is being prepared and will be forwarded to you upon completion.

    I will be pleased to provide you with any additional information you may require.

    Please accept my best wishes for your future success.

    Yours truly,

Hon. Doug Lewis, P.C., M.P.

Enclosure

Ottawa, Canada K1A 0P8

Old Style Pardon

Government          Gouvernement
         of Canada           du Canada

         Parole Board        Commission des libérations
         of Canada           conditionnelles du Canada

         Ottawa, Ontario     Ottawa (Ontario)
         K1A 0R1             K1A 0R1

## PARDON

The Parole Board of Canada hereby awards to

a pardon under the Criminal Records Act.

AND this pardon is evidence of the fact that the Board, after making proper inquiries, was satisfied that the said

has remained free of any conviction since completing the sentence and was of good conduct and that the conviction(s) should no longer reflect adversely on his/her character and, unless it ceases to exist or is subsequently revoked, requires the judicial record of conviction to be kept separate and apart from other criminal records and removes any disqualification to which

is, by reason of the conviction, subject by virtue of any Act of Parliament or a regulation made thereunder.

Given at Ottawa, this 11th day of April, 2012

Harvey Cenaiko
Chairperson

Canada

**PROTECTED B**

New Style Pardon

| Government of Canada | Gouvernement du Canada |
| --- | --- |
| Parole Board of Canada | Commission des libérations conditionnelles du Canada |
| Ottawa, Ontario K1A 0R1 | Ottawa (Ontario) K1A 0R1 |

Date: 2012-04-26

Pardons Canada          BULK
45 St. Clair Avenue West
Suite 901
Toronto, Ontario  M4V 1K9 Canada

Application File: ▆▆▆▆▆

Request for a Record suspension under the *Criminal Records Act* (CRA) for ▆▆▆▆▆

The Parole Board of Canada (PBC) hereby informs you that a record suspension, under the *Criminal Records Act*, has been ordered for the conviction(s) mentioned in the attached schedule. The formal Record suspension document is also attached.

The resulting Board decision means that the criminal record held by federal departments and agencies will be sequestered from other criminal records. Please note that while many provincial and municipal agencies, when notified, choose to comply with the CRA by restricting the disclosure of the criminal record, it is possible that they do not. If this is the case it is your responsibility to inform them and request that they comply with the CRA.

A record suspension ordered under the CRA may not be recognized by a foreign government, nor will it necessarily ensure entry or visa privileges. It is recommended that should you wish to travel that you obtain procedural requirements with the embassy or consulate of the country you wish to visit. You can also obtain information from Foreign Affairs and International Trade Canada at http://www.travel.gc.ca or by calling 1-800-267-6788 or (613) 944-6788.

Please be advised that a Record Suspension will not remove, or eliminate, the effects of a prohibition order made under section 109, 110, 161, 259, 490.012, 490.019 or 490.02901 of the *Criminal Code*, subsection 147.1(1) or section 227.01 or 227.06 of the *National Defence Act* or section 36.1 of the *International Transfer of Offenders Act* — or of a regulation made under an Act of Parliament.

It is important to note that the Board has the authority to revoke a record suspension if you are subsequently convicted of a summary offence; that you are no longer of good conduct; that you knowingly made a false or deceptive statement in relation to the application.

1/2

Canadä          **PROTECTED B**

New Style Record Suspension cover letter

-2-

Further, the record suspension ceases to have effect, meaning the criminal record will be reactivated should you be convicted of an indictable offence (there are exceptions, please refer to section 7.2 of the CRA); or if you were ineligible at the time it was awarded.

For an official version of the CRA please visit http://www.pbc-clcc.gc.ca. Should you have additional questions please contact the Clemency and Record Suspension Division at 1-800-874-2652.

Regards,

Denis Ladouceur, Director
Parole Board of Canada
Clemency and Record Suspension Division
410 Laurier Avenue West
Ottawa, ON  K1A 0R1
1-800-874-2652

Canada

**PROTECTED B**

New Style Record Suspension cover letter

Government
of Canada

Gouvernement
du Canada

Parole Board
of Canada

Commission des libérations
conditionnelles du Canada

Ottawa, Ontario
K1A 0R1

Ottawa (Ontario)
K1A 0R1

## Record suspension

The Parole Board of Canada hereby orders to

a record suspension under the Criminal Records Act.

AND this record suspension is evidence of the fact that the Board, after making proper inquiries, was satisfied that the said

has remained free of any conviction since completing the sentence and was of good conduct and that the conviction(s) should no longer reflect adversely on his/her character and, unless it ceases to exist or is subsequently revoked, requires the judicial record of conviction to be kept separate and apart from other criminal records and removes any disqualification to which

is, by reason of the conviction, subject by virtue of any Act of Parliament or a regulation made thereunder.

Given at Ottawa, this 24th day of April, 2012

Harvey Cenaiko
Chairperson

Canada

**PROTECTED B**

New Style Record Suspension

SCHEDULE OF OFFENCE(S)

RESPECTING A RECORD SUSPENSION UNDER THE CRIMINAL RECORDS ACT

NAME: ▆▆▆▆▆▆▆▆

DATE OF BIRTH: ▆▆▆▆▆▆

FPS: ▆▆▆▆

RECORD OF OFFENCE(S):

1986▆▆▆▆▆▆▆▆▆▆
Driving with more than 80 mgs of alcohol in 100 ml of blood
Reference: ▆▆▆▆

FILE: ▆▆▆▆▆              PAGE: 1 of 1
DECISION: Record Suspension Ordered    DATE RECORDED: 2012▆▆▆▆

Canada            **PROTECTED B**

New Style Schedule of Offences forming part of the Record Suspension

## 34. Do employers ever pay to remove their employees' criminal records?

Yes, sometimes. When a criminal record gets in the way of an excellent employee doing his or her job—if, for example, they are unable to travel, be bonded, or obtain a career certification—the employer may decide to pay for the removal of the criminal record. Many employers consider this a cost of doing business, where the benefit of keeping the employee outweighs the cost of the application.

> Many trucking companies pay for their drivers' criminal records to be removed.

## 35. Will government assistance programs pay for someone's RS application?

Yes, at their discretion. Police records checks are legally required for many careers and are part of standard screening for many other jobs. Therefore, if someone is receiving government assistance benefits (such as welfare or employment insurance), the government worker usually has some discretion to pay for the cost of the RS application, if they feel the criminal record is a significant *barrier to employment*.

## 36. Is a lawyer or agent needed to make an RS application?

Technically, a lawyer or representative is not required in order to make an RS application. That said, it has always been my policy that people should seek the help of experts when making important, life-altering applications such as this.

Although the applicant may have been told that he or she does not need assistance in preparing an RS application, the record removal process is often quite complicated. Determining where to get a proper and complete copy of the criminal record and then analyzing it is often too confusing, overwhelming, and re-traumatizing for most people.

Now, with the recent changes in the RS process, it has become even more daunting. Equally as important, a criminal record can affect so many aspects of a person's life that it is advisable to obtain proper guidance about those things at the same time. Many people find the responsibility of handling the paperwork and making decisions on their own so stressful that they abandon the application altogether. Having professional help also will reduce the risk of having the application rejected.

## 37. What problems could people face by preparing their own RS application?

For an RS application, the individual has to deal with many different government agencies—such as the RCMP, courts, charging police services, and Immigration Canada—each with its own rules, procedures, policies, and forms. Furthermore, the entire process is usually spread out over ten to twenty-four months. Within this lengthy process, individuals doing their own RS application are almost certain to face one or more of the following setbacks:

- **Not initiating the process.** To embark on the process of removing one's own criminal record will mean reliving what are almost always very painful memories. Gathering documents and putting together the pieces of a traumatic time can lead to stress, emotional upset, and sometimes physical illness. After some preliminary research, many people are too confused and emotionally re-traumatized, so they do not even begin the process.
- **Initiating and then abandoning the process.** Some people begin the process of removing their record, then, after looking at their RCMP report, they embark in some misguided direction. They may even go so far as to submit some type of an application. When their application is rejected (for any one of a multitude of reasons), they get discouraged and give up.
- **Submitting the wrong application** for the type of criminal record they have.
- **Getting lost in the legal system.** To successfully complete the application process, people will need to educate themselves on some of the complicated and varied elements of the justice system, much of

which has its own unique language, policies, and procedures.

- **Panicking when reviewing documents.** Reviewing documents alone at home or at work can be a traumatic and frustrating experience that people need to prepare themselves for.

- **Getting buried in the application process.** Collecting documents in the wrong order, not collecting all the required documents, or collecting the wrong documents can slow down the RS process significantly.

- **Sharing information with the wrong people.** Another major pitfall is inadvertently sharing the criminal record information with the wrong law-enforcement or government agency, when there was no obligation to do so.

- **Thinking a criminal record is gone when it is not**. People often can be misled into thinking that they don't have a criminal record if they receive an RCMP report indicating that there are no convictions on file. This could happen when: (i) people do the *wrong type* of RCMP search, whereby *non-conviction records* are *not* disclosed, or (ii) even though the RCMP report may not show a charge, it may still be available at the local police service.

- **Unwanted discovery.** By using the services of an expert, the applicant can avoid receiving indiscreet letters from the RCMP, local police, court, etc., to their home or office, which could accidentally fall into the hands of a co-worker, neighbour, or child.

- **Submitting a deficient application.** The chart below shows that only 75 percent of the 328,447 applications received by the PBC from 1998 to 2011 were accepted for consideration. This means that about 82,000 of the applications were deficient or incorrect in some material way.

- **RCMP, police, court, and PBC policies and timelines keep changing.** This is the really tricky part. Unless you are dealing with these organizations on a day-to-day basis, you wouldn't know what the latest time-frames are, whether the supporting documents being submitted are sufficient, which steps should be done and in which order. It's like trying to hit a series of moving targets, each of which can impact the other.

## Percentage of Pardon Applications Accepted 1998-2011

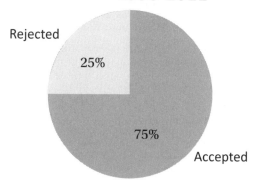

Parole Board of Canada, 2012. The term *accepted* means that the application was accepted for consideration, not that the Pardon was granted.

## 38. Evaluating criminal record removal providers

Those looking for assistance in removing their criminal records may want to consider the following factors when making their decision:

- The PBC, courts, police services, etc., process the paperwork at the same rate no matter who submits it.
- Understand the costs. Do they include *taxes, disbursements* and *other costs* (e.g., court fees)? Do they say *plus disbursements*, or *plus costs*? This can be very confusing as costs and disbursements can add up to more than the advertised fee.
- How long has the company or organization been in operation?
- What qualifications do they have? Are the employees properly trained? Do they have legal training? Are lawyers involved? How are their systems set up?
- Do they have any connection to the government or any other helping organizations? For example, do they provide the government with information, seminars, and materials?[27]
- Does the company have an office where the applicant can attend in person, or is there simply a Web site?

- Do they provide employment or immigration support letters? Will they speak to employers or CIC on behalf of the client?
- Do they provide support with affidavits when required by the PBC?
- Does the applicant own his or her own file contents or does the company withhold the person's file or original documents for any reason?
- Is the company in compliance with privacy laws? Do they have a written privacy policy?
- Will the company destroy all information about the applicant and the application after completion? Is there a process in place for information destruction?
- Does the company provide the names of owners, directors, and officers who are ultimately responsible for the successful processing of the file?

## 39. How many Pardon applications did the PBC process each year?

The number of applications received by the PBC has fluctuated over the years, reaching a record high of 35,784 applications in 2009. Of those applications received by the PBC, on average, 25 percent were rejected for various reasons, including that a Pardon was not required, documents were missing or were stale-dated, and the remaining 75 percent were accepted for processing. The following charts show the number of applications received, accepted, and processed for each year from 1998 to 2011.

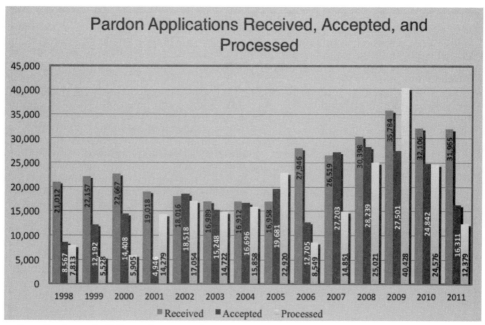

Parole Board of Canada, 2012[28]

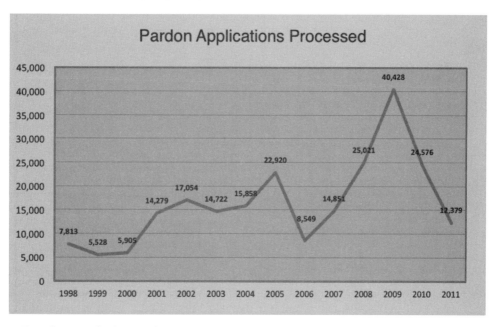

Parole Board of Canada, 2012

The 2011 figure of 12,379 files processed is low because about 17,000 additional files had been received by the PBC but had not yet been processed.

## The PBC application review process

There are five main steps that the PBC undertakes in reviewing RS applications.

| PBC Review Process | | |
|---|---|---|
| 1 | **Screening** | Upon receipt of an application, the PBC screens it to determine if it has all the elements necessary to be accepted for processing. The PBC officer will check such things as whether the application has been properly completed, if the processing fee was included, that all necessary supporting documents were submitted, and whether the applicant is eligible. |
| **Accepted** If the application is accepted, the processing fee will be deposited and a letter will be sent to the applicant (or their representative) saying that the application is "in process." | | **Rejected** If the application is rejected, the application will be sent back to the applicant (or their representative) with an explanation as to what is wrong with the application. The applicant is permitted to correct the deficiency and immediately send the application back to the PBC (unless the applicant has not waited long enough to meet the eligibility requirements). |
| 2 | **Assignment** | After an application is accepted, it must be assigned to a PBC officer for processing. |
| 3 | **Investigation** | Once a file is assigned to a PBC officer, that officer is responsible for completing the investigation process, determining if the person was of "good conduct," and whether the application will be successful. The PBC officer will contact the RCMP, Canadian police services, and courts to ensure that the applicant has remained crime-free and that there are no outstanding charges, investigations, warrants, fines, and so on. From time to time, the PBC may make further requests from the applicant. |
| 4 | **Decision** | If, after reviewing an application, the PBC officer is satisfied that the applicant has met all the necessary criteria, an RS will be ordered. Otherwise, the PBC officer will propose to deny the application. |
| | **Record Suspension Ordered** If the RS is ordered, the applicant (or representative) will be notified in writing. | **Proposal to Deny** If the PBC proposes to deny the application, the applicant (and, if applicable, the representative) will be sent a letter stating this fact, and told the reason(s) why. At that point, the applicant will have an opportunity to address the concerns raised by the PBC. |
| 5 | **Notification** | The final decision of the PBC will be mailed to the mailing address provided in the application. If an RS is ordered, there is no further action required on the part of the applicant. The PBC will notify the RCMP, all Canadian police services, and the courts that the RS was ordered, and will ask that they, too, seal their files. |
| | | If the RS is denied, the applicant must wait at least one year from the date of the denial letter before reapplying. |

Following are samples of:

- a PBC letter sent to applicants (or their representatives) when an application has been accepted for processing, and
- a letter from the NPB to the court notifying it that a Pardon had been awarded.

Government of Canada | Gouvernement du Canada

Parole Board of Canada | Commission des libérations conditionnelles du Canada

Ottawa, Ontario K1A 0R1 | Ottawa (Ontario) K1A 0R1

Date: 2012-04-03

[redacted]
Pardons Canada BULK
45 St. Clair Avenue West
Suite 901
Toronto, Ontario M4V 1K9 Canada

Application Reference: [redacted]

<u>Request for a Record suspension under the *Criminal Records Act (CRA)* for</u> [redacted]

This acknowledges receipt of your application for a record suspension and the $631 processing fee. You must quote the reference number provided in all future communications with the Parole Board of Canada.

Please be advised that a Record Suspension will not remove, or eliminate, the effects of a prohibition order made under section 109, 110, 161, 259, 490.012, 490.019 or 490.02901 of the Criminal Code, subsection 147.1(1) or section 227.01 or 227.06 of the National Defence Act or section 36.1 of the International Transfer of Offenders Act — or of a regulation made under an Act of Parliament.

If applicable to you, please find attached documents that are being returned for your personal records as they are not required for the decision-making process of your application.

Regards,

Michael Cyr
Clemency and Record Suspension Division
Parole Board of Canada
410 Laurier Avenue West
Ottawa, ON K1A 0R1
1-800-874-2652

Canada PROTECTED B

Parole Board of Canada Letter stating that the application has been accepted for processing

Government     Gouvernement
of Canada     du Canada

National     Commission nationale des
Parole Board     libérations conditionnelles

Ottawa, Ontario     Ottawa (Ontario)
K1A 0R1     K1A 0R1

Our File:     ▓▓▓▓▓▓
Your File:

Date:   2002/04/05

Clerk of the Court     BULK MAIL
Provincial Court (Criminal Division)
7755 Hurontario St., Suite 100
Brampton ON  L6W 4T6

Dear Sir / Madam:

RE: ▓▓▓▓▓▓▓▓▓▓▓

This is to inform you that the person mentioned in the attached Schedule has been awarded a pardon for the conviction(s) mentioned therein.

We would like to draw your attention to section 6 of the *Criminal Records Act*. The term "judicial record of conviction" is interpreted as including certificates of conviction and, in the case where the trial has been before a superior court of criminal jurisdiction, would also include the entries of conviction made by the judge in the bench book and by the clerk of the court in the court calendar.

Subsection 6(2) applies only to federal departments or agencies. Further, the *Criminal Records Act* has jurisdiction only in respect of offences under Acts of Parliament or regulations made thereunder. The assistance of departments or agencies which are not within federal jurisdiction is, nonetheless, greatly appreciated in implementing the spirit of the legislation. Therefore, we would suggest that you keep your records separate and apart from other records.

Your co-operation in this matter is appreciated.

Yours truly,

C.M. Galipeau, Pardon Officer
Clemency and Pardons Division
410 Laurier Avenue West, Ottawa ON  K1A 0R1
(800) 874-2652
Enclosure(s)

 Canada

**PROTECTED**

National Parole Board Letter asking the Court to seal its records since a Pardon was awarded

PBC REVIEW PROCESS
# 40. How long does it take for the PBC to process an application?

Recent figures from the PBC show that, in 2010, it took an average of 2.4 months for a Pardon application to be processed and issued. These figures, however, do not take into account the idle time during which applications accepted by the PBC had not yet been assigned to an officer for processing. As of 2011, the PBC figures showed that there were over 17,000 Pardon applications that had been submitted and accepted for processing but that had not yet been processed.[29] During the past ten years, there have been periods in which the average time that applications were with the PBC was well over twenty-four months. This includes the time prior to the file being assigned, as well as the processing time. That being said, following is a chart of the average processing times as reported by the PBC.

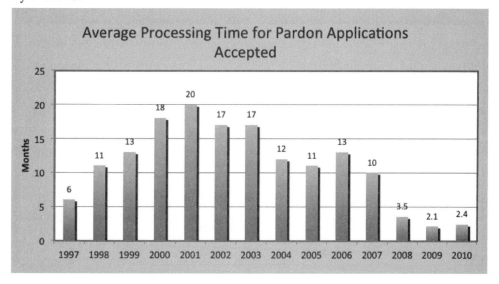

Parole Board of Canada, 2012[30]

Over the years, I have known the total time an application is at the PBC to fluctuate from one to twenty-four months. The processing time varies in each particular case and may depend on the type of offence(s) contained in the criminal record. For example, the less serious summary conviction offences committed many years ago may not require as extensive an investigation and could be processed faster than a more serious indictable offence. Also, other factors can affect the processing times, such as delays in receiving court responses, and investigations into behaviour reported to the PBC from local police or the RCMP.

Worth mentioning is that the six to fifteen months it takes to prepare an application for submission is not part of the PBC's functions, and is, therefore, not included in the PBC processing time figures.

## 41. Does the PBC grant urgency status?

Not anymore. In the past it was possible for the PBC to process some applications in priority to others if there was evidence of a significant opportunity that would be lost if the Pardon were delayed (e.g., unique job opportunities, deportation from Canada, etc.).

Now, the PBC processes the files in the order that they are received. Keep in mind, however, that this does not mean that the first application received is going to be the first RS completed. Those files requiring more extensive investigations, or for which court responses are delayed, may end up taking longer to process than other files that were submitted later.

Following on p. 250 is a letter from the Solicitor General's office, dated 2000 (when the granting of urgency status was still possible), confirming that priority processing had been approved.

## 42. When someone applies for an RS, will the police go to the applicant's home or work?

Almost never. All communications with the police and other government departments will be electronic, through the mail, or, where necessary, the applicant might have to appear at the police station (e.g., to pick up their *LPRC*).

## 43. How likely is it that an RS will be approved?

If the individual had waited the requisite time period after the sentence imposed by the court was completed, if all the proper supporting documents had been prepared and submitted, and if the person had been of good conduct, then the PBC almost always granted the Pardon. Historically speaking, only 1.6 percent of the Pardon applications processed by the PBC have ever been denied, giving an approval rate of 98.4 percent. Whether this will be true with RS applications remains to be seen.

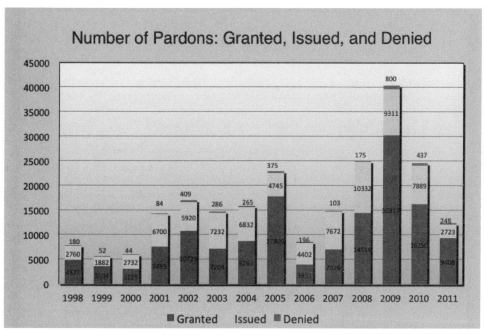

Parole Board of Canada, 2012[31]

## 44. What is the difference between a Pardon "granted" and a Pardon "issued"?

Under the previous Pardon rules, a Pardon that was approved was either *granted* or *issued*. Both terms mean that the individual was successful in their Pardon application. For practical purposes, once approved, the Pardon had the same effect whether granted or issued. The difference in terminology depended on the seriousness of the offence being pardoned.

- **Pardon *Granted* for Indictable Offence:** For indictable offences, the PBC used different and more comprehensive screening processes

Solicitor General
of Canada

Solliciteur général
du Canada

Ottawa, Canada K1A 0P8

The Honourable Charles Caccia, P.C., M.P.                    JUN 1 2 2000
House of Commons
Ottawa, Ontario
K1A 0A6

Dear Charles:

    Thank you for your letter of May 23, 2000, concerning a pardon under the provisions of the *Criminal Records Act (CRA)* for your constituent, Mr. ▓▓▓▓▓▓▓▓.

    To date, the Clemency and Investigations Division of the National Parole Board (NPB), the agency within this Ministry that is responsible for the administration of the *CRA*, has not received an application for pardon for Mr. ▓▓▓▓▓▓.

    In view of the special circumstances described in your letter, NPB will grant priority status to Mr.▓▓▓▓▓▓'s case, upon receipt of his complete application providing that the eligibility requirements of the *CRA* are satisfied. Please have your constituent forward a copy of this correspondence to the Clemency and Investigations Division, in order to ensure that his request is processed expeditiously.

    I trust that you will find this information to be helpful.

                  Sincerely,

*Lawrence MacAulay*

              Lawrence MacAulay, P.C., M.P.

JUN 1 3 2000

# Canada

Letter from the Solicitor General of Canada to a local MP confirming that the constituent's Pardon would be granted priority status

than for summary convictions. The PBC would: (i) confirm that the applicant was eligible, (ii) verify through the RCMP and local police services that there had been no further convictions, and (iii) investigate the applicant's behaviour after completing their sentence to determine if they had been of good conduct. In light of this evaluation, a Pardon was granted or denied.

- **Pardon *Issued* for Summary Offence:** For summary conviction offences (less serious), the PBC did not have the same discretionary powers as for indictable offences. Here, once the PBC confirmed that the applicant was eligible and that there had been no further convictions, a Pardon was issued.[32]

## 45. Will a Local Police Records Check (LPRC) reveal that a Pardon or an RS was awarded?

No. Excluding Pardons or Record Suspensions obtained for certain sexual offences, when someone has a Pardon or an RS, the record is sealed and kept separate from other criminal records in the RCMP's data bank. Similarly, the local police services will also remove these records from their active data bank. Therefore, a police records search for it will return a finding of no criminal record.

## 46. Are pardoned or suspended sexual offences disclosed on an LPRC?

In certain cases. Pardons or Record Suspensions related to sexual offences are flagged in the RCMP's automated criminal conviction records retrieval system.[33] This allows members of any Canadian police force and others who are authorized to know if there is a record of a conviction for a sexual offence involving children or youth, even if it has been pardoned or suspended.[34] Even if the criminal record is no longer listed on the federal Sex Registry because a Pardon or an RS was ordered,[35] the record will still be accessible for vulnerable sector police records checks.

If any organization or person responsible for the well-being of a vulnerable person—including children, the elderly, the disabled—requests this information from the police, it will be given to them, provided that: (i) the position applied for is one of trust or authority toward the vulnerable person, and (ii) the applicant has consented in writing. See p. 253 for a copy of the RCMP criminal records check request form for those wishing to work with vulnerable persons.

## 47. Who can legally disclose a criminal record if a Pardon or an RS was awarded?

Under the *CRA* (and except for certain sexual offences), only the federal Minister of Public Safety (formerly the Solicitor General of Canada) has the authority to disclose information from a pardoned or suspended record. Such disclosure only will be made in exceptional circumstances. Practically speaking, as long as the person does not reoffend, no one will ever be able to gain access to the criminal record.

## 48. What happens if an RS application is denied?

To understand what happens if the PBC denies an application, it is first important to know the difference between an application's being *rejected* and being *denied*.

- **Accepted or Rejected**. When an RS application is submitted to the PBC, it is reviewed to see if it is complete and if the person is eligible. If both of these criteria are met, the application is *accepted* for *processing*. If the application is not complete or if the eligibility waiting-period has not been met, the application will be *rejected* and sent back to the applicant. Historically, about 25 percent of the Pardon applications submitted were rejected.
- **Denied**. Having an RS *denied* means that the application was *accepted* for *processing*, and that the PBC officer, after completing his or her evaluation, *determined* that it should *not* be ordered. Almost all denials are based on the PBC officer's discovering something that shows the

 Royal Canadian  Gendarmerie royale
Mounted Police   du Canada

Form 1

## CRIMINAL RECORDS - CONSENT FOR CHECK FOR A SEXUAL OFFENCE
## FOR WHICH A PARDON HAS BEEN GRANTED OR ISSUED

This form is to be used by a person applying for a position with a person or organization responsible for the well-being of one or more children or vulnerable persons, if the position is a position of authority or trust relative to those children or vulnerable persons and the applicant wishes to consent to a search being made in criminal conviction records to determine if the applicant has been convicted of a sexual offence listed in the schedule to the *Criminal Records Act* and has been pardoned.

### Identification of the Applicant

| Surname | Given Name(s) |
|---|---|

| Sex    ☐ Male   ☐ Female | Date of Birth (yyyy-mm-dd) | Place of Birth (city and province) |
|---|---|---|

| Home Address | City | Province | Postal Code |
|---|---|---|---|

Previous addresses, if any, within the last 5 years

### Reason for the Consent

I am an applicant for a paid or volunteer position with a person or organization responsible for the well-being of one or more children or vulnerable persons.

| Description of the paid or volunteer position | Name of the person or organization |
|---|---|

Details regarding the children or vulnerable person(s)

### Consent

I, _____ consent to a search being made in the automated criminal records retrieval system maintained by the Royal Canadian Mounted Police to find out if I have been convicted of, and been granted or issued a pardon for, any of the sexual offences that are listed in the schedule to the *Criminal Records Act*.

I understand that, as a result of giving this consent, a search discloses that there is a record of my conviction for one of the sexual offences listed in the schedule to the *Criminal Records Act* in respect of which a pardon was granted or issued, that record shall be provided by the Commissioner of the Royal Canadian Mounted Police to the Minister of Public Safety, who may then disclose all or part of the information contained in that record to a police force or other authorized body. That police force or authorized body will then disclose that information to me. If I further consent in writing to disclosure of that information to the person or organization referred to above that requested the verification, that information will be disclosed to that person or organization.

**Fingerprint: For card scan submissions only.**

| Contributing Agency |
|---|

| Signature of Applicant | Date (yyyy-mm-dd) |
|---|---|

Finger: _____

RCMP GRC 3923e (2009-12)

Canadä

applicant is not of good conduct, such as being involved in subsequent criminal activity.

Before an RS is denied, the PBC officer sends a letter to the applicant stating that it is proposing to deny the application. The letter will explain the basis for the denial and give the applicant a sixty-day time-frame in which to respond. It is up to the applicant to give a compelling reason as to why an RS should still be ordered.[36] If the PBC ultimately denies the RS application, the applicant must wait at least one year from the date of the PBC decision to reapply.

## Average Percentage of Pardons Denied or Granted: 1998-2011

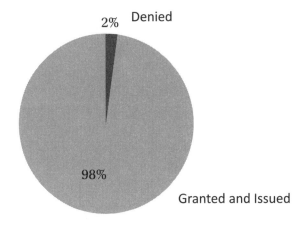

Parole Board of Canada, 2012, percentages vary slightly due to rounding.

## 49. If people who have a Pardon or an RS are asked, "Have you ever been convicted of a criminal offence?" what should they answer?

By granting a Pardon or an RS, the Government of Canada is saying that the "... conviction should no longer reflect adversely on [the person's] character ..." To help accomplish this, the *Canadian Human Rights Act* forbids discrimination based on a conviction for which a Pardon or an RS has been awarded.[37] This prohibition against discrimination applies to the provision of services that a person needs, such as living accommodations or employment. No employer, landlord, or other service provider is allowed to ask whether a person has a criminal record that has been pardoned or for which an RS was ordered. They may only ask: "Do you have a criminal record for which a Pardon or an RS has not been awarded?" The answer to that question is "No."

### WHEN A PARDON OR RECORD SUSPENSION CEASES
## 50. When can a Pardon or an RS be revoked or cease to have effect?

- **Revoked**. Generally, a Pardon or an RS *may* be revoked by the PBC if:
  - ◊ the person is subsequently convicted of a summary offence under a federal act or regulation of Canada
  - ◊ the PBC finds that the person is no longer of good conduct
  - ◊ the PBC learns that the applicant knowingly made a false or deceptive statement or relevant information was concealed at the time the application was made.
- **Ceases to Have Effect**. A Pardon or an RS ceases to have effect if a person is subsequently convicted of a hybrid or an indictable offence under a federal act or regulation of Canada, or if the PBC is convinced by new information that the person was not eligible for a Pardon or an RS at the time it was awarded.[38]

In either case, the criminal record will be returned to the RCMP's active data bank and will once again be disclosed on police records checks.

### SUCESS OF PARDON PROGRAM
## 51. How often do people with Pardons reoffend?

Almost never. Pardons can be revoked or cease to have effect if the individual reoffends. As previously mentioned, PBC statistics show that only a small percentage of Pardons have ever been revoked (4 percent), proving that once people get their Pardons, almost all remain crime-free.

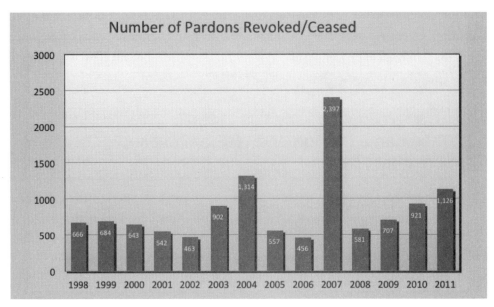

Parole Board of Canada, 2012

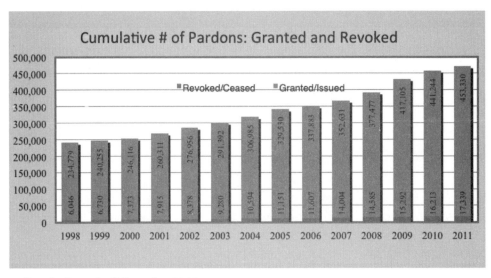

Parole Board of Canada, 2012

# Percentage of Pardons Revoked/Ceased: 1970-2011

Revoked/Ceased

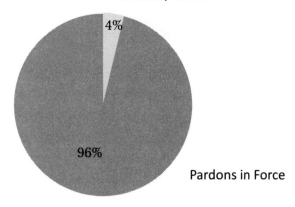

Parole Board of Canada, 2012

## Quiz

**1. What is the effect of a Pardon or an RS?**
    a. It erases a person's criminal record
    b. It removes, seals, and prevents disclosure of a criminal record held by the RCMP
    c. It guarantees the person entry into a foreign country
    d. It cancels prohibition orders
    e. It prevents disclosure for offences of a sexual nature

**2. Why should someone clear his or her criminal record?**
    a. To be more competitive for an employment or volunteer position
    b. To overcome obstacles in immigrating to Canada or becoming a citizen
    c. To prevent future discrimination from employers, police, courts, and others
    d. To feel a sense of freedom from the stigma of having a criminal record
    e. All of the above

**3. If a criminal case is "withdrawn" or "dismissed" ...**
    a. It means there is no finding of guilt
    b. It will usually show up at the U.S.A. border during a standard computer search
    c. It will almost always show up on a police records check
    d. The police service that laid the charge has discretion as to whether to destroy the person's fingerprints, photographs, and charge records
    e. All of the above

**4. If someone received a conditional discharge, what does it mean?**
    a. The person was convicted
    b. The case was thrown out of court
    c. The person was found guilty but not convicted
    d. The RCMP will purge the record after 5 years from the final court date
    e. None of the above

**5. The Parole Board of Canada:**
    a. Has absolute authority to, grant, deny, and revoke Pardons and Record Suspensions under the *Criminal Records Act*
    b. Is an agency within the Ministry of Public Safety
    c. Has granted over 400,000 Pardons since 1970
    d. Is responsible for deciding parole application reviews
    e. All of the above

**6. True or False:**

a.  All criminal records go away automatically
b.  Police services have jurisdiction over charges with not-guilty outcomes
c.  Probation orders and Prohibition orders are essentially the same
d.  The effect of both a Pardon and an RS are the same
e.  Because of the new Pardon law, it can now take a total of 7-13 years (after the final court date) for a person to complete his or her sentence and receive an RS.

Answer Key: 1 (b), 2 (e), 3 (e), 4 (c), 5 (e), 6 false, true, false, true, true

# End Notes

1. Youth records that have been *locked in* with adult records are not automatically removed. They must be sealed with a Pardon or Record Suspension.

2. The criminal record will remain in the RCMP Identification data bank even beyond this point (until one hundred years of age), if, for example, the person has been sentenced to life imprisonment, has been designated a dangerous offender, is still subject to an unexpired prohibition order, or is subject to an outstanding warrant.

3. When reference is made to charging police, in this book, it means the local police service that charged the individual.

4. Some police services charge fees for destructions.

5. Some reasons for refusal include situations where the applicant has (i) a conviction, (ii) an unexpired discharge on file, (iii) an unexpired peace bond, and so on.

6. The *CRA* states that "... a discharge referred to in section 6.1 may be disclosed to a police force if a fingerprint, identified as that of the person, is found
(*a*) at the scene of a crime during an investigation of the crime; or
(*b*) during an attempt to identify a deceased person or a person suffering from amnesia."

7. While the *CRA* mainly deals with record suspensions, it also sets out the law for the purging of discharges in sections 6.1 (1) and 6.1 (2).

8. Consequential Amendments to other statutes include: *Canadian Human Rights Act*; *Contraventions Act*; Criminal Code; *DNA Identification Act*; *Immigration and Refugee Protection Act*; *National Defence Act*; and the *Youth Criminal Justice Act*. These *Acts* were changed so that the word *Pardon* was replaced by the term *Record Suspension*.

9. The word *Pardon* and the term *Record Suspension (RS)* will be used as follows:
• When discussing *new* applications, the term *Record Suspension* or RS will be used
• When reviewing historical data, the word *Pardon* will be used
• When discussing matters that apply to both the over 400,000 Pardons in existence and to Record Suspensions being ordered now, both will be used.

10. The exception to this is that if someone received a Pardon or an RS for a Schedule 2 sexual offence, then that fact will be disclosed on vulnerable-sector checks.

11. Mr. Harvey Cenaiko, Chairperson, National Parole Board, at the Senate Standing Committee on Legal and Constitutional Affairs, 3rd Session, 40th Parliament, June 22, 2010.

12. Standard Pardon cover letter from Mr. Yves Bellefeuille, Director, Clemency and Pardons Division, National Parole Board, 2004.

13. Examples of federal laws include the *Criminal Code* and the *Controlled Drugs and Substances Act*.

14. PBC, Record Suspension and Clemency Division, 410 Laurier Avenue West  Ottawa , Ontario  K1A 0R1

15. www.pbc-clcc.gc.ca, 2012.

16. The exception to this rule is if the convicted person was not in a position of trust toward the victim; the victim was not in a relationship of dependency with him or her; the person did not use, or threaten to use violence; and the convicted person was less than 5 years older than the victim. (Section 4(3), *CRA*). The convicted person must meet all of the above-listed criteria.

17. CRA, section 4(2).

18. Calculated as follows: Summary offence typical sentence is one year probation + five-year waiting period + one year at PBC (seven years total). Indictable offence often includes a jail or probation time of about one to two years + ten-year waiting period + one year at the PBC (thirteen years total). Please note, the PBC time period includes the evaluation for accepting the application, and also the time before the application is assigned plus the actual processing time.

19. *CRA*, section 2.1: "The Board has exclusive jurisdiction and absolute discretion to order, refuse to order or revoke a record suspension."
———, section 2.2 (1): "An application for a record suspension shall be determined, and a decision whether to revoke a record suspension under section 7 shall be made, by a panel that consists of one member of the Board."

20. *Criminal Code* section 748.

21. In addition to reviewing clemency applications, the PBC can also cancel or vary the unexpired portion of a prohibition order made under s. 259 of the *Criminal Code*.

22. Based on Cumulative Figures from 2000 to 2010. Numbers add up to more than 100% due to rounding.

23. If fingerprints are taken by the local police, it will be up to the individual to send the prints to the RCMP (with the proper processing fee) for certification. The individual must also ensure that the correct type of report is requested (i.e., for RS purposes).

24. For information regarding the digital fingerprinting office nearest to you, contact L-1 Identity Solutions: www.L1id.com/pages/564

25. www.pbc-clcc.gc.ca

26. The definition of the word "*sequestered*" refers to the separation of jurors or the seizure of property.

27  For over twenty years, while at Pardons Canada, Ian Levine provided over four hundred government and community Outreach Education Seminars. He educated all levels of government and other helping organizations with respect to the creation, effects, and removal of criminal records. Refer to www.pardons.org and www.record-suspension.org.

28. In some years, more Pardon applications were processed than were received. This occurred because, due to backlogs, not all applications were processed in the same year that they were received.

29. Calculated as follows: Number of Pardon applications accepted minus the number of Pardon applications processed, during the period 1998–2011 (247,057 - 229,883 = 17,174).

30. The 2010 average processing time was calculated by taking the average processing times of both summary offences (1.2 months) and indictable offences (3.5 months): 1.2 + 3.5 / 2 = 2.4 months. The 2007–2010 averages do not include processing times for Pardons that were denied, which took significantly longer, 9-15 months.

31. Calculated as follows: Number of pardon applications denied divided by the number of pardons granted + issued (3,604/145,097 + 81,132 = 1.59%).

32. Hybrid offences—which may be prosecuted by indictment or summarily—were treated as indictable offences unless the applicant submitted proof that the prosecutor proceeded summarily.

33. Schedule 2 of the *CRA* lists the sexual offences for which a notation can be made.

34. Note that under the new Pardon law, an RS can still be ordered for a Schedule 1 offence if it falls under the exemption.

35. *Sex Offender Information Registration Act,* section 8.1(1), *Criminal Code* 490.02 (2)(c); *Christopher's Law,* (Ontario ) section 9.

36. Although it is possible, with the PBC's approval, to make these representations in person, it is not done often. *CRA* section 4.2(4)

37. *Canadian Human Rights Act,* section 3 (1).

38. *CRA*, sections 7, 7.1, and 7.2.

Chapter Eight

# Criminal Record Statistics

This book would not be complete without some statistical analysis about people with criminal records. From raw data supplied by the RCMP, and factoring in the crimes not included in that data bank, it is estimated that, in Canada, *over 4 million people have a criminal record*. If we include those who have had their records pardoned or suspended, or removed by other legislation, it is likely *over 4.5 million people*—about one in five Canadian *adults*.

What are the demographic characteristics—age, sex, and racial group—of those people? Unfortunately, there can be no definitive answers to these and other questions. Not only is there limited data, but difficulties such as categorization into racial groups or variations in the way the criminal charges are recorded and categorized by different government departments across the country make it impossible to offer a complete and accurate picture.

Furthermore, the policies and trends of law-enforcement and the judicial system, together with the limited resources available to those working in the criminal justice system, make it difficult to get an accurate picture of what is really going on. Too many court cases means that not all of them can be prosecuted. Many will be stayed or settled by way of a plea bargain. This affects the statistics relating to the number of convictions for particular crimes. Obviously, the more serious crimes will be prosecuted, while many of the less serious crimes may be withdrawn or plea-bargained. This process will give an inaccurate representation of how many *less serious* crimes may have resulted in convictions. Similarly, in the case of law-enforcement, limited resources make it necessary for the police services to concentrate on more serious crimes. Unfortunately, no complete Canadian criminal record data bank exists. Given the nature of what a criminal record is, published figures typically underestimate the number of people who have a Canadian criminal record.

That said, a partial picture does exist. Although it may look like this chapter contains a lot of numbers, don't let that deter you. The graphs are straightforward and I focus on the key facts and explain what they mean.

# 1. Sources of Data

**RCMP**

The RCMP is the federal police of Canada. In order to assist with this chapter, Yves Marineau, RCMP Access to Information and Privacy Coordinator, and Cpl. Mel Abramovitch generously provided me with raw information from the RCMP Identification data bank. The data contained information of approximately *3,250,000 people with criminal records* in existence in that data bank in 2010. This is a cumulative figure and should not be confused with the *number of people* committing crimes each year, or the *number of crimes* committed each year.

Personal identifying information—such as names, fingerprints, and addresses—was *not* disclosed. The data included information such as age, sex, race, whether the person was a juvenile, and the criminal record information. Among other things, the criminal record information included the offence (but not how many times the person was charged with the same crime); the disposition (outcome), but if someone was charged with more than one crime we can't tell which the disposition refers to; and whether a DNA sample was collected.

The RCMP Identification data bank has some shortcomings however, and does *not* include all those who have ever committed a crime. There are several reasons for this:

- Only charges supported by fingerprints are included in the RCMP Identification data bank. Therefore, less serious offences (i.e., strictly summary offences), cannot be recorded in that data bank because fingerprints are not legally allowed to be taken for this category of offences. However, these charges and their outcomes will likely be on record at the local police.
- Except for youth charges, police departments are not required to report criminal charges or their outcomes to the RCMP.
- Some crimes are never detected, never reported to police, or reported to the police but the person responsible is never caught. We have no way of knowing how many crimes were not detected, or how many were detected but not reported.

- Criminal records have been removed from this data bank due to:
  ◊ the granting of Pardons or Record Suspensions (over 400,000)[1]
  ◊ RCMP purges (approximately over 300,000), and
  ◊ destruction of files by local police services (over 500,000).[2]

The result, therefore, is that the RCMP data bank provides an underestimate of the number of crimes committed and the number of people who have criminal records in Canada. A more accurate estimate of the number of people who have a Canadian criminal record, together with those who have had their records removed, is likely over 4.5 million.

## Pardons Canada (www.pardons.org)

Pardons Canada is a federal non-profit organization specializing in the removal of criminal records. As the co-founder of this organization, I oversaw the analysis of thousands of criminal records during the past twenty years. From time to time we conducted statistical reviews of the criminal records in the various Pardons Canada data banks.

For this chapter, Pardons Canada provided me with a random sample of 450 criminal records of people in their data bank in 2011. Although at first glance this may seem like a relatively small sample, you will see that the results of this random sample are consistent to a great extent with the results of the data provided by the over 3 million RCMP records. In removing criminal records, Pardons Canada deals with both new and old records originating from crimes committed across the country, and the RCMP reports used by Pardons Canada are both requested and processed at different times. Therefore, a random sample is quite accurately representative of the extensive information in the Pardons Canada data bank.

The random sample group has been used to determine such things as: the number of men and of women; the number of Pardons or Record Suspensions (RS), purges, and fingerprint and photograph destructions; the type of crimes committed; the number of crimes committed; the number of people also applying for U.S.A. Entry Waivers; and the number of people who reoffend after their Pardon is granted. Pardons Canada has found that the statistics have remained fairly consistent over the years in terms of: the percentage of crimes committed by men and by women, the percentage of people with Pardons who reoffend, and the number and type of crimes.

**Statistics Canada**

Statistics Canada is Canada's national statistical agency. This agency is required by law to "collect, compile, analyze, abstract and publish statistical information" relating to many aspects of Canadian life, including financial, social, and economic. The statistics produced by Statistics Canada are meant to be in a format that will help Canadians better understand their country. Although this agency strives to provide objective and accurate information, they are limited by the information provided to them, and also by legislative changes, new crime categories, and so on. For example, in the 2010 crime statistics, "sexual offences against children" was a relatively new crime category, making it impossible to be compared directly with prior years. Further, the police-reported crime statistics can be influenced by social and demographic factors, as well as the practices and policies of local police services. Having said that, however, the results provided by Statistics Canada can provide a general idea of the type and number of crimes reported by the police.

## 2. Number and type of crimes

Throughout this chapter, a number of broad terms will be used to categorize types of crimes. This is done to make it easier to compare numbers and keep the graphs easy to read. Following is a list of the category terms and some of the offences included in each category:

**Property Crime**: theft, possession of stolen property, theft of motor vehicle, fraud, breaking and entering, arson, etc.

**Violence**: homicide, murder, sexual assault (all levels), assault (all levels), robbery, forcible confinement, etc.

**Other** (used by Statistics Canada): counterfeiting, weapons violations, child pornography, prostitution, etc.

**Other** (used by Pardons Canada): fail to appear, mischief, fail to comply, impersonate, etc.

**Driving**: drive or care or control of motor vehicle while impaired, with over 80 milligrams of alcohol in 100 millilitres of blood, dangerous driving

**Drug**: possessing, trafficking in, distributing, producing, growing, or cultivating a controlled drug or substance

**Other Federal Statute** (used only by Statistics Canada): specific statutes and offences were *not* listed

**Youth:** crimes committed by those at least twelve years old and under eighteen years of age and prosecuted under the *Youth Criminal Justice Act*

**Sex** (used by Pardons Canada): communicate for the purpose of prostitution, inmate of a bawdy house, found in bawdy house

Unfortunately, because of the different methods used by the RCMP, Statistics Canada, and Pardons Canada to present their information, very few direct comparisons between the data are possible. General observations, however, can be made.

### Statistics Canada

Statistics Canada figures state that there were a total of 2,377,171 crimes reported by the police in 2010.[3] Looking at the categories and numbers provided in the Statistics Canada report, we can produce the following graph.

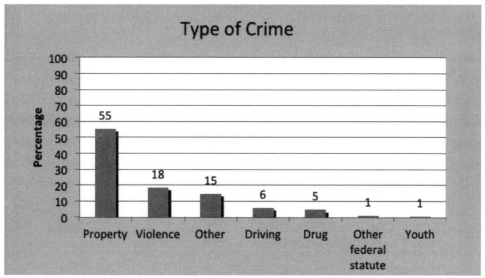

Statistics Canada Police-reported crime statistics, 2010, p. 29

This report shows that the most prevalent type of crime *reported by the police* was property crime. In fact, there were approximately three times as many property crimes as crimes of violence (the second largest number). Of the property crimes reported, 66 percent were relatively minor crimes comprised of 40 percent minor thefts (theft under $5,000), and 26 percent mischief.

# Property Crime Breakdown

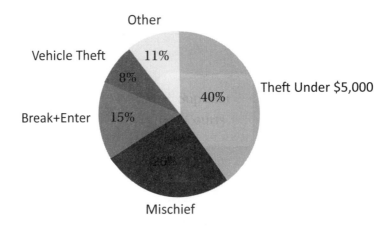

Statistics Canada Police-reported crime statistics, 2010, p. 29

## RCMP Data

How does the Statistics Canada 2010 crime report compare with the information in the RCMP data?[4] The adult crime rate derived from the RCMP data (see the following graph) produces similar results to the Statistics Canada report for the top two crime categories, that is, property and violence. Although the graph shows property as the most common crime category and violent crimes as second, the percentage difference between the two is much smaller than the spread between the two categories in the Statistics Canada report.

# Type of Crime

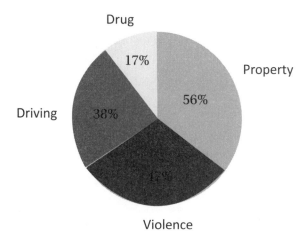

RCMP data, 2010[5]

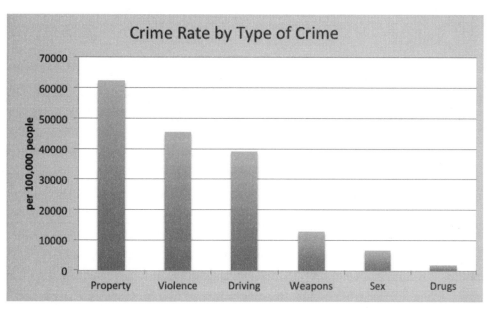

RCMP data, 2010[6]

In the RCMP data, the lowest number of charges per person is one and the highest is eight. If we look at the charges presented previously in the chart, we can calculate the average number of charges per person to be about 1.7.[7] This number, however, underestimates the actual number of charges because of the way the information was presented. Since multiple charges for the same type of offence (called counts) were only counted as one charge in the RCMP's raw data as given to us, it is no surprise that the figure of 1.7 crimes per person is well below the averages derived from both the Pardons Canada data (5.8) and the Statistics Canada average (4.8). These figures are calculated in the Pardons Canada section that follows.

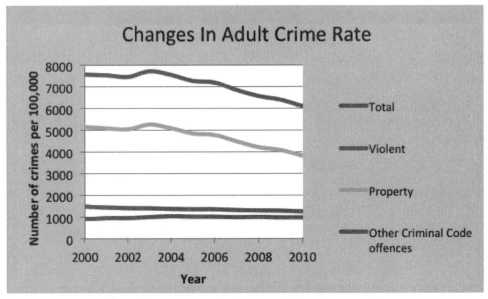

Statistics Canada Police-reported crime statistics, 2010, p. 29

Looking at the Statistics Canada Uniform Crime Reporting Survey, there may be some good news. According to this survey, the crime rate reported by police[8] (excluding drug and traffic crimes and provincial offences), has been declining. A decrease in property crimes was mainly responsible for the decline,[9] while drug offences went against the overall trend and increased by 10 percent. In 2010, the crime rate decreased by 5 percent compared to the previous year, reaching the lowest level since the 1970s.

This statistic was quite surprising to me. My understanding had always been that as a population increased and urban areas became denser, the crime rate would go up due to overcrowding and all that that encompasses. Since the government is reporting that the crime rate has decreased to its lowest level in forty years, there must be significant reasons.

My guess is that, today, people are discouraged from committing crimes for two main reasons: the likelihood of getting caught is greater, and the chance of the criminal record's being discovered by third parties is higher. Technology is largely responsible for these new realities. For example:

1. Widespread video use by police and private citizens (cameras on streets, buildings, homes, in stores, schools, malls, cell phones, taxi cabs, etc.)
2. Fast and inexpensive criminal record searches by potential employers, immigration office, etc., and
3. Transferral of information between police services in other jurisdictions, including the U.S.A.

### Pardons Canada

In contrast to the way the RCMP information is presented, the Pardons Canada data contains information about the total number of times a person has been charged with a crime. From the random sample of 450 people, there were a total of 2,622 charges laid. From this, we can calculate how many charges have been filed in each category for each person.

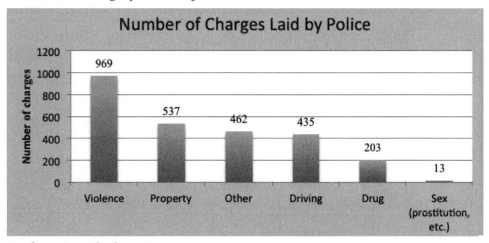

Pardons Canada data, 2011[10]

The Pardons Canada raw data showed that the number of offences per person ranged from 1 to 71, with an average of 5.8 crimes per person.[11] This figure is close to the average of 4.8 crimes per person that is derived from the 2010 Statistics Canada report.[12] Not all charges in the Pardons Canada sample resulted in convictions. The number of convictions ranged from 1 to 52 with an average of 3.77 convictions per person.[13] If we look at the nature of the crimes committed by the group as a whole, we see that 37 percent (969 out of 2,622) of the total charges were violent crimes, making that the most common category.

It is impossible to make an accurate comparison amongst the three sources of data, however, because of the way the number of crimes are recorded (and not recorded) and because of the way the crimes are categorized. For example, at first glance, it would seem that the Pardons Canada results are different from the other two sources of data.

If we re-categorize the offences, however, and include the same type of offences under the same categories—such as adding the weapons offences to the violent crime category in the RCMP data—we find that both the Pardons Canada information and the RCMP data show violent crimes as being the most common. By contrast, the 2010 Statistics Canada crime report showed property crime as the most common. That said, the information from all three sources—Pardons Canada, the RCMP, and Statistics Canada—show that property and violence are the most common crime categories in Canada.

The graph on p. 273 shows what percentage of the Pardons Canada sample group were charged with which type of offence. Interestingly, while 45 percent of the group was charged with a driving offence, that offence only ranked fourth most common in the number of charges that were laid by the police. From the Pardons Canada data we can discern that those charged with a criminal driving offence were charged with two driving offences.[14] From experience in dealing with criminal records, we know that almost every time someone is charged with a driving offence, the police will charge the person with a second driving offence to ensure that the elements of the crime can be proved for at least one, thereby securing a conviction. Crown prosecutors will prosecute the charges they feel they can get a conviction for and withdraw the others. As a result, although 45 percent of the group was charged with a driving offence, in almost all cases both charges were laid at the same time.

In comparison, while only 36 percent of the group was charged with a property crime, they must have been charged with an average of about 3.3 property crimes each, making that the second most common crime category.[15]

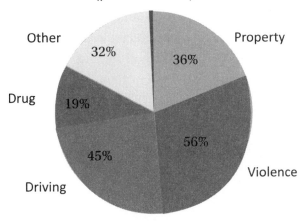

## Type of Crime
## (by percentage of group charged)

Sex (prostitution etc) 1%

Other 32%

Property 36%

Drug 19%

Violence 56%

Driving 45%

Pardons Canada data, 2011[16]

## 3.  Number of people committing crimes

In 2010, approximately 3,250,000 people with criminal records were recorded in the RCMP *Identification* data bank. This figure is cumulative and represents people who acquired their criminal records in different years. As mentioned earlier, an estimate of the percentage of people ever charged with a crime (regardless of whether the record was removed or never transferred to the RCMP) is about *20 percent of the Canadian adult population.*

The number of entries in the RCMP data bank will increase as new people are entered, and decrease as existing files are removed pursuant to the Pardon, Record Suspension, purge, and file destruction processes, and other federal legislation. If someone who already has a record in the data bank commits a subsequent crime, the new information is added to the individual's existing file. In such a case, only the number of offences for the individual increases, not the number of people recorded in the RCMP data bank.

Worth mentioning is that the number of people recorded in this data bank has remained relatively stable over time. In 1985, there were about 2.9 million records in the data bank.[17] A 1996 study by the Privacy Commissioner of Canada showed that, on average, there were about 2.5 million records in the data bank at any given point. In 2005, it contained approximately 3 million records.

What this information doesn't tell us, however, is, on an annual basis, how many people are being charged with crimes. From Statistics Canada reports over the years, we know that each year in Canada, over half a million people are charged with a crime.[18] The exact figure fluctuates, for example, from a low of 379,338 persons charged in 1977 to a high of 753,743 persons charged in 1991. From the following graph, we can see that in 2008 a total of 566,143 people were charged with a Criminal Code offence. Of those charged, 87.4 percent were adults and 12.6 percent were youths.

## Crimes: Adult and Youth

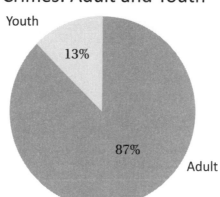

Source: CANSIM Table 2520014, 2008 (Adult 494,796 crimes, Youth 71,347 crimes)

## 4.  Crimes by men and by women

**Percentage of Crimes**

Of those people in the RCMP data, 80 percent were men and 20 percent were women. Information about the person's sex was not recorded for a very small percentage, (less than 1 percent). Those records were not included in the following graph.

# Crimes by Men and by Women

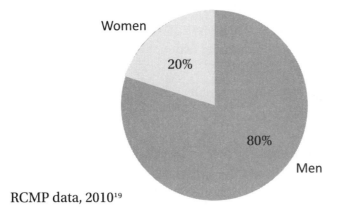

RCMP data, 2010[19]

Below are the numbers from Pardons Canada. From the sample, 82 percent were men and 18 percent were women. This is almost exactly the same as the ratio derived from the RCMP data. Therefore, it would seem that the percentage of men and of women seeking to remove their criminal records (those found in the Pardons Canada data) is consistent with those who actually have a criminal record (those found in the RCMP data). Since the statistics from both data banks are consistent, we can infer that men and women with criminal records are equally likely to take steps to have their records removed.

# Crimes by Men and by Women

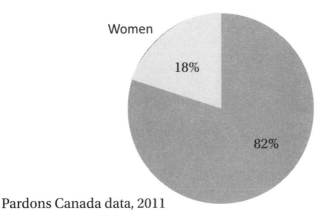

Pardons Canada data, 2011

### Type of crimes committed by men and by women

Do men and women differ in the nature of the crimes they are charged with? To correct for the fact that the RCMP data contains far more men than women, we will look at the crime rate and use the number of people charged with an offence out of every 100,000 in the data provided.

If we look at men and women and see which crimes each is charged with, we get the results in the following graph.

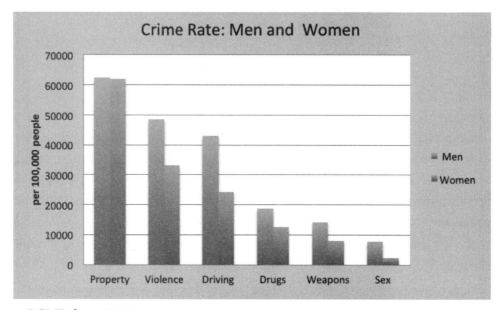

RCMP data, 2010[20]

Comparing the crime-rate statistics, we can see that for both men and women, the RCMP data show property and violent crimes are the most common, while driving offences are third.

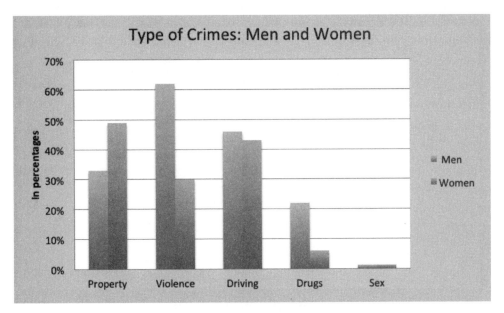

Pardons Canada data, 2011

From the Pardons Canada data, we see that men are most likely to be charged with violent crimes but women are most likely to be charged with property crimes. This differs from the RCMP data where both men and women were most likely to be charged with property offences. Interestingly, the second most common crime category in the Pardons Canada sample, for both men and women, is crime related to driving.[21]

## 5. Race and crimes

Many people think that race is a well-defined and completely objective fact. It isn't. There is no objective test that can determine what race a person is. The various racial classification systems that have been developed also cannot handle mixed races. Groups that have attempted to come up with racial classification systems have not been successful.

One reason that racial classification systems are doomed to fail is that they try to assign people to rigid categories that do not really exist in nature. For example, some classify people as Black, White, or Oriental, but where do people from India, Mexico, or the Middle East fit into this scheme? They don't.

When it comes to race, in the RCMP data, people were classified as White or Non-white. We do not know how this decision is made. We do not know, if we had two observers classify the same group of people, how often they would agree on racial status. How is the police officer recording this information trained to make this determination, and is it the same training nationally? It is understandable that a detailed description of a person charged with a crime is needed, however, it seems that the limited categories of White and Non-white would be only marginally helpful for identification purposes, given Canada's diverse racial population.

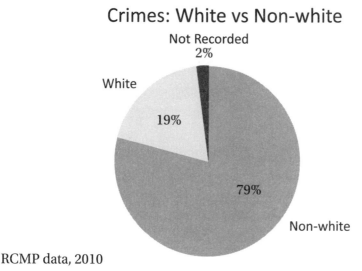

## Crimes: White vs Non-white

RCMP data, 2010

Out of the records supplied to us, 78 percent were classified as Non-white, 19 percent as White, and 2 percent did not have their race recorded. This method of categorizing race is quite limited in comparison to the method the RCMP data listed for categorizing eye colour, which provided twenty-eight different options.

## 6.  Young offenders

If we look at the total percentage of crimes committed by youths and adults, we get the following graph.[22]

# Crimes: Youth and Adult

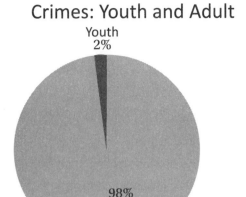

Youth
2%

98%

Adult

RCMP data, 2010

Given the concern about youth crime, it is interesting to see how many young offender criminal records are in the RCMP data. As it turns out, in 2010, youth records only comprised 2 percent of the criminal records held in the RCMP Identification data bank. In comparison, in 2008, Statistics Canada reported that 13 percent of all crimes committed in that year were by youth.[23] The difference in these 2 statistics may stem from how young people are dealt with under the criminal justice system. Although the young person may have been involved in crime, since the Youth Criminal Justice Act came into effect, more and more youth are dealt with outside of the police and courts and their fingerprints are not taken. Young offenders who commit minor crimes are less likely to be charged than adults (in many cases the police simply contact the parents and allow them to discipline the youth at home); and youth records are removed from the RCMP Identification data bank once the charges have reached the non-disclosure date. Further, in order for a record to be included in the RCMP Identification data bank, fingerprints must be submitted. This means that those youths who did not have their prints taken would not appear in the RCMP Identification data bank and, consequently, are not represented in the previous chart. In 2011, 57 percent of youth were dealt with outside of the formal justice system while 43 percent were formally charged.[24]

According to the Uniform Crime Reporting Survey by Statistics Canada, the crime rate for crimes committed by young people decreased by 7 percent between 2009 and 2010,[25] and 18,100 fewer youth were charged with a Criminal Code offence in 2011, than in 2010.[26]

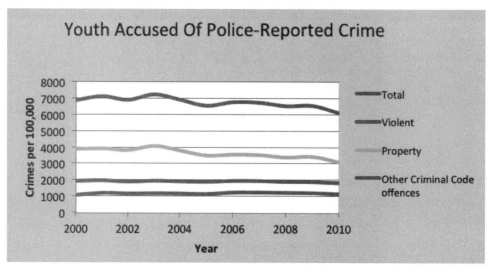

Statistics Canada Police-reported crime statistics, 2010, p. 35

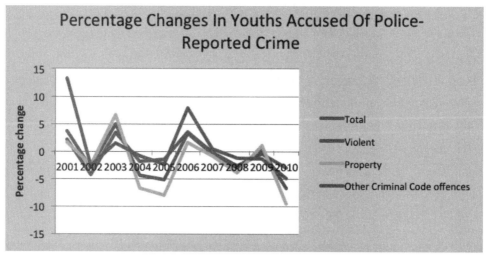

Statistics Canada Police-reported crime statistics, 2010, p. 35

If we calculate the crime rate for adults and youth, we obtain the following graph.

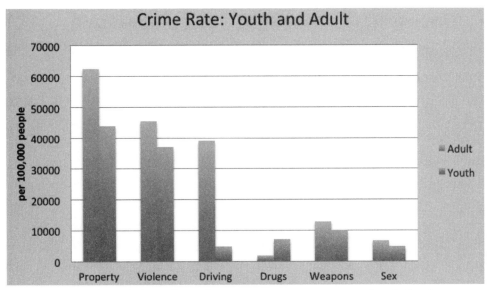

Comparing the adult and youth crime rates, we can see that in both groups, property is the most common offence and violence is second.

## 7.  DNA sample

It might come as a surprise to crime-show aficionados that a DNA sample was only available for 6 percent of those in the RCMP data. The percentage is low because the taking of a bodily substance for law-enforcement purposes must be done within the framework of the Canadian constitution. Therefore, strict rules exist as to the circumstances under which samples can be taken, and also as to the retention of the DNA information.

## DNA Sample Provided

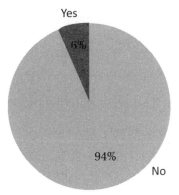

RCMP data, 2010

## 8.  Disposition of charges

What was the outcome of all the charges found in the RCMP data? The majority of people received a conviction. However, due to the way the data was provided, we cannot tell which of the charges led to the convictions. For example, if someone were charged with auto-theft and also a driving offence, we would only know whether that person received a conviction. We cannot tell if that person was convicted of both charges or of just one. And, if that conviction is for only one charge, we cannot tell which.

It is not surprising that most charges lead to convictions because of the process by which charges are laid. The police strive to be certain that someone committed an offence before charging them, and they often lay more than one charge. They do this for three main reasons:

1.  The actions of the accused may be elements of more than one crime of a similar nature (e.g., driving while impaired, care and control of motor vehicle while impaired). Since at the time of the arrest the police can't be certain which crime can be proved, they will usually charge the person with both crimes to increase the chance of securing at least one conviction.

2.  The accused may be thought to have committed more than one offence at the same time, (e.g., driving while impaired, theft of motor vehicle, possession of illegal substance).

3.  The primary offence might be a *strictly summary* offence for which fingerprints can't be taken. In such cases, the police may charge the individual with a related offence for which prints can be taken. Having fingerprints will greatly assist the police in their identification and investigation of the accused.

## Disposition

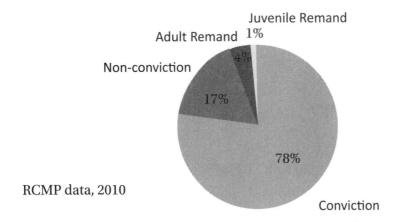

RCMP data, 2010

## Disposition

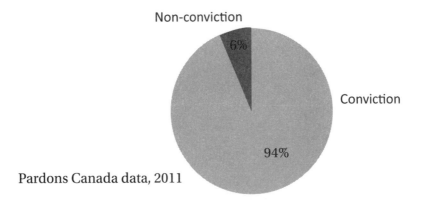

Pardons Canada data, 2011

The graph above, derived from the Pardons Canada sample group, shows a very high conviction rate of 94 percent. Although both the RCMP and Pardons Canada data show similar results, the Pardons Canada results for convictions is much higher.

A possible reason is as follows: Throughout our experience in removing criminal records, we have found that people who have been convicted of a crime clearly know they have a criminal record whereas people who have received non-conviction dispositions (e.g., discharges, withdrawn or dismissed charges, peace bonds, etc.) are led to believe that they do not have a criminal record.[27] Although this is not true, many people with non-convictions, believing they have no criminal record, do nothing about it. As a result, many of those with non-convictions would not seek the help of Pardons Canada and would not be part of the Pardons Canada data bank. Consequently, most people seeking assistance from Pardons Canada would be those with convictions, resulting in a very high percentage of those in the sample group.

## 9. Highlights

The data from the three sources—the RCMP, Pardons Canada, and Statistics Canada—were compiled and presented differently. This created some difficulty in making direct comparisons. Having said that, however, we are still able to draw some interesting observations. In Canada:

- The number of criminal charges, per person charged, per year, is about five.
- Men are charged with 80 percent of crimes.
- The RCMP data did not provide meaningful information with respect to race and crime.
- The majority of people with a criminal record will receive at least one conviction.
- The greatest number of crimes committed—both by adults and by youths—is in the property and violence categories.
- Only about 6 percent of people charged with a crime are required to provide a DNA sample.
- The crime rate has been declining, and in 2011 it reached its lowest rate since the 1970s.
- About 20 percent of Canadian *adults* have a criminal record.

A SPECIAL THANKS

Dr. Kent A. Campbell is an experimental psychologist with a four-year BSc from the University of Toronto and a PhD from McMaster University. His main area of interest is health psychology / behavioural medicine. Dr. Campbell has extensive experience in data analysis on a wide variety of projects. He has won two teaching awards for his undergraduate statistics courses at Ryerson University and an award for graduate-student supervision at the University of Toronto. I would like to offer my sincere gratitude to Dr. Kent A. Campbell for his insight and analytical work in this chapter. His ability to take raw information from over 3 million records and turn it into something we can all understand is truly a gift.

## Quiz

**1. In any given year, how many people are charged with a crime in Canada?**

    a.  2 million

    b.  10% of the adult population

    c.  About 500,000 adults

    d.  Increases by 5% per year

    e.  None of the above

**2. With respect to youths with criminal records:**

    a.  Statistics Canada reported: Youth crime decreased from 2009–2010

    b.  Police reported that about 153,000 youths were accused of committing crimes in 2010

    c.  RCMP data showed about 2% of people with criminal records were youth

    d.  Statistics Canada reported: Youth committed more property crimes than any other type of crime

    e.  All of the above

**3. Crime: Men and Women**

    a.  Men comprised about 80% of those in the RCMP data

    b.  Women comprised 18% of those in the Pardons Canada sample

    c.  Women were more likely to commit a property crime (Pardons Canada sample)

    d.  Men and Women are equally likely to take steps to remove their criminal records

    e.  All of the above

**4. Number and Type of Crimes:**

    a.  In 2010, police reported approximately 2.4 million crimes in Canada

    b.  Property and violence were the top crime categories

    c.  According to Statistics Canada, minor thefts accounted for over 40% of the property crimes in 2010

    d.  In the Pardons Canada sample, 45% of the people were charged with a driving offence

    e.  All of the above

## 5. Race:

a. The RCMP data only showed 2 race categories: White + Non-white
b. There is no national standard process to categorize race
c. In contrast, the RCMP showed 28 "eye colour" categories
d. (a) and (b)
e. (a), (b) and (c)

## 6. True or False:

a. The RCMP Identification data bank holds all Canadian criminal record information
b. Criminal Records that have been pardoned or suspended no longer appear in the RCMP Identification data bank
c. By far the most crimes committed in Canada, as reported by Statistics Canada in 2010, are related to property
d. The individual police services in Canada transfer all their criminal record information to the RCMP
e. The majority of people in both the RCMP and Pardons Canada data received at least one conviction

Answer Key: 1 (c), 2 (e), 3 (e), 4 (e), 5 (e), 6 false, true, true, false, true

## End Notes

1. Parole Board of Canada, 2011

2. RCMP purges refers to the purging of *discharges* pursuant to the *Criminal Records Act*; and police destruction refers to the destruction of fingerprints, photographs, and incident files by local police services throughout the country, pursuant to the policies of the individual police service. Refer to Chapter 7 for more information about the different ways criminal records can be removed and/or destroyed.

3. Police-reported crime statistics in Canada, 2010, by Shannon Brennan and Mia Dauvergne, released July 21, 2011. Component of Statistics Canada catalogue no. 85-002-X Juristat. Source: Statistics Canada, Uniform Crime Reporting Survey.

4. In the RCMP data, although someone may have been charged with multiple counts of the same crime, it will show up as only one occurrence of that type of crime. So someone who has committed motor vehicle theft once or a thousand times would look exactly the same in the way the data was provided—they would have a "yes" for theft of motor vehicle.

5. Since people are often charged with more than one type of crime, *the same person* can have crimes reported in *more than one category*. This accounts for the above percentages adding up to more than 100 percent. For example, let's assume five people are charged with crimes. If four of the five are charged with a criminal driving offence, that would be recorded as 80 percent of the group having a driving charge. But if three of the five also have a theft charge, that would mean 60 percent of the people have been charged with a property crime. If you add those percentages together, you will get 140 percent.

6. The RCMP: "Adult Crime Rate by Type of Crime" graph shows the crime rate of those in the RCMP data as opposed to the general population. That is, how many people per 100,000 in the RCMP data were charged with a particular crime.

7. Calculated as follows: Sum of crimes in all categories per 100,000 (62407 + 45482 + 39180 + 12853 + 6638 + 1757), divided by 100,000 people.

8. When reviewing crime-rate statistics, it is important to understand what crime rates are. The crime rate is not the same as the actual number of crimes. Crime rates are similar to percentages; percentages are based on the number of events per 100 people, while crime rates are based on the number of crimes per 100,000 people. So a crime rate of 50 means that a crime was reported 50 times for every 100,000 people in the population. This method of reporting ensures that the crime rate is not influenced by the number of people in the population.

9. The homicide rate also dropped dramatically in 2010.

10. In this graph, crimes involving sex were recorded either in the violent crime category (i.e., sexual assault), or in the sex category (e.g., prostitution).

11. Calculated as follows: Number of charges, 2,622, divided by the number of people in the sample group, 450.

12. Calculated as follows: Number of crimes reported, 2,377,171, divided by the number of people committing crimes each year, (approximately) 500,000.

13. Calculated as follows: Number of charges resulting in convictions, 1695, divided by the number of people in the sample group, 450.

14. Calculated as follows: Number of people in study group (450), multiplied by the percentage of people charged with a driving offence (45%) = 202.5 people charged with a driving offence. If about 202 people received 435 driving charges, that means each person was charged with about 2 driving offences (435 charges divided by 202 people).

15. Calculated as above: 450 people x 36% = 162 people charged with a property crime; 537 property crimes divided by 162 people = 3.3 property crimes per person.

16. As with the RCMP Type of Crime graph, the percentages in the above graph add up to more than 100 percent because the people were charged with more than one type of offence.

17. Source: David H. Flaherty, "Protecting Privacy in Police Information Systems: Data Protection in the Canadian Police Information Centre" (Spring, 1986), *University of Toronto Law Journal*, Vol. 36, No. 2, p. 146, Appendix 1.

18. CANSIM Table 2520014

19. Percentages may not add up to exactly 100 percent due to rounding.

20. A total of 6.6 percent of records (213,526) in the RCMP data contain a sex offence. Of those 213,526 records only 1,063 (0.5 percent) have received a pardon (1,063 / 213,526 = 0.5 percent).

21. To calculate the Pardons Canada percentages, we adopted the same system used by the RCMP, that is, we just looked at whether the individuals were charged with a crime, *not* the actual number of charges per type of crime.

22. Under the *Youth Criminal Justice Act, Youth* is defined as children from twelve up to and including seventeen years of age. For criminal-law purposes, once a person reaches the age of eighteen, he or she is considered an adult. For more information about youth criminal records, refer to Chapter 3.

23. Source: CANSIM Table 2520014, 2008: Adult 494,796 crimes, Youth 71,347 crimes.

24. Statistics Canada, Police-reported crime statistics in Canada, 2011

25. In 2010, police reported almost 153,000 youth accused of crimes. That figure includes both those youth who were charged with an offence and those referred to a community program, or only given a warning. Statistics Canada, Police-reported crime statistics, 2010, p. 18.

26. Statistics Canada, Police-reported crime statistics in Canada, 2011

27. For information about what is considered a criminal record, refer to Chapter 1.

# Index

## A

## C

# D

# E

# F

# S

# T

weight-loss, 49, 71, 82, 84, 89, 129, 133, 136-139, 141, 146, 151, 175, 183-184-193, 233, 291
weightlifting (lift weights), 117, 122, 215, 232, 235-236, 244-245, 349
weight training, 117, 188, 232
Women's Single Sculls final, 211 (See also Laumann, Silken)
World Health Organization, 78, 277

Y

Yerkes-Dodson, 285, 286

# ABOUT THE AUTHOR

Dr. Dwight Chapin, B.Sc(H), D.C., is an award-winning chiropractor and co-owner of High Point Wellness Centre, Team Chiropractor for the CFL's Toronto Argonauts, and onsite clinician for *The Globe and Mail*.

A corporate wellness innovator and experienced clinician and public speaker, Chapin has spoken extensively to corporations across Canada on a variety of health topics. He is also the co-author of a five-part webinar series on Mental Health at Work for the Canadian Centre for Occupational Health and Safety (CCOHS).

As a Health Advisor, Chapin's original work has been featured in *The Globe and Mail*, where he also operates an onsite repetitive strain injury prevention clinic for Globe employees.

Awarded the 2018 Chiropractor of the Year by the Ontario Chiropractic Association, he is also a two-time Grey Cup champion as a member of the Toronto Argonauts' medical staff.

Dr. Chapin has made it his life's mission to care for, educate, and inspire others in their journey toward optimal health. In his first book, *Take Good Care: 7 Wellness Rituals for Health, Strength & Hope*, he brings the science of preventative medicine to life.

## FOLLOW DR. CHAPIN ONLINE:

www.**7WellnessRituals**.com